# The Sketches of Erinensis

Also by Martin Fallon

ABRAHAM COLLES: 1773–1843
Surgeon of Ireland

# THE SKETCHES OF
# *Erinensis*

### Selections of
### Irish Medical Satire 1824–1836

#### edited by
## MARTIN FALLON
O.B.E., M.A., M.Ch., F.R.C.S., F.A.C.S.

SKILTON & SHAW
52 Lincoln's Inn Fields, London

"Satire no doubt has its advantages when levelled against folly
and knavery."

"Sir, there are rascals in all countries."

Dr. Johnson

© MARTIN FALLON, 1979
ISBN 0 7050 0082 6
Printed in Great Britain for Skilton & Shaw
(Fudge & Co. Ltd.), Sardinia House,
Sardinia Street, London WC2A 3NW

# ACKNOWLEDGEMENTS

As Editor I am much indebted to my sister, colleagues and friends — Jessie Dobson, Sir Donald Douglas, Kathleen Fallon, Sinclair Gauldie, Bryan Guinness (Lord Moyne), Professor G.P Henderson, Edward Kermode, Professor Stanley McCollum, Professor R.M. Ogilvie, and Donald Southgate, who have either read, checked, corrected, translated, illustrated or typed the following pages.

I am also indebted to the Royal College of Physicians of Ireland, and the Royal College of Surgeons in Ireland for permission to reproduce portraits, busts and other items from their collections.

MARTIN FALLON
Longforgan,
Perthshire.

The University of Dublin, often known by the name of its single college — Trinity College Dublin sometimes appears in this book simply as Trinity.

## COMMILITONIBUS ERINENSIBUS

Bernard Fallon (1876–1955.)
Head Constable, Royal Irish Constabulary.

John Bernard Fallon (1907–1970). M.A., T.C.D.
Colonel, Duke of Wellington's Regt.,
The Arab Legion, and The Oman Scouts.

Thaddeus Fallon (1913–1964). B.A., M.B., T.C.D.
Captain R.A.M.C., B.E. Force,
W.A. Force and Burma Command.

# CONTENTS

| | |
|---|---|
| *Foreword* | xi |
| *Introduction* | 1 |
| 1. The Royal College of Surgeons in Ireland | 15 |
| 2. Mr. Colles | 19 |
| 3. Mr. Todd | 26 |
| 4. Dr. Stokes | 35 |
| 5. Mr. Kirby | 43 |
| 6. Mr. Crampton | 54 |
| 7. Mr. Jacob | 70 |
| 8. Mr. Macartney | 82 |
| 9. Dublin Hospitals | 97 |
| 10. Mr. Carmichael | 107 |
| 11. Stevens' Hospital | 117 |
| 12. Mercer's Hospital | 128 |
| 13. Letters from Eminent Characters with Comments etc | 147 |
| 14. Mr. Wilmot | 156 |
| 15. Mr. Harrison | 163 |
| 16. Dr. Jacob's Introductory Lecture | 173 |
| 17. The Private Schools of Dublin | 184 |
| 18. Opening of the Medical Session in Dublin | 198 |
| 19. The Dublin College of Surgeons and Erinensis | 210 |
| 20. Mr. Cusack, Park Street School | 216 |
| *Appendix* | 225 |
| *Notes* | 228 |
| *Bibliography* | 243 |
| *Index* | 245 |

*The line drawings at the chapter heads are by*
*Sinclair Gauldie, C.B.E.*

# FOREWORD

*"We may our ends by our beginnings know"*.

*(Sir John Denham 1615–1669)*

The device on the title page of this book will serve to remind the reader when and where medical education in Ireland officially began.

Trinity College produced few medical graduates in the first century of its turbulent existence, but in 1711 it opened its first medical school — the oldest in the British Isles — with lectures in Medicine, Anatomy, Botany and Chemistry. In that small building the amiable Scot, George Cleghorn, laboured for many decades.

The Physicians' College was founded by Trinity in 1654 and subsquently received Royal Charters from Charles II and from William and Mary which legally entitled them to control all medical practice in and within 7 miles of Dublin City.

In the succeeding century the two Colleges did not co-operate in harmony but were forced by events to come together in 1785 to form a combined medical school — The School of Physic. This, however, did not produce the hoped-for results as it failed to provide a Clinical School, and hundreds of Irishmen were necessarily forced to seek this training in Edinburgh where they usually acquired an M.D. degree in that University. Meanwhile, the Dublin Surgeons, long dissociated from the Barbers' Company and now conscious of their respectability and inspired by the success of the Paris Surgeons, acquired their own Royal Charter in 1784 and developed their own medical school. This latter was an immediate success, especially under the dynamic leadership of Abraham Colles.

Side by side with all this, in Dublin, in London and elsewhere, were the private medical schools. Dublin was favoured in the supply of adequate anatomical material from the huge Hospital Fields burial ground at Kilmainham: it was the age of the 'resurrectionists' who thrived and even developed a valuable export market!

The certificates of the private medical schools were accepted by the Service Departments, by the Dublin and London Colleges of Surgeons and by the Scottish Universities. The Trinity Medical School did rise again with the appointment of James Macartney to its Anatomy and Chirurgery Chair, and his new medical school built in 1825 was the only serious rival to Colles in the Surgeons' School but, in general, medicine in Dublin, as elsewhere, was a free-for-all. There were no standards in medical training and registration until 1858 although Wakley had proposed this some 12 years before. Reforms were necessary: Thomas Wakley and his friends and fellow-parliamentarians Daniel O'Connell and William Wilberforce were likewise engaged in their respective missions. We were, after all, in the Regency and the reign of George IV! Martin Fallon, a loyal son of Trinity where he taught Anatomy and surgery in his own inimitable style, is a distinguished Fellow of the Royal College of Surgeons in Ireland, where he is especially remembered for his excellent biography of Abraham Colles published in 1972.

He now presents us with a selection of the sketches of "Erinensis", Wakley's man in Dublin. They tell us of the characters of the men and the institutions they served in that bygone age, of their freedoms and their enterprise. It is all satire and very amusing, yet the reader is left with the feeling, nostalgic perhaps, that in our own modern age of economic stress, technology and bureaucratic control, a new Wakley and "Erinensis" will have to be born to restore the dignity and freedom of a great profession.

STANLEY T. McCOLLUM
Regius Professor of Surgery
in the University of Dublin

Past President of the Royal
College of Surgeons in Ireland

# INTRODUCTION

IN AUGUST 1820, a doctor practising in Argyll Street, off Regent Street, London, was brutally assaulted and his fine house burnt to the ground, by persons unknown. It subsequently transpired that the victim, Thomas Wakley, had been mistaken for the masked scaffold attendant who decapitated Thistlewood and four others, after their public hanging at Newgate on May Day 1820. The mistake may have been the result of similarity of build, both men were strong physical types, but more likely, the expertise of the actual decapitation suggested to the enraged onlookers that the perpetrator must be a medical man, or at least someone with a knowledge of anatomy. Sprigge, in his biography of Wakley, confidently asserts that the masked scaffold attendant was Tom Parker, a well known character in the underworld as a 'resurrectionist', and a dissecting-room porter employed in Grainger's private medical school, where, long afterwards, he used to demonstrate his 'secret method of cutting off a head'.

Thistlewood and his fellow conspirators at Cato Street had come within an ace of assassinating the whole Cabinet (then accustomed to meet 'over the port' in the houses of various members in some sort of rotation), and represented in an extreme form that Radicalism which had existed before the French Revolution, was accentuated by it, and suppressed as a result of it. It lay, on the whole, dormant during the Napoleonic Wars, only to burst out again in a post-war inflation and depression, so that repressive measures were introduced by the Tory administration of Lord Liverpool, in view of tumultuous meetings such as 'Peterloo' when the Manchester mob was fired on, conspiracies such as Thistlewood's, and the undeserved popularity of the noxious Queen Caroline. These represented a popular protest against that royal rascal, Regent since 1811, who was proclaimed King George IV on January 31 1820, two days after the death of his father George III, the licentiousness of his Court, and his incurable extravagance, the remoteness of the Tory administration and the ineffectiveness of the Whig opposition.

1

Whatever his political errors of judgement, George III had been (until finally incapacitated in 1811 by 'madness' to which was added blindness) a chaste, conscientious, and respectable man, most interesting to the medical profession in the 20th century because of recent diagnosis of his intermittent, and finally chronic incapacity as *Porphyria* (from which Macalpine *et al.* suggest George IV also suffered, on inheritance from Mary Queen of Scots), and in the eighteenth and nineteenth centuries because of unique contacts between politicians and physicians resulting from his recurrent 'mania'.

These Royal doctors, and there were many, were formed by the age to which they belonged; their art was as old as their science was young. As a profession they were then, as always, independent, conservative, and never failing to protect their own interests. At a Thanksgiving Service for the King's recovery at St. Paul's Cathedral in April 1789, medals were distributed bearing the Royal image, and 'Lost to Britannia's Hope, but to her Prayers Restor'd' on the reverse. The King's physician, Dr. Robert Darling Willis, with a keen eye on publicity, also had a medal struck with his own likeness, and its reverse inscribed, 'Britons Rejoice, your King's Restored'. Much later, when the King became a recluse at Windsor, and more or less abandoned by his Queen and his family, his doctors were not neglectful in their attendance — 35 guineas for a daily visit, £35,000 per annum, and a grand total of £276,691 18s. 0d.! Hillaire Belloc, in a later age and in another context penned some apposite lines:

> Physicians of the utmost fame
> Were called at once; but when they came
> They answered, as they took their fees,
> 'There is no cure for this disease'.

In that tragic and final decade of his life, George III would not have known of the continued disgraceful careers of the Regent and the Royal Dukes. 'My God, they are the damnedest millstones about the necks of any Government as can be imagined', was Wellington's remark about them. Nor would the King have been aware of Wellington's victory at Waterloo, of Caroline's wild escapades in her Grand Tour of European resorts and the Near East, of Princess Charlotte's death in childbirth in 1817, of the great Race for the Succession in 1818, and of the birth of Princess Victoria in 1819.

Although Lord Liverpool was Prime Minister, and Lord Sidmouth, Home Secretary, it was Castlereagh, an Ulsterman and brilliant Foreign Secretary, who was Leader of the House of Commons which passed the repressive measures which more or less coincided with the Accession of George IV in 1820. This made him the special target of the mob, and he had to bear the brunt of much of the odium against the Government. When this unfortunate man committed suicide in 1822, his burial service at Westminister Abbey had to be curtailed on account of the cheers of the mob, and their idolised poet Byron pursued the object of their hatred even beyond the tomb with this brutal epitaph:

> Posterity will ne'er survey
> A nobler grave than his;
> Here lies the bones of Castlereagh;
> Stop, traveller and piss.

But revolution it was not to be, England's political genius prevailed and REFORM became the watchword of the hour. Of the many reforms that were now to follow, commencing under the aegis of Liverpool with another semi-Irishman George Canning (who succeeded Castlereagh), only those related to the medical profession concern us here. For these we introduce a remarkable figure, who, if not the great medical reformer as he is often stated to be, at least made his contribution to the spirit of the age. This was the man the assault upon whom was noticed at the beginning of this Introduction.

Thomas Wakley was born in 1795 at Membury in Devonshire. He was the 8th and youngest son of a substantial farmer, and received his early education at local grammer schools. At the age of 15 he chose medicine as a career and was apprenticed to a local apothecary. But desiring to advance himself in his profession, he transferred to London in 1815, becoming a pupil of the United Borough Hospitals of St. Thomas's and Guy's, which he was to 'walk' for a further two years before becoming a member of the Royal College of Surgeons. The system of medical education then prevailing in the Capital shocked and embittered this country lad with a strong puritanical streak.

Although he paid fees to certain official teachers, they were extremely lax in providing any instruction in return, and like all medical students of that age he had to acquire his professional knowledge in the private medical schools. The realisation that he could never rise to the top of his profession, because he had not the financial resources necessary for apprenticeship to a leading London surgeon, and was destined for the rank and file of his profession made him a Radical. To him, the medical profession was static, resisting change, enjoying monopoly, pomposity, patronage and privilege, with nepotism abounding in medical corporations and hospitals.

In 1817, Wakley now a member of the Royal College of Surgeons returned home to begin his career as a general medical practitioner, in competition with the licentiates of the Royal College of Physicians, and with the Apothecaries who were then encroaching on the practices of both. But the idea of a country practice was soon dissipated by a love affair which recalled Wakley to London, and for two years he had a small practice in the City. Wakley married on February 1820, and his wealthy father-in-law purchased for him a fine house and lucrative practice in Argyll Street, off Regent Street, where, within months, the assault due to mistaken identity took place.

Wakley now broken in health and fortune, had understandably a grudge against society. Furthermore, as he had succeeded in his court action against the insurance company who had refused to pay for the fire damage, the law courts were never again to hold any terrors for him. In this unsettled period of his life Wakley became a friend of William Cobbett, Editor of the *Weekly Political Register*, and leader of a group of Radical reformers who were to inspire Wakley in his new venture. He launched his new weekly medical journal on October 5, 1823.

*The Lancet*, which has been in continuous production for over a century and a half, may well carve its name with pride; it has outlived and outclassed all its competitors, and is now the leading British medical weekly, respected at home and abroad. Its title was not without significance. A lancet was sharp and cutting, the tool of the surgeons, and employed in bloodletting and the opening of abscesses. From its first number onwards, the new journal was an immediate success, and its great attraction was the publication of

Sir Astley Cooper's lectures, which any student could now read for an initial outlay of sixpence. Later, in deference to the wishes of his old teacher, Wakley agreed to have Sir Astley's name removed from the title pages. But when John Abernethy's lectures were likewise published without permission, Abernethy obtained a court injunction, which however was later removed on Wakley's successful submission that the lectures were not private, that they were public lectures given in a public place, and in the same category as parliamentary and legal reports. Wakley and Abernethy, both strong-willed men were now to engage in a life-long feud. Wakley's next step was to publish hospital reports of clinical cases, again without permission. This action brought him into open conflict with every surgeon in London, and he was debarred entry to St. Thomas's Hospital.

The editorial and other features of the earlier volumes of *The Lancet* make incredible reading in our polite age, but it is well, however, to remember that the scurrility of the journals and pamphlets of the early 19th century is always a matter of surprise to non-historians, and the number of libel actions well understandable. The reader is spared the Billingsgate, coarse ribaldry, invective and personal abuse levelled at the surgical leaders of the metropolis, which were now to feature in *The Lancet* columns. There were many court actions for libel; the most sensational resulted from *The Lancet* report of a bungling lithotomy operation which Bransby Cooper took 55 minutes to perform, failing to find the stone, and losing his patient. Cooper sued Wakley for £2,000, but was awarded only £100, and this was immediately collected for Wakley by public subscription; indeed, the appeal was over-subscribed, and Wakley in a generous gesture donated the excess to the widow of the unfortunate patient. This court action brought into sharp focus the nepotism prevailing in the appointments to hospital staffs, where a good connection or sponsor counted more than real merit for professional advancement. Sir Astley Cooper was then to admit to being a *pater familias* to the surgical staffs of St. Thomas's and Guy's Hospitals — seven of its members were his former apprentices, three of these were his nephews, and one his godson! Henceforth, in *The Lancet* language they became the 'nephews and the noodles', the 'ninnyhammers', the 'cock-sparrows' and much worse.

At the same time, *The Lancet* opened up a second front against the Royal College of Surgeons in London. This was triggered off by a new regulation of the R.C.S. which recognised only the lectures of certain teachers (their own examiners) and those of the universities of Aberdeen, Dublin, Edinburgh, and Glasgow. Wakley was quick to denounce the R.C.S. Charter of 1800, in which the College Council could themselves fill their own vacancies, which were life appointments, and from these choose their own Court of Examiners, without any reference to the vast body of the college — the members. Wakley led a demonstration of members to the college during a Hunterian lecture and was bodily ejected from its hall. He extended his campaign with attacks on the Royal College of Surgeons of Edinburgh — the oldest college, and against the Royal College of Surgeons in Ireland — next in seniority. The Royal College of Physicians of London did not escape censure — they were dubbed the 'Old Ladies of Pall Mall East', and their distinguished President, Sir Henry Halford was referred to as the 'Halfordian Humbug'. The Apothecaries Company of London was ridiculed as consisting of the 'Old Hags of Rhubarb Hall'. The lowly Dublin Apothecaries Company, who apparently were charging high apprenticeship fees, were chastised with this irreverent anecdote. A man brought an ass to be ordained by the bishop. His mit'red reverence, in a fit of choler, vociferated, 'Begone, you rascal, how dare you insult the mysteries of our religion'. The man was quietly leading his animal away, when the bishop perceiving a purse of gold tied to his tail, immediately cried out, 'Stop, friend, though your animal be an ass *before*, he will make a very good priest *behind*.' Also under attack were the ancient universities of Scotland, in particular Edinburgh with its famous medical school, accused of producing the 'Sangrados of the English provinces'.

The continued success of *The Lancet* naturally had its effect on other contemporary medical journals; a dozen or more of the smaller ones quickly folded their parchments and faded away. Three of the long-standing journals who were strongly supported by medical establishment — *The London Medical Repository* edited by James Copland, *The Medico-Chirurgical Review* edited by James Johnstone, and *The London Medical* and *Physical Journal* edited by Roderick Macleod, turned round to fight a fierce literary battle before they too were liquidated. No language like this was ever used before or since by medical men, and it lowered the standing of the profession in public estimation and respect, though at a time when every institution from the Throne, the Lords, the unreformed Commons, and ancient universities was similarly abused.

Wakley mellowed as the years entered the respectability and greatness of the Victorian age; we leave his subsequent career to his able biographers. When assessing his place in the history of medical reforms, it may be recorded that his attempt to establish a London College of Medicine in opposition to the Royal Colleges ended in dismal failure. His advocacy of an Anatomy Bill also failed, even though supported by the public outcry which followed the Burke and Hare murders; it required another gruesome murder by Bishop, Williams and May to break down the resistance of the Archbishop of Canterbury and his fellow peers to allow Henry Warburton's second Anatomy Bill of 1832 to reach the statute book. The Royal College of Surgeons in London, though irritated, was not unduly influenced by *The Lancet* strictures. It, in its own time, secured a new Charter in 1843, changing its title to the Royal College of Surgeons of England, and establishing a new class of senior members to be known as Fellows who were to elect the Council of the College. The Dublin College in its own new Charter in the following year also adopted the term Fellow instead of Member for holders of the senior diploma. Finally, although Wakley as a vigorous Radical Member of Parliament introduced a Bill for the registration of medical practitioners in 1846, it was not until 1858 that the Medical Act incorporating many provisions originally proposed by Wakley became law under Government sponsorship.

Wakley obviously had many able assistants contributing to the remarkable success of his new journal, many of these are unknown to us now. 'Scotus' and others who conducted the Scottish 'campaign' have not been identified. William Lawrence initially gave Wakley powerful support against the Royal College of Surgeons, but on his election to its Council five years later, he abandoned Wakley and *The Lancet* for ever. As Sir William Lawrence he reached eminence in his college and in his profession. James Wardrop, a Scot, who in London also rose high in his profession to become Surgeon to George IV was apparently the 'Brutus' who

attacked the Royal College of Surgeons, and was later considered
to have been the author of those famous 'intercepted letters'
against Sir Henry Halford and the Physicians' College. But in
descriptive writing, literary brilliance, and native wit, none of these
correspondents could compare with *The Lancet's* man in Dublin.

> ... Erinensis, 'the Irish vagabond, the half rebel, half
> surgeon' as he had been called by the pious Dr Copland some
> twelve months ago, is showing in intellectual verdure, 'the
> might that slumbers in a Paddy's arm'...
>
> *The Lancet*, 1828

Erinensis was the pseudonym of the author of a brilliant series
of sketches and letters contributed to *The Lancet* on the Irish
medical scene during the years 1824–1836. Like Junius of the
century before his effectiveness was undoubtedly his anonymity.
'To him who knows his company,' remarked Dr. Johnson, 'it is not
hard to be sarcastic in a mask'. But the mask was necessary; its
removal would certainly have led to prosecution or worse.

In his amusing style, Erinensis teases us with his own identity:

> ... so capricious is that spirit of conjecture which has made
> me in succession, Mr. Cross, Dr. Macartney, Professor Kirby,
> a rejected candidate, a puffing Apothecary, a Popish editor, a
> Protestant reporter, a Green-horn of Mercer's, Sir Astley
> Cooper, Mr. Jacob, a Phrenological Madman, Mr. Jones
> Quain, a Witch, a Woman of the Town; and of course, it will
> be duly discovered, that in addition to all these, I am the
> 'terræ filius' of the next institution I may chance to give a
> description. The enjoyment of the privileges of immortality
> on alternate days, by the twin Sons of Leda, or the contor-
> tions of Proteus in the hands of Aristæus, were but plain
> matter of fact transactions, compared with these mere mytho-
> logical transformations of character.

Erinensis admitted only to being an Irishman and a Christian.

Who was he? Sir Charles Cameron, in his History of the Royal
College of Surgeons in Ireland, stated, 'Through the courtesy of
Dr. Wakley, proprietor of *The Lancet* I have ascertained that the
writer of these letters was an Irishman. Dr. *Herris Greene*, who was
for eighteen years a member of *The Lancet* staff, and whose
anonymity was carefully preserved.' This is undoubtedly a typo-
graphical error, which unfortunately, though not untypically, has
been repeated by later historians. Professor Alexander Macalister

in his biography of James Macartney stated unequivocally that Erinensis was Dr. *Peter Hennis Green*, and the present writer sees no reason to challenge this identification. There are records of a Trinity student of that name and of that period, who was a Scholar of the House, and later a graduate in arts and medicine of the university. In a paper in *The Lancet* in 1832, Dr. Peter Hennis Green stated that he was for many years an assistant and Demonstrator to Professor James Macartney in the University of Dublin, and from whose department he published a small book on '*The Varieties of the Arterial System*', and was about to publish another volume on '*The Anatomy of the Nerves*'. In the early 1830's, P. Hennis Green (now usually dropping his first name or confining it to an initial) was in London, where incidentally he acquired the M.R.C.S. diploma, and was contributing papers to *The Lancet* on the pathology of malignant cholera. Later, he was to write from Paris, where he lived for about a year, visiting children's hospitals, and writing extensively on pediatric pathology. He translated French and German medical literature for *The Lancet*, and in a letter dated May 1839 he described himself as a sub-editor of that journal. We also see his name as a member of the B.M.A. Council in 1838, and finally as co-editor (with Dr. R.J. Streeton of Worcester) of *The Provincial Medical and Surgical Journal* (forerunner of *The British Medical Journal*) in 1840.

As *The Lancet's* man in Dublin, Erinensis was bound to carry out the policy of his London Editor, in seeking out evidence of maladministration, monopoly, favouritism, patronage etc in the Dublin medical corporations. The Royal College of Surgeons in Ireland, in particular, became his special target; its Council, Court of Examiners, the apprenticeship system, and the Surgeons' School were the theme of many critical sketches. Likewise, he was to write on the University of Dublin, the Physicians' College and the private medical schools. In his sketches of the Dublin hospitals, he was seeking for any trace of nepotism in their staff appointments, and for any irregularities or mismanagement in them as public institutions. Erinensis also wrote on the Anatomy Bill, on the 'resurrectionists' activities, on the gruesome export trade in dead bodies crated and labelled 'salted herring' to the medical schools of England and Scotland. Finally there are some interesting sketches on other Dublin institutions, the Royal Dublin Society, the Royal

Zoological Society, etc — cultural bodies then much closer to the medical profession than they are today.

The noteworthy success of these sketches of the Dublin medical scene caused particular interest, if not concern, to the medical profession in London, when the following editorial note appeared in *The Lancet* on October 31, 1829:

SKETCHES OF THE MEDICAL PROFESSION IN LONDON.

This is a fit undertaking for the accurate, classic, and poetical pencil of our excellent friend Erinensis, by whom, in fact, it will be commenced, and, we hope, accomplished.

A work of this description requires much time and labour. The artist has not only a great quantity of materials to collect, but he must have frequent opportunities of *seeing* his subjects; for, without being *seen*, many of them cannot be sufficiently admired. The accuracy and beauty of our friend's Dublin sketches, have been the theme of universal penegyric, and his genius might seem to justify a speedy commencement of his graphic labours in this metropolis; but Erinensis informs us, that both animal painting and morbid delineations are somewhat new to him; hence, a careful study of the elements of both of these branches is indispensable. Thus qualified, the Owls, Bats*, Oysters, Funguses and Excrescences, will incur but little risk of misrepresentation, or false colouring. As we are exceedingly anxious that the pallet of the artist should be well furnished for giving his various subjects their peculiar and almost numberless tints, we entreat those of our readers who are in a condition to supply us with any portion, however small, of *colouring material*, to transmit it forthwith to the office of this Journal. The private character of the Editor of *The Lancet* having been treated by his opponents with great delicacy, propriety, and truth, he is anxious to show his gratitude for so much kindness and liberality, in the only way by which its intensity can be displayed.

Subjects to be sketched: Hospital Surgeons and Physicians; Authors, successful and unsuccessful; Editors; Ex-editors; Plasterers; Compilers; Dubs, and Hacks; Bats, learned, Cyclopean and Astonian; A Middlesex Owl, and one Oyster.

An account of any interesting circumstances connected with these *pretty* objects would be highly acceptable to the artist. Pedigree, professional relationship, electioneering anecdotes, and the means by which any BAT obtained his first flight, would be deemed matters or importance.

*Prostitutes favouring the night. (Partridge).

There is no evidence that Erinensis contributed to that particular project; he would scarcely have known his subjects well enough, and also was unlikely to lower his literary standards to that invective which *The Lancet* then employed against the medical profession in London.

But Erinensis *did* supplement *The Lancet's* campaign against contemporary medical editors, though in this correspondence he rarely departed from his own particular style of good-humoured raillery:

### JEMMY COPLAND

... in publica commoda peccem,
Si longo sermone merer tua tempora COPLAND.

my Dear James,

You must excuse the brevity indicated in the motto to this address. The labour of reading or writing long letters in this warm weather should be as strictly prohibited by the laws of fashionable etiquette as the dangerous exercise of dancing waltzes or quadrilles. Summer, you are aware, is the season of the body, not of the mind — of corporeal repose, not of intellectual exertion. It is a time sacred to idleness, and should not be profaned by any species of mental or manual operation. It is the grand 'Passover' of authors, when they exchange their books for brooks; emerge from groves of chimneys to enjoy the 'green-wood' shade. Hence you may have observed, that all periodicals decline in wit as the sun takes a higher station in the heavens, and that, for some time before and after the solstice, the genius of the age, like the songsters of an eastern grove at noon, seems to be in a state of suspended animation. There is, indeed, a degree of irreverence offered to Nature, if not of personal risk too, incurred, in disturbing the animal economy during this great sabbath of the year, by the tumult of argumentation, or in rousing the mind from its luxurious torpor, at a time when to think is labour, and to write is pain; when the effects of an antithesis might prove fatal from over excitement, or in epigram might operate on the brain like a *coup de soleil*. Instead of extending the limits of physiology, or deciding the fate of some new aspirant to medical fame, I should expect to find you *lentus in umbra*, at some villa in the vicinity of London, discussing may-duke cherries, or strawberries and cream...

It is so probable that Erinensis was also responsible for some of *The Lancet* editorials on the Dublin medical scene that a few of these are listed in the Appendix.

But when all these contributions of Erinensis are assessed, we have recourse once more to Dr. Johnson's lines — 'It is the personal alone, Sir, that interests mankind'. It is those personal data, pen-pictures, biographical brevities, anecdotes, and epigrams on Dublin medical men — characters all in a city ever known for its characters, that make the writings of Erinensis so valuable for the historian. Thus he reviews, like John Gilborne did in the poetic muse a half-century before, in his panegyric on the Faculty of Dublin, Physicians, Surgeons, and Apothecaries, marching in procession to the Temple of Fame. As the new generation pass by, we stand with Virgil:

> *Et tumulum capit, unde omnes longo ordine possit*
> *Adversos legere et venientum discere vultus\*.*

ABRAHAM COLLES. 'Ah! Aby, I knew thou wert ever a lucky fellow, and thou hast won the start.'

CHARLES HAWKES TODD. '... full, fat and forty.'

WHITLEY STOKES. '... who presents in his person the rare combination of the Patriot, the Scholar, and an Irishman.'

JOHN TIMOTHY KIRBY. '... they go to hear him for a certain purpose — to be amazed.

PHILIP CRAMPTON. '... of his ancestors, by far the most illustrious that we could hear of were Adam and Eve. From this venerable couple he is descended in a direct line.'

ARTHUR JACOB. '... harnessed in a pair of spectacles, so admirably fitted to the prominences and depressions of the orbitary processes, that we might have mistaken the whole optical apparatus as the natural production of the parts, or an expansion of the cornea spread out upon a delicate frame of silver wire.'

JAMES MACARTNEY. '... a very singular, if not an extraordinary personage, upon whom the panegyrist might safely lavish a portion of his art, without any risk of satirising by a misapplication of praise.'

RICHARD CARMICHAEL. '... a name which, to all acquainted with the person whom it represents, is synonymous with many excellent qualities of the head and heart.'

---

\*Then takes a rising Ground, from whence he may View the long train and every Face survey.

SAMUEL WILMOT.   '... whose powers of speech had previously
   been seldom extended beyond the Parliamentary standard in
   saying "Yes" or "No" in a case of consultation.'

ROBERT HARRISON.   '... one of those elastic persevering votaries
   of fortune, whom no coolness or procrastination of the goddess
   can repulse from her worship.'

JAMES WILLIAM CUSACK.   '... to fill up the hours of languid enjoyment between waking and rising, and preferring the couch to the
   rostrum, for delivering his discourses, the epicurean philosopher
   calls his pupils around him, removes the curtains, and, after a
   deep-drawn yawn, and a comfortable stretch, with his face
   bathed in oratorial diaphoresis commences the laborious task of
   instruction.'

These then are Erinensis' characters; there was not a genius
among them, but they were more than respectable, and equal to, if
not greater than their contemporaries in any other capital. What is
more, they were the builders of an age, never known before or since
in their country — The Golden Age of Irish Medicine.

MARTIN FALLON

'... the universitality of the sons of Erin is truly wonderful. Had Parry discovered the North-West Passage, or
Sadler succeeded in reaching the moon, there can be no
doubt, such is the diffusibility of this singular people,
but colonies of them would have been found there. They
are, to the rest of the world, what the Greeks were to the
Romans in the days of Juvenal, administering to the
necessities, the pleasures, the vices, and the instruction
of mankind. In killing or curing, lecturing or lampoon-
ing, mixing mortar or manufacturing magazines, they
are without competitors. Wellington at Waterloo, and
Burke at Edinburgh; Mr. Abernethy at St. Bartholomew's Hospital, and Dr. Shiel at the Freemasons'
Tavern; the contributors of wit to the press, and the
carriers of bricks to the buildings of London; these give
us some idea of the versatility and omnipresence of the
inhabitants of Erin; in short, wherever we turn we are
sure to see the national genius in some shape hovering
before us, like the manes of an unburied corse, through
neglect or persecution at home.'

*The Lancet*, 1829

THE ROYAL COLLEGE OF SURGEONS IN 1810.

# 1

# THE ROYAL COLLEGE OF SURGEONS IN IRELAND

BY WAY of prelude to my future operations, I shall lay open the short history of the Institution, the name of which stands at the head of this paper. Many, perhaps, of your English readers may have never so much as heard of this establishment, the members of which, with the exception of a few, are not over solicitous about what is called making a noise in the world. Perfectly content with the profits of their profession, they are not troubled with a 'longing after immortality'. The rest of the medical world they look upon as a sort of *Jackal*, formed for their use; but they have no idea of quitting the old *lair* of routine and custom, in quest of enterprise and discovery. If others have the labour of invention, the advantage derived from putting in practice what is new satisfies their ambition. Alive only to the impulses of self-interest, they seem to borrow the tone of their character from the heartless rapacity and monotonous scene of desolation by which they are surrounded, for here there is but one struggle between the avarice of the aristocracy and the poverty of the people. It is no wonder then, that men who aspire to belong to the former class of individuals should be found deeply tinged with their vices. But to resume the proposition with which I commenced: As late as the year 1806 the proceedings of the Royal College of Surgeons in Ireland, which was first chartered in 1784, were conducted in an outhouse situate in the midst of a scene

15

of matchless misery, at the rear of Mercer's Hospital, in Stephen-street. The concern at that period, although proportionate to the existing wants of the Society, was upon a small scale, being princi-pally confined to one apartment, which served the two-fold purpose of a lecture and dissecting room. A few seats of plain pine, temporarily put together, without even the embellishment which the painter bestows on those occasions, accommodated the limited audience, while they were separated by this means from the 'High Priest', who officiated in the centre. 'Twas here in a noonday twilight, when the sun's rays were entangled in the meshes of invio-lable cobwebs, or excluded by the impenetrable dust of the windows, that Dease, whose bust of 'polished Parian' now presides, in the majesty of contemplative attitude over the treasures of the New Museum, was wont to give his 'little Senate laws'. 'Twas here, in the midst of crowded and crumbling ruins, that Irish surgery drew its first breath, and afterwards issued forth in the person of Professor Halahan, swaddled in native *frieze*, and with one spur to stimulate his Rosinnate, to the great delight of the citi-zens. Such was the origin of the subject of the present memoir — an Institution, nurtured in the lap of filth; but which now basks in the sunshine of at least Irish popularity.

Here then let oblivion for ever rest upon the old establishment, and the obscurity of its birth; henceforward we shall only speak of a neat little structure which suddenly arose upon the scite of the Quakers' burial ground, at the corner of York-street, Steven's-green. On the 17th of March, 1806, the usual ceremony of laying the first stone was performed by the Lord Lieutenant, and as it now stands it reminds one very strongly of the appearance of these people, whose relics it has sacrilegiously supplanted, it looks for all the world like the genius of Quakerism personified in stone. Solid and substantial, no gewgaw of the Sculptor's art disfigures the sim-plicity of its style. With a facade of six pillars of Portland stone resting upon a basement of mountain granite, and supporting a cornice terminating in an angle at top; it stands the pride of Irish surgery, and the terror of many a candidate, whose fate often depends upon its decrees. Nothing can be more elaborately finished than the mere architectural appointments of this building — it is securely slated — accurately glazed — the doors are chinkless — everything in fact wears the look of comfort and prosperity —

while a flight of steps, by which we are just about to ascend to the front entrance, proclaims by their unsullied whiteness, that few have access to this Mansion of Corporate Exclusion. Would that the soul which should animate this structure were equal to its architectural excellence. But the proverb says, that 'Corporations have no spiritual appendages', nor does this establishment promise to impugn the veracity of the adage. Having gained admission, our attention is divided between two objects, a hall, which with a little more elevation would be grand, and a gentleman in black, with snowy temples — raven voice — and a *wild Irish* physiognomy — who perambulates here with an air somewhat unsuited to his avocation. This is no less a personage than Sir P–r C–y, the clerk of the College — a bustling, restless, talkative sort of being, who derives his titular baronetcy from his politics, which are ultra tory. Ah! Sir P–r, you little thought when last we saw you *crossing* your forehead, and *smiting* your bosom behind a poor papist's back, that we would chastise you for your tricks; but we respect your better qualifications, and will only laugh at your foibles. The remainder of the furniture of the hall is easily disposed of; it consists of a bust of George the Third, (a type of our loyalty,) and opposite to it, where the stairs commence, rises, of gigantic dismensions, a cameleopard, the present, I believe, of one of your countrymen, to the members of this Institution. On this floor is the library, containing an excellent collection of books, destined, as it would seem, for the worm and not the student, as the place is only accessible in company with a member or a licentiate. A hard case to be sure; '*Sed. quid ego, hæc autem nequicquam ingrata revolvo*'. For brevity sake, then, I will suppose that we are together in the museum, which, if report says truth, eclipses all other repositories of this kind, in the number, rarity, and excellence of its anatomical preparations, and specimens of morbid anatomy. It consists of one apartment, about the size of an ordinary bed-chamber, with one window to supply it with light. This trifling inconvenience could be easily got over, if the persons were admitted there: but, like the books underneath, it is kept more for ornament than use. It would be a superfluous task to enumerate the contents of this place; they are just such as are always found in similar places, and only valuable in proportion as liberality extends the means of studying them to advantage. Adjoining the museum is the board-room, where the examinations are latterly held. At each end of this splendid apartment there are two full-length portraits of Doctor Renny and Surgeon Henthorn, vying with each other in brilliancy of carmine, and pomp of gilding. What endowments of the mind, or charms of the person, could have induced the *pictorial* muse to exhibit thus their forms to the admiration of posterity I cannot say, for neither one or the other has left, or is likely to leave any memorial that would justify the presumption of appearing on the canvass. If such be the models which the college proposes for the imitation of its future members, it will not be difficult for them to come up to those standards, who have so easily earned an oil and colour immortality. — Patience for one moment longer, and the *topography* of our sketch is finished. Distinct from all we have been describing are the anatomical concerns, and the theatres of the professors — all well arranged and convenient for their size. The anatomical theatre is said to be capable of containing 800; four, I believe, would be nearer the truth. Behind the part appropriated for the Students is a gallery intended for the public, to witness the dissection of malefactors; but they have no chance of admission now; the doors, which were on the outside, being hermetically sealed with brick and mortar: lest I suppose the back-bone of a whale, that sleeps there in venerable dust, should escape to his natural element. But the bell rings — Mr. C's carriage is at the gate — the benches fill — confusion in all its fantastic forms of juvenile levity prevails throughout the scene. The whole artillery of confectionery, from *canister* lozenges to the heavy *grape*-shot of spice nuts, is flying on all sides — while other aspirants for anarchial reputation eagerly contend for the aromatic ammunition. On another side some musical amateur amuses the audience with the fashionable song or quadrille of the day. Thus every one contributes something to increase this scene of unphilosophical tumult. Here I must cease — the folding doors open — and in hurries Mr. C — with a slip of paper, twisted round his *index* finger — a simultaneous burst of applause greets his welcome entry, but modestly declining the honour intended him, he instantly proceeds, without even returning the salute, 'Gentlemen, at our last meeting'. &c. &c. — When we meet again we shall consider the remainder of the performance. — Adieu.

ERINENSIS
January 11, 1824

## 2

## MR. COLLES

TO THE labours of Spurzheim we are partly indebted for a new
and fashionable art, which promises to divide the laurel with the
more ancient ones of painting, statuary, and engraving. By the
reduction of the German's theory to practice, the verbal draughts-
man has been armed with many resources to give effect to his
designs. He no longer appears in the limited capacity of a historical
recorder of the mere treasures and qualities of the mind; his pencil
takes a wider range, and in its lawless excursions brings home to the
canvass, with unerring fidelity, the corporeal as well as intellectual
beauties and deformities of human nature. A portrait of a Scottish
philosopher, by the facetious Peter Morris, or a Sketch of an Irish
Barrister, in the 'New Monthly', requires only the addition of
framing and gilding to rival the exertions of a Lawrence in the accuracy of characteristic delineation. — Nay more, these ingenious
productions of the pen possess many advantages over those of the
pencil, for we are not only made acquainted with every peculiarity
in the expressions of the countenance, but the mind itself is reduced
to a palpable form, and its causes explained, in those graphic
efforts of description. Does not this compound species of composition, in which an attempt is made to explain mental phenomena
upon mechanical principles, as by tracing depth of judgment to an
expanse and elevation of forehead — richness of fancy to an arch
spanning the frontal region — measuring, in short, a man's genius,
by applying the tape to his head — does not all this, taken along
with the pleasure which such performances afford to the public,

19

look like an acquiescence in the doctrine of thought being the consequence of organization? We are far from thinking lightly of this beautiful acquisition to modern discoveries, which seems to be founded upon the common consent of mankind; for who is there who has not observed the similitude that exists between the inward and the outward man? Or who has not beheld, with silent veneration, the grandeur of those architectural proportions which usually enshrine the majesty of intellectual greatness, and predicted from the lustre of the eye the intensity of that internal fire of which the former is only a feeble emanation? Those exterior marks, however, of superiority upon the 'human face divine', which challenge our admiration, we look upon at most as the effects or concomitants, and not the causes of genius, as presumed in the speculations of Phrenology. But have we been all this time describing the art of description, or attempting to 'break a lance' with Phrenologists? No, surely not; for we are just about to admit that an examination of the mental and personal characteristics of the subject of the present sketch, if it do not increase, it cannot diminish the probability of their specious hypothesis. Any person who has contemplated for a moment the contour of Mr. Colles's head, could not but make a pretty correct guess at the contents. Plain and commonplace, no eminences break the surface of this almost hairless globe, as smooth and as even as any turnip that Mr. Cobbett ever reared to mature rotundity. Precisely of the same description is the spirit (shall we say?) that resides within. One would be induced to suppose that the cause which reduced the exterior to a tame uniformity of circumference had formed the interior to correspond. To use an agricultural phrase, Nature seems to have laid down this Gentleman's head more in the *broad-cast* than in the *drill style* of cultivation. It may be for this reason that the crops which it produces are less luxuriant, and of a more average description, than if the soil had been raised into fertilizing mounds and elevations.

The jargon, however, of metaphor apart — you will please to recollect that when we had the honour of addressing you last, we supposed that you were seated beside us on one of the benches of the great theatre of Anatomy at the Royal College of Surgeons in Ireland, surrounded by one of the largest classes that has been at this Institution since the peace, in all perhaps about two hundred, a hundred and fifty of whom have dissected, or intend to dissect, this season. We also told you, that they were very noisy and ill-behaved. More than three parts of them are apprenticed to surgeons, and being neglected by their masters, and suffered to do as they please by the College, many of them must, of course, be guiltless of any knowledge of their profession! The conduct of youth thus left to themselves, without any restraint to check their levity, cannot be expected to be decorous or attentive. Their mere appearance is our present concern, and as they sit in the living panorama before us, they do not much accord with the notions which might be formed of a body of medical students. The same number of young men taken from the various counting-houses or haberdashers' shops through town, would present as much of the elements of genius, as much of the deep traces of thought, and as much of every thing else which gives a studious character to the countenance, as this blue-frocked, black-stocked, Wellington-booted assemblage of medical dandies. Gold-rings, broad and bright, glitter here and there among the artful labours of the friseur, as the hand supports the head, thrown into the attitude of mental abstraction; steel-guard chains, often without watches to protect, sparkle almost in every breast, and quizzing-glasses hang gracefully pendent from every neck; in short, the whole paraphernalia of puppyism are displayed here in the greatest possible profusion. Such is the foreground of this chequered medley of thoughtless beings, who have withdrawn our attention from the principal object of the scene.

Short as our digression has been, Mr. Colles has already de-scribed the symptoms, and detailed the treatment of, perhaps, five or six different forms of disease, and having unloaded his memory of a variety of information, he has laconically consigned the hope-less case to the grave. In this dogmatic effusion, books, authors and authorities are all run over, to arrive at the one arbitrary and everlasting conclusion, 'the truth is, gentlemen, those men knew nothing of the matter!' What an inducement to a class to read! But perhaps he has not reflected on the dangerous consequences of thus indiscriminately censuring, before a youthful audience, the labours of the living and the dead; if he had, we are sure, the innate recti-tude — the *mens conscia recti*, which is no less conspicuous in all his actions than on the azure of his carriage door, would have pre-vented him from falling into so obvious an error. He should recollect that while he is battering down the reputation of others, he is sapping the foundation upon which his own authority rests. It has been justly remarked, that man is an imitative animal; a circumstance in his natural history which Mr. Colles seems to forget, or he would not teach, by his own example, a doctrine which, had he inspected the countenances of his auditors, he must perceive was often turned against himself. Few of his pupils who have sat out his Lectures for a season, that do not make allowances for those occasional bursts of invective and exaggeration in which he delights to indulge. There are many peculiarities in his manner of lecturing; or, perhaps, his manner is in every respect peculiar to himself. We know not whether he composes his discourses or not, but certain we are that arrangement forms no part of his system of composition. So completely destitute are they of order, that no person, however versed in medical science, or the history of disease, could guess, from one sentence, what might probably follow. One transition succeeds the other wih a rapidity and abruptness which must surprise every auditor whose mind has been accustomed to move in the measured pace of regularity. He is never at a loss for appropriate terms to express his meaning; and though he evidently labours to comprise a great deal in a short space, the very effort is often at the expense of offensive diffuseness. Having premised some general principles, fiction or reality supplies him with a case. This offspring of his fancy he places in as many points of view as his invention can suggest. He seems to think that his observations should be all original, and they usually are so, merely because he wishes they should differ from every other authority. — As he proceeds in his narrative — gloomy as if the spirit of Monk Lewis had breathed upon every period, the clouds darken, dangers thicken, things grow worse; try every expedient, make use of what remedies you please, 'tis all in vain, for the melancholy spectre of his brain was predestined to destruction, and the unfortunate case only detailed to terminate in death: 'but from what cause he cannot tell'. Extremes, it is said, meet, and after having brought his patient, 'per tot discrimina rerum', to the verge of dissolution, lo! he recovers, and again the student is consoled with another 'why he cannot tell'. Thus from one end of the discourse to the other, does our learned Professor labour in an intermittent of scepticism and despondency, or sink into the *coma* of paralysed astonishment. A ray of confidence or hope seldom glimmers through the dark vistas of this Gentleman's lectures. His instructions are mostly of the negative kind: he tells you every thing you ought to avoid, seldom any thing you should follow. It is singular he places no reliance on the efficacy of medicine while in the lecture room; yet his prescriptions in private practice would seem as if he took into consideration the destitute state of our numerous Apothecaries. Contrast is another weapon which Mr. Colles wields with peculiar dexterity. For this purpose, he disinters from the grave of antiquated practice some absurd proposals, perhaps the offspring of closet meditations, and placing them beside some improvement or discovery in modern Surgery, it is quite amusing to hear him comment upon the ludicrous comparison, and to see with what a gusto he enjoys the imaginary triumph. It is only on those emphatic occasions that his leucophlegmatic countenance ever betrays any symptoms of internal agitation, or that a rush of the vital current of the heart diffuses a blush over the habitual and marble-like paleness of his face. — Having seized, however, on some unfortunate theorist, a momentary flash of indignation lights up his rigid features, and like one of those birds peculiar to the Irish shores, that soars into the clouds to destroy its prey, by letting it fall upon the rocks below, he gradually poises himself upon the wings of self-sufficiency and fancied superiority, until his vengeance, from exertion, becomes expended, and then dashes out his victim's·brains upon some rugged common-place of contumelious reprobation. To him the surgical practice of every person and every country seems obnoxious; but that of France is his aversion. The latter prejudice, however, is not confined to him alone; for every thing Continental has an antimonial operation on the orthodox nerves of the profession in Ireland. It is a littleness which deserves to be treated with silent contempt. If the nature of our subject did not preclude the introduction of politics, we could easily assign a reason for this hatred of *popish* surgery.

We believe the opinions of Mr. Colles, upon the subject of professional education, are opposed to those entertained by the majority of the body to which he belongs. But we are not a little surprised that he has not taken some active means of effecting what he considers would be so conducive to the interests of society, and the reputation of the College. The remedy is in his own hands whenever he chooses to make use of it, for we have no hesitation in declaring, that if he withdrew his services from that institution, his secession would be its ruin; for there is not another individual in the profession here capable of supplying his place. Who, for instance, could have the patience to sit out the drawling of a Todd, or abide the flatulent phraseology and oratorical form of Mr. Kirby? Crampton, to be sure, might give us the poetry of surgery clad in his double mail of Siberian furs, but we doubt much if the weight of a professorship would not crush the flimsy frame of wire and whalebone that supports his studied pomposity. And should the College, in its folly, ever elevate our renowned demonstrator, Mr. Harrison, to the chair, who could withstand his torrent of words, and calmly listen to bones and splints, remedies and disease, all harmoniously arranged in jig-time to the '*tune of the Grinder*'? Under these circumstances, why does not Mr. Colles commence the work of reform? He has only to act decidedly, and success must attend his exertions. The field is open to him; let him therefore proclaim for the opening of the Museum, the establishment of a library, and education by classes. Supported by the strength of public opinion, the petty tide of monopoly and exclusion would roll harmless at his feet, as the wave dashes innocuous against the rock. While our heart can feel, or our hand direct a pen, he may be assured of our support. As to the little we have done on a former occasion, its beneficial effects are already beginning to appear; but we advise those gentlemen* who would fain appear regardless of our efforts to be more on their guard, for our labours have only commenced.

We have dealt pretty freely with the faults or rather the foibles of Mr. Colles' character: but who, in this benighted part of the world, possesses in such abundance the qualities of redemption? Without what may be called the philosophy of his art; without a particle of that enthusiasm which reconciles to the errors of a great man, without many books, and paying less attention to their contents, he is still the laborious shrewd, observing, matter-of-fact, and practical surgeon. As an operator he has many equals and some superiors; but in advice, from long experience and a peculiar

---

*When we come to treat of the Dublin Hospitals, we shall take an early opportunity of returning Dr. Graves our thanks for his gratuitous notice of the sketch of the R.C.S. in '*The Lancet*'. As he is too minute an object himself for the pencil, we shall merely point him out as a *molecule* in the mass of * * * that preside over the New Meath Institution.

tact of discovering the hidden causes of disease, he has scarcely a rival. If the case were otherwise, it were to be wondered at indeed. Any person who has spent so long an apprenticeship to his art, and under circumstances so favourable to the acquisition of knowledge, must profit by such advantages. His opportunities were of the first order for improvement, — an early education under an eminent surgeon, at an extensive hospital at which he became resident, and, subsequently, visiting surgeon, along with an extensive private practice, and a professorship of about twenty years' standing, must confer upon any individual so favoured advantages the most substantial. His labours seem to have little impaired a constitution which promises to keep for many years in sickening suspense the ambitious expectants of office, who, of course, await his removal in anxiety, to ascend another link in the scale of professional eminence. Many anecdotes, illustrative of his character, and the difficulties which he experienced in early life are in circulation, but they are not worth the trouble of recording. Perseverance, however, and connection, ultimately turned the scale in his favour, and he now stands at the head of his profession in Ireland, a living exemplification of the truth of the old adage —

'*Labor omnia vincit improbus.*'

ERINENSIS
Dublin, February 15, 1824

# 3

# MR. TODD

NEXT TO Mr. Colles in official importance, Mr. Todd presents himself, 'full, fat, and forty', for biographical consideration. His robust frame, rustic features, and ruddy complexion, along with other corresponding charms, would do equal honour to the hale member of a farming society, or the beef and claret amateur of a city corporation. His sleek, well-fed person, is a most appropriate illustration of the *ventri obedientia* of Sallust. The head, more distinguished by what it is not than by what it is, rises above his 'brawny shoulders, four feet square', by an unusually short cervical interval, and possesses many of the characteristic beauties of the Paddy Carey family. It is partially covered by a few surviving filaments of lank hair, thinly spread over its surface, which seem, notwithstanding the richness of the soil, to be perishing for want of nutriment. The eyes large, and though not sparkling with the pure flame of the diamond, yet glisten with the soft and subdued lustre of the best French paste composition. If it be true, as it has been asserted, that the mind in moments of excitement sallies through those spiritual spy-holes, a conclusion unfavourable to its activity might be drawn in the present instance, from their slow and heavy evolutions. From what we know of Mr. Todd's mental energy to the contrary, the observation does not apply in his case; but logicians say that the exception proves the rule. His forehead, denuded to a considerable extent for the years of the man, may be said to be of the composite kind, in which no particular organ predominates. A nose somewhat Roman in shape and dimension completes the personal outline of the subject of the present sketch. It is any thing but the *beau ideal* of a professor's head. As it is probable that Mr. Todd is not destined to be an object of much interest with posterity, the place of his birth, his parentage, and education, may be safely omitted. The natal incidents and juvenile propensities of great men only are worthy of record, as it is pleasing to trace through their various stages the development of those powers which astonish in the maturity of life. Presuming, therefore, that it is with the public as with ourselves a matter of the most perfect indifference in what parish our professor's cradle was rocked, or what spectacled school-dame had the honour of teaching him the alphabet, we shall pass at once, even at the risk of a breach of precedent, to an examination of Mr. Todd as he is, and leave to others if they choose to descant upon the circumstances of his nativity.

Having served a tolerably long noviciate in the drudgery of the dissecting room, he has lately emerged from the obscurity of that situation, being called by the consent of the College to the dignity of a Professorship. While he discharged the duties annexed to the former office, he was much and deservedly esteemed for the accuracy of his anatomical knowledge, and for the clear concise manner in which he communicated that knowledge of his pupils. So minute, indeed, were his demonstrations, that it is said here, that the vertebral and other ligaments expanded to a degree beyond what nature had intended. It was his worst fate, however, to have been educated under a system the contagion of which was irresistible, and to possess facilities of ascending to that pinnacle of eminence, on which the most aspiring would be satisfied to rest, without that fair competition which tries the strength of candidates for professional honours. Had he been unassisted by extraneous aid, and left to his own resources, 'tis probable he would now have escaped the ordeal of criticism; but at present he holds a situation that precludes him from neglect, and exposes him to that discussion to which all public characters are subject. The day is past when office and merit were coupled together in men's minds as cause and effect, and when the gown of a Professor, like the ark, was considered inviolate. This revolution in public sentiment is a glorious triumph over the prejudices of our blindfolded predecessors, for though the consequences of undue influence are still manifect in most institutions, yet the cynical race of the present day are not to be duped by the splendour of a name, or the length of a title. We therefore much doubt the propriety of an individual risking the quiet of his mind, by giving up a situation in which he was respected, and accepting of another where success was dubious. The transition from demonstrating to lecturing seems so easy, that the person who performs the one well might naturally expect that he would do justice to the other with equal facility; but the train of duties which the later department of surgical tuition brings along with it makes it much more difficult than the former, and he that would have the good sense to consult his own powers, and to observe the great distinction between those branches of education, would illustrate by his conduct the truth of those observations we have just advanced, and would never be afflicted with the *lumbago* at the approach of the first Monday in November. That men can excel in that situation only for which they have a strong predilection there are to many melancholy instances. There is no individual, however humbly endowed by nature, who cannot by industry, exerted in a proper sphere, ensure respect, and if he cannot command our applause, he may pass without provoking censure. It is only when men by inordinate ambition and the injudicious interposition of friends, are elevated of offices unsuited to their capacities that they excite our contempt, and become the objects of merited ridicule. A paviour, as long as he follows his own avocation of arranging stones in due order, is a very useful member of the Commonweal; but if, instead of the mallet, the sceptre is committed to his hands, is it to be wondered if he should be as worthless as one of the Holy Alliance? So it is with those who, outraging the intentions of nature, would fain ascend upon the Pelion and Ossa foundations of vanity and presumption, to those situations where none should ever presume to preside without the credentials of genius. But in a country, or to limit the application of our remarks in a body where every thing surprises without giving delights — where the ends are all, and the means nothing — where intrigue seems the soul that animates the mass, and candour is sneered at as the attribute of fools — surely in such a labyrinth of designed complexity the high-mindedness of genius stands no chance with such ungenerous competition. Such is the Surgical College of Dublin, presenting the extraordinary circumstance of the absence of men distinguished by a single discovery in modern Surgery, that cannot be otherwise explained than by a consideration of the prescriptive principles upon which it has been founded. Established at an era when science of every description was making a rapid progress towards its present perfection, but more especially that department of it which this Institution was exclusively founded to cultivate, it is somewhat singular, that the projectors did not take such measures as would ensure success. Unlike other establishments of a similar kind, this has not to contend with the dogmas of authority, or to break through the shackles of precedent. Under skilful architects, it might have assumed a form of unrivalled excellence. Instead, however, of extending its basis for the greater diffusion of its utility, it was contracted into a narrow circle of corporate monopoly. The system of education adopted was much better calculated to suit the convenience of the teacher than to advance the interests of the student. These reflections we are well aware may be by some considered irrelevant to the nature of our undertaking, but as our manner is of the rambling, digressive kind, we wish to turn even our faults to some advantage, by giving our professional readers upon the other side of the Channel some idea of a state of things here, which, we understand, they mean shortly to make a subject of Parliamentary investigation. We wish they may do so, but with feelings differing widely from theirs, 'for our first best country ever is at home.' The measure which they propose, if successful, will lead to results the very reverse of those indended, and precisely what we wish of all things should take place, — a re-action in the persons concerned in the professional education in Ireland.

Of the system, at which we have only glanced, Mr. Todd, we are sorry to say, is an ardent admirer and an able champion, if we take as indications of his sentiments and powers the elaborate eulogiums which he lavishes upon this institution in his introductory lectures. It happened to be on one of those solemn occasions, at the opening of the winter session, when the effluvia of musk and lavender, combined with the jetty lustre of kid gloves and silken hose, confer additional interest upon the person of a professor, and give a sensual delight to the intellectual banquet prepared from an Encylopædia, that we first had the pleasure of hearing Mr. Todd hold forth with an enthusiasm quite amusing, upon the transcendant superiority of his own beloved institution — the Surgical Corporation of Dublin. To us the exhibition was no less amusing than it was new, but even the charms of novelty were soon lost in those feelings excited by some opinions of the grave speaker. Had we been less versed in the history of our profession, we might have supposed that the Colleges of Paris, Edinburgh and London were but planets of a minor order, and that the *Alma Mater* of York-street was the glorious sun round which they revolved at an immeasurable distance. When we recollect the serious composure of countenance with which he warned his junior auditors, as he called them, against the horrors of foreign surgery, and when we recollect that on the following day in his discourse upon that eternal common-place of introductory flourishing — digestion, he was compelled to borrow from those sources which he had so lately and so wantonly attacked, we know not whether to weep for his ingratitude, or to smile at his presumption. Surely it is not well to turn thus upon our professional parents, of whom we are but the degenerate offspring, or the servile imitators — 'tis not well to revile those men, the repetition of whose experiments, and the detail of whose labours, confer upon us a temporary semblance of learnedness — 'tis not well, after having made ourselves masters of our neighbours' treasures, to raise our puny hands and tear from their brows the laurels which they have so dearly earned, and in the genuine spirit of legitimacy, defend our spoil 'by the right of conquest'. — No! the philosophic mind shrinks from the disingenuousness of detraction — it recommends with caution — censures with reluctance — and if it discovers any perfection beyond its own attainment, it envies not, but admires. It knows no distinction but that which merit constitutes. It is not influenced by any of those petty local prejudices which sway the ordinary mass of society. It embraces within the sphere of its benevolence every scientific man of every country, and considers them as so many coadjutors in the one grand undertaking — the diffusion of knowledge for the amelioration of the sufferings of the human race. It should be recollected, and it must strike every person who reflects upon the history of the past, that the systems which are now the fashionable standards, may appear to future generations as visionary as those of a century back seem to us; that they are but the 'Cynthias of a minute' to be lost in the 'heliacal rising' of some future discovery.

Digressions, like crimes, generate others. Nature, ever capricious in the distribution of her favours, gives to some personal, to others mental advantages; to few only a combination of both. The

accomplished speaker and the man of deep research are seldom
found united in the same person. To make a strong impression
upon the minds of an audience, a conjunction of these requisites is
necessary, and in no case, perhaps, is a graceful delivery more
essential than to a Professor. The dry details of Anatomy, and the
abstract speculations of Physiology, require no small share of ornamental illustration, to fix the attention upon subjects of so uninvit-
ing a nature. One of these requisites Mr. Todd possesses in an
eminent degree, in the other he is lamentably deficient. In other
hands the fund of knowledge which he possesses might be
expanded into all that is beautiful and useful in surgical discourses.
Perhaps it is to the *regime* of that system, with the principles of
which he seems so deeply imbued, more than to his physical defects
and cold temperament that his spiritless manner ought to be attributed. In an atmosphere of competition, where the nerves of the
mind become vigorous from the collision of ambitious rivalry, he
might appear a different man. His manner, however, which comes
more immediately within the sphere of our duty, we shall
endeavour to describe, for we would not wish to be understood as
deciding upon the professional merits of any individual. We only
touch upon the surface of things, — upon looks, words and ges-
tures, and give them, if we can, a permanency in the mirror of
description. Since the publication of 'Letters by an apprentice', in
which the system of education of the College of Surgeons was justly
censured, Mr. Todd has taken good care to obviate many objections of that writer, by giving the class an opportunity of taking a
cursory glance at the treasures of the museum. The table behind
which he stands is no longer a *tabula rasa*, with nothing to relieve
the eye from the uniformity of the scene save the refreshing verdure
of some green baize. It is now daily strewed with those rarities
which, forsooth, excel, in point of execution, even continental
ingenuity; all which Mr. Todd arranges 'in gay theatric pride', with
as much precision as an experienced butler collocates the intricate
furniture of an epicure's dinner service. To this array of morbid
preserves a watch is added, as if the speaker was about to run a race
with time, or to measure his discourse by the revolution of the
minute hand. Every thing being at length adjusted to the
professor's satisfaction, he patiently waits until the Exquisites have
drawn up their spear-pointed shirt-necks — frizzed up their curls —

settled their umbrellas — and until the last echoes of brazen boot-heels and clanking of chains have died away among the benches. The moment of inspiration commences — the speaker emunges his nose with all his might — a doleful voice, scarcely audible, something like the melancholy moan of the midnight breeze, which so few have heard, informs you that the person whom you might have supposed destitute of the organs of speech, possesses in some respect the faculties of speaking. As yet all is little more than dumb show and pantomimic solemnity. By degrees a few deep inspirations bring the vocal organs into a more perfect state of modulation, while each word, separated from its fellow by a considerable *hiatus*, is followed up, *pari passu*, with a delectable accompaniment, reverberated through the mazy labyrinths of the nose. The invariable monotony of the Gregorian note only can rival the *sing-song* solemnity of this surgical ditty. In vain you expect that the importance of the subject, the presence of an audience, and the situation of the speaker, would call forth some animated exertion. But his narrative is never enlivened by any of those practical anecdotes and *double entendres* with which Mr. Colles occasionally sets his hearers in roars of laughter. He does not possess the same colloquial fluency or tact of discrimination which are the principal attractions in the Lectures of the latter gentleman. Yet with these defects the student who will be satisfied with mere instruction, such as a candidate going in for his examinations, as it is termed here, will be much improved by attending Mr. Todd's lectures. But to do so requires no small share of patience, along with a flow of animal spirits, or he will enter the lecture room as gloomy as if he had been on a visit to the cave of Trophonius. Independent of the delivery, it is to be regretted that there are many virtues in these lectures which, by bad management, turn out downright blemishes. Unlike Mr. Colles in this respect, this gentleman seems to have some notion of the utility of arrangement, but from a confusion of parts tolerably well executed the same results follow as if no idea of order had existed. There is in general a *proem*; it may be, and sometimes is, a good one, but either itself or its echo will surely be repeated twice or oftener, during the remainder of the discourse. So with the other parts of the lecture, until the 'Diruit, ædificat, mutat quadrata rotundis' of the Roman poet is most satisfactorily elucidated. This mixing and combining, saying and unsaying, repeating and recapitulating, loses all the effect intended to be produced upon the mind, for instead of being impressed with one connected whole, it is ultimately stupified by the frequency with which the same subjects are forced upon its attention. It is as if an architect wished to give us an idea of some particular order, and that he presented us with a model in which the same pediments, pillars, and volutes, were every where incrusted upon its surface; or, like the Indian who broke the mirror to multiply its reflections.

In the quarterly meetings of the College, Mr. Todd's voice is particularly influential, for being of those principles in academic politics which are best described by the word *ascendancy*, he is sure that his propositions will meet with the approbation of his professional brethren. So seldom indeed does any man of spirit come forward upon these occasions, that opposition is out of the question. This want of spirit is to be attributed, in a great degree, to the fear entertained by the junior members of the College, of drawing upon them the wrath of the elders. The state of Society too has no inconsiderable influence upon the destinies of Irish Surgery. Innovation in matters even purely scientific is looked upon with a jealous eye, and the member who would dare to speak his sentiments freely would be next suspected of a secret alliance with Captain Rock.

There are only two other situations to be considered, in which Mr. Todd's character is involved: his connexion with the Richmond Hospital, and the 'Dublin Hospital Reports'. The London College, in enacting a law which compels pupils from this country to attend this institution, or Stephenson's, have been much out in their calculation; for we can assure them, that from the manner in which these students are treated at either of these Hospitals, they have but little chance of acquiring a competent knowledge of their profession. We have had frequent opportunities of witnessing what we assert, in following Mr. Todd through the wards of the Richmond, wedged in, as he usually is, between a phalanx of his own pupils, while those intended for the London diploma-shop, as he politely calls it, follow in the rear at a respectable distance. How can persons thus circumstanced, repulsed on the one side by the *hauteur* of the master, and on the other by a privilege order of students, gain any information? The thing is quite impossible, particularly as there are never any clinical observations delivered. We therefore have no hesitation in saying, that any of the minor Hospitals of the city are preferable to those unwieldy Institutions. There are two medical periodicals in Dublin; of the principal one, the 'Dublin Hospital Reports', Mr. Todd is one of the Editors, and a constant contributor. If an illustration of the want of energy in the surgical profession in Ireland were required, this publication would offer in itself a most satisfactory corroboration of the remarks we have made upon this body. It is published but once a year, so that its visits are like angels', 'few and far between', and seems to be got up for no other purpose than to register, in capital letters, the names and titles of thirteen or fourteen surgeons and physicians at the head of the same number of articles. When it is considered that there are annually admitted into the Dublin Hospital from eight to ten thousand patients, and that out of this vast number there are but some twenty cases reported, astonishment is by no means an unnatural feeling; nor can censure be misapplied. Look here, you who annually waste the 'midnight oil' in preparing invectives against the Institutions of every other country — look here into this mirror of your own making, and learn from your insignificancy to appreciate at least, if you cannot rival, the example of others. Oh! for some men to break the lethargic spell by which the profession of Ireland are bound, and to infuse into their torpid veins some portion of that spirit which animates every country but this. Shall we ever see the fetters that bind the Irish genius struck off by some superior intellect? Shall we ever behold in the profession of our country a man possessed of this sublime daring of a Cooper, — the philosophic research of a Home, — and the accomplished genius of a Lawrence, no less distinguished for his scientific attainments than by the fearless independence with which they are promulgated, and the scorn he would feel for any thing like a mean and mercenary retraction of opinions? To expect such a change would be to speculate farther than sober reason would warrant, as long as the present order of things exists. We therefore be content with hoping for more auspicious times.

ERINENSIS
Dublin March 21 1824

# 4

# DR. STOKES

A WRITER whose name we cannot recollect, informs us that every duty has its concomitant evils, a truism not without meaning when applied to ourselves, as we find that the office of biographer is not wholly exempt from unpleasant consequences. For be his pen steeped in the 'milk of human kindness', or saturated with the gall of asperity; let him flatter where merit does not exist, or censure where abuses provoke chastisement; 'tis all the same, he is sure not to please his implacable world. The undiscriminating who see perfection in all things, ask for still more praise, while the malignant whom nothing short of injustice will satisfy, cry out — lay on the lash with a bolder hand. On the other side, the morbid thirst of vanity for applause is not to be slaked — no more than the ambition of mediocrity can bear to be reduced to its proper level. It is one of the inseparable failings too, of men in power, not to forgive any thing which their self-love may construe into an injury. They prize their persons and their pretensions as a Jew does his beard, and are not to be approached but with veneration. In this respect they resemble royalty, amenable to no laws, and above public opinion. The halo of importance with which their pride invests them, is to suffer no obscuration from comparison. As long as their name is inflated with by an official title, the bubble is not to be burst by the rude hand of examination. Yet these men will pay an artist to perform that which they deny our right of executing gratuitously, and will challenge all whom it may concern, by an advertisement in a newspaper, to witness the extent of their learning and the powers of their genius. Strange inconsistency! but, knowing the necessity of these assumed appearances to veil the nakedness of pretension from the gaze of derision, we are less disposed to quarrel with the almost pardonable craftiness of impotence. Ever since it was our lot to dip our hands in ink, our ears have been stunned by the murmurs of discontent or amused by the silly conjectures of sundry individuals, as to the identity and intention of the author of the 'sketches in *The Lancet*'. Poor Sir Peter* *ululates* plaintively as an Irish Banshee over the fate of the College; but his sorrows have been latterly somewhat consoled by the sympathetic sighs of Mr. Colles, who with a vindictiveness, of which we could not suspect him, has made common cause to discover the aggressor; and as for Mr. Todd whom the approach of the first of May was beginning to revive, he has a confirmed relapse of the Lumbago. One will have it, that our remarks have been written to gratify the rage of disappointment. Another with much about the same accuracy, but with more charitable feelings, attributes them to the overflowing of bilious malignity; a third accuses a rejected candidate, of speaking so lightly of the merits of the Surgical Corporation; while a fourth put the crime to the account of an irritable little gentleman, merely because his inditing of a few medical pamphlets gives a colour to such a suspicion. To those diviners, whose guesses are about as correct, as the responses of the sybilline leaves, we deign not to explain our motives, or to apologise for our conduct. They will both answer for themselves. 'Tis not therefore to allay the fever of the curious that we have touched upon this question, but to set aside in future all conjecture, and to protect the innocent from the penalty that should only fall on the guilty. We assure them that in secreting our name, we will at least in this one respect imitate the immortal Junius, and that their suspicions, like the labours of the Danaides will be unavailing in the end. We will only add to what we have said upon this subject, that it is not against persons, but a system we inveigh — a system that has converted the temple of science into a mart of imposition and intrigue, — that has profaned the purity of her altar by the elevation of a 'Lama' to the exclusion of the true divinity of Genius.

Even in the desolateness of the desert there are spots of vendure and of shade, where the weary traveller may repose, and cool his

*Sir Peter Courtney.

lips with the waters of some refreshing spring — where the song of some solitary wanderer like himself will harmonize his feelings to the contrast of past suffering with present enjoyment, and reconcile him to the endurance of toilsome and perilous futurity. On the sterile chart too of criticism, through which we have to steer our course, it is some consolation that there are objects to which we can turn with pleasure, and contemplate with unmixed delight. Such is the subject of the present essay, a man who can never be looked upon without respect, or known without being admired. Already beginning to stoop to the influence of time, like a sear leaf bent upon its stem in autumn, we approach him with a deferential feeling inspired alike by his virtues and his years. A blue roquelaire, hanging carelessly from his shoulders, conceals beneath its classic folds, a form of slender proportions, unincumbered by *sartorial* embellishment. But under this unstudied simplicity of appearance so conformable to the habits of studious old age, we may say with the poet: '*ingenium ingens latet hoc sub corpore*'. And as he now hurries on before us in imagination from the Lecture room to bury himself once more in the beloved solitude of the library, he seems as if unconscious of all around him, and that his thoughts were fixed upon something ulterior to the earth on which he treads. The patriachal repose of his aspect and the unaffected dignity of his demeanor are enlivened by those finer tints of feeling contracted from a long communion with the spiritualities of Creation. — Ascending from the effect to its cause, he seems to have only commenced his enquiries, where others conclude theirs, and to have by an insatiable curiosity directed by reason and assisted by a powerful mind, penetrated the mysterious ways of providence in the distribution and production of its works. In this arduous voyage, wherein so many have failed from the tenuity of an ideal atmosphere, he has happily reached that point of science attainable only to the few. There is none of the trickery, none of the artifice of would-be philosophy about him — he is what he would pass for, 'An honest man, the noblest work of God', and a living satire upon the majority of the medical profession in Ireland. We need not inform our readers here at least, that the person whom we have been attempting to describe, is their venerable countryman Dr. Stokes.

Of the early history of this distinguished individual, we regret to say our information is limited. It would be a pleasing task to trace

him through all the gradations and vicissitudes of life, to walk with
him in the morning of existence, when hope first put forth its vernal
shoots — to sympathise with his sorrows is disappointment — to
contemplate the vigour of his mind in the maturity of manhood —
to mark by what exertions he became a proficient in every department of science, — and to learn from his patient, uncompromising
independence to persevere against persecution and adversity. But if
this pleasure and improvement be denied us in the absence of the
first pages of his history we have the moral of his labours to recom-
pence us for the deficiency which we cannot supply. As early as the
year 1788, he became a fellow of Trinity College, and continued in
the discharge of his duties in a manner no less profitable to his
pupils, than honourable to himself, up to the memorable era of
1798. From this period to 1802 there was little tranquility in
Ireland. Its inhabitants tortured into madness by persecutors
numerous as the patronage of an heartless Government multiplies
those pests of society, were compelled at length to vindicate themselves by opposing force to force. If in this natural struggle for self-
preservation, there were implicated characters otherwise respectable, it is less to be wondered at than if there had not. Accordingly
we find, that in this last effort of suffering humanity, to extricate
itself from the deadly grasp of that serpent, in whose coils it had for
centuries been patiently entwined, persons in every department of
society participated. The senate, the bar, the medical profession,
and even the protestant Church itself, poured forth its votaries to
the cause of independence who could relinquish the certain enjoyment of bloated benefices, for the dubious success of revolutionary
warfare. In short there were persons of all professions either openly
connected with, or who secretly sanctioned the enterprize into
which their harassed into which their harassed countrymen had
embarked. The park of freedom elicited by the collision of contending parties having next fallen into the University, was soon
fanned into a threatening flame by the declamations of many an
embryo Brutus. — During this period however, the notorious
Clane* happened to be Vice-Chancellor of the College. To purify
the hallowed sanctuary of religion from the taint of sedition, and
pike-errantry, he expelled many of the students, and condemned

*Lord Clare

Dr. Stokes to three years of probationary degradation, as a penance for a crime of which there was no proof, except that which existed in the suspicion of his lordly inquisitor. Struck with the injustice of the sentence pronounced on their esteemed associate, the Fellows of the College resolved upon presenting a petition praying a mitigation of the punishment. The voice of the whole body was in his favour, except William Magee, at present the Archbishop of Dublin, and now pretty well known here by the name of Doctor Syntax, to which ideal personage it is said he bears a strong resemblance. In this shameful transaction, at all events, the said Syntactical Doctor gave proofs of his qualifications to set out on a pilgrimage in search of the *sublimities* of this world. Against the wish of all the Fellows he refused to sign the petition — he triumphed in his mercenary speculation, — obtained the next senior Fellowship, which Doctor Stokes would have been elevated to, had he not been the victim of unmerited persecution. But the same liberality of sentiment which exposed him on former occasions to the abuse of power, doomed him to still severer trials, for we find he became again the butt of intolerance, being compelled, in consequence of some objections to his religious opinions, as there could be none to his virtue to relinquish altogether a College life, after holding a Fellowship for thirty-four years. Fortunately for him, however, he possessed those resources over which his enemies could have no control — the accumulated treasures of nearly half a century's laborious study. Since the late change in his circumstances, he has exclusively practised as a physician, and with considerable success notwithstanding the silly prejudices which exist in this country on the incompatibility of literary pursuits with professional avocations. A few years back he was appointed Professor of Natural History to the Medical Department of the University — a situation which could not be committed to abler hands. From one who possesses every requisite for the study of this beautiful science: — such as a knowledge of most languages — the advantages of foreign travel — and above all, an enthusiastic admiration of the works of nature, a display of no mean type might be expected. To the improvement to be derived from those lectures, the pleasure of attending them gratuitously is superadded; for during their delivery in the Natural Philosophy Hall of the college,

'No surly porter stands in awkward state,
'To spurn th' imploring *student* from the gate',

the worthy professor generously permitting all who wish to attend
his discourses. Of course we have taken advantage of this
immunity; and as often as an advertisement from the Academic
Portal informed us of Dr. Stokes's twelve lectures, on some
subjects of Natural History, we hastened to enjoy the treat. It is
here perhaps the best idea of his manner and powers may be
formed; for in discussions of this nature he is quite 'at home'. His
world in miniature being arranged previous to his entry, he walks
forward modestly but manfully with nature's own credentials
stamped upon his brow, and centered in his looks, addresses his
audience — 'Gentlemen, the object of this lecture is profit, the
subject &c. &c.' giving its name whatever it may be. You would
perceive at once, even before he opened his lips, that he is not of the
common mould. The forehead, awful to a degree from its magnitude, is finely formed, and intellectual in the extreme; the eye rolling in its liquid element of benevolence, tells you in language not to
be misunderstood, that here is a tear for misfortune, while the
native energy of its fire still beaming from under the time-drooping
lids, would seem, like a beacon in the storm, to invite the houseless
to a home; and then the halo of philanthropy that encircles his
whole countenance, concentrating in its conciliating softness all
you could expect from the ablest artist in realizing upon the canvass
'another kiss of peace'. Never was the triumph of the soul in its
tracings and impressions upon the temple of its abode, more
manifest than in the physiognomy of Dr. Stokes. His is a true copy
of the '*os sublime*' — in him the happy definition of the bard is
fully realised. His delivery, or rather his reading, for he writes upon
all his subjects, presents little to warrant any particular description.
His voice is weak, so that it cannot be heard at a great distance, and
is occasionally interrupted, as if the organs of speech were not
under the influence of volition, or as if the flow of ideas was too
rapid for distinct enunciation. Besides the excellence of the matter
in his discourses, the composition is invariably correct — sometimes beautiful and sublime, as the subject admits. From the
meanest reptile up to the last link which reasoning man forms in the
chair of creation, every object is sketched with a masterly hand.

The secrets of the earth are explored by a descent into some fathomless mine — mountains are ascended, their height calculated, and their production accounted for upon the volcanic principle with a hypothetical accuracy quite surprising. But if in this comprehensive view of the Universe, any thing bearing upon the state of his country or the malignity of man should present itself, it is then every fibre of his heart vibrates to the theme, and his noble feelings rush in a torrent of indignant digression. In a moment the 'green hills' of his country that now lie blasted beneath the service of oppression, are clothed with bleating flocks, and re-echo the 'piping' of happy shepherds — the valleys that are doomed by the present order of things to produce a tenth of their fruit, to be confiscated in the name of God, pour forth the superabundance of their fertility into granaries for the relief of the poor — the mines of Wicklow only wait the hand of industry to bring back another 'Age of Gold' — and even the bleak heights of Connemarra were already beginning to feel the genial warmth of blazing coal-fires, eviscerated from those mountains by the application of steam. Robert Owen himself, in his brightest dreams of regeneration, might *envy* the protractor of so blissful a scene. The

> *'Flumina Jam lactis, jam flumina nectaris ibant',*
> *'Flava que de viridi stillabant ilice mella'*

of the silver-tongued Ovid falls short of his promised land of milk and honey. For awhile he smiles upon his Elysian offspring of his fancy — but doubts soon begin to rise — he casts a scowling glance upon the incorrigible mar-plot man — the vision melts from his agonizing gaze — and hope itself becomes ultimately the parent of despair. Nor does the culprit pass with impunity — his abuse of power, perversion of intellect, and dangerous ambition, are all chastized in a manner no way flattering to his vanity as lord of the universe. The frugality of the ant teaches him temperance; the social habits of the beaver instruct him in domestic tranquillity; and the pure virtues of the Indian, in his native wilds, are called to bear witness against the perfidiousness of civilization. Digressions of this nature often bring the Lecturer to a favourite subject — Political Economy, a science in which he is profoundly skilled. His knowledge in this respect is profound, for we believe he could without any great exertion of memory, state the relative bearings

not only of British commerce and manufactures, but of those of
every other country where they are cultivated. Of the correctness of
his views we cannot pretend to speak, but sure we are that they are
opposed to be legislative views which have reduced this country to a
colony of paupers, and have the merit of being on the side of
humanity. Having concluded his lecture, he lays aside the didactic
formality of their Profession; the elevation of the Naturalist subsides into the dignified familiarity of the companion — seated upon
the end of his table, he is surrounded by his pupils, and inculcates
by a practical illustration those amenities of life of which he is so
warm an advocate, and so perfect an example. Oh it is a pleasing
prospect thus to behold the virtues of old age amalgamating with
the feelings of youth, and rendering them divine even for a
moment, by the contagion of a sympatheic communion. But there
are things which will not melt into description even in the most
skilful hands, and our admiration warns us to beware. We trust our
silence therefore will be more eloquent than words, since neither
our limits nor capacity will allow us to enter at greater length into
the merits of this talented individual, who presents in his person,
the rare combination of the Patriot — the scholar — and an
Irishman.

ERINENSIS
Dublin, April 10, 1824

# 5

# MR. KIRBY

THERE ARE few names in the Medical world, better known than
that of John Timothy Kirby, if we except those which occupy a
standing place in the daily Journals — such as Solomon and James.
Well might this singular individual exclaim, '*Quæ regio in terris
nostri non plena laboris*', for in every habitable clime, from the
Equator to the Pole, where the genius of Irish emigration could
find a resting place, there are thousands dying of his precepts, or
daily restored to health by the judicious re-application of his skill.
It is no small tribute to his laborious industry, that his fame is commensurate with the glory of the British arms: into whatever part of
the globe they have carried victory and desolation, the scions of his
surgery have ramified, while the parental stem twining its roots in
the kindred soil of the Coburg Garden, Harcourt-street, still luxuri-
antly flourishes in all the pomp and vigour of undiminished exuberance. Long may it wear its leafy honours, and put forth its annual
blossoms, so full of promise and disappointment. '*Non semel deci-
mus, io triumphe!*' — That interesting portion of Ireland, which in
these happy times, goes by the name of the 'South', and which now
bids fair to be long the inheritance of 'Rack', and misrule, has the
honour, we are told, of giving birth to the subject of this memoir,
as it has of being the nurse of many other adventurers, who, if
traced to their '*domus Ilium*', might be found employed in the
alternate avocations of translating Homer and footing turf. From
the democratic floor he ascended at an early age to be 'attics' of a
College dormitory, a transition by no means uncommon in this
country, where instead of 'Moll Flanders', as lately asserted by one

of her 'faithless sons' in the House of Commons, the classics are often taught under the shade of the hawthorn. About the same time he commenced his Surgical studies under the auspices of Professor Halahan, and was one of the twenty-five, who then composed the class of the Royal College of Surgeons in Mercer-street. Having kept his terms in the usual way, and with the usual improvement, he obtained the degree of Bachelor of Arts. His whole time however was not devoted, it seems to Parnassian lore, or to his 'Anatomia Britannica', for we find that at another school he was still more successful than at the temple of the muses, since instead of his courtship being rewarded with the sterile enjoyment of stamped parchment, he contrived to win the heart of a more substantial Euterpe — the fair daughter of a Mr. Rose, who was returning to enjoy in his native land, the 'showers of Barbaric gold' he had accumulated in the East. The *ci-devant* nabob's talents not having fructified, as Mr. Kirby had anticipated, he was of course thrown pretty much upon his own resources, and the event proves that they were not unequal to his hopes. He lost no time in preparing himself to commence the world, and shortly after his nuptials he became a licentiate of the College, to which he was subsequently appointed assistant demonstrator, and is at this time, President. From servitude however his elastic mind rebounded, and he determined to become master himself. Possessed in no mean degree of the '*ingenium velox*' and '*audacia perdita*' so necessary for such an enterprise, and having a keen anticipation of the time when his paternal ears were to be greeted with 'Papa, Timmy wants new shoes', he thought he could not do better than turn lecturer. Many circumstances, however, besides the mere impulse of ambition, and a presentiment of the wants of lisping infancy, conspired to fix him in this choice, and to inspire him with the hopes of success. But a dispute with a deceased professor, as it separated him from the College and annulled his expectations of preferment in that quarter, confirmed him more fully in this resolution. Much about this time, too, the 'demon of Corsica' had 'let slip the dogs of war' upon the Peninsula; but that Providence which 'tempers the wind to the shorn lamb', seems to have raised Mr. Kirby as an antidote to the impending desolation, and, perhaps, he felt himself, by some internal inspiration, that he was reserved for this high destiny. Be this as it may, to him, the firing of the first gun that announced the passing of the French army over the heights of the Sierra Morena, was music of that agreeable kind, comprising the '*utile dulce*', and the succeeding cannonades, telegraphed from the Isle of Leon, were pregnant with meaning, for he sapiently conjectured that where there was so much noise, it was not too much to presume that there were some bones broken also, and that they would of course require 'surgical assistance'. Besides these manifestations of fortune in his favour abroad, the goddess condescended to make known her divine will at home, as there was shortly after a commission received by the principal practitioners of this city to send out such of their pupils as they considered competent to the important duties of cutting adhesive plaster and of attending as nurses upon the sick. — His 'vision' of future success was now no longer, 'baseless' as this confirmation of its correctness placed it upon a stable foundation. To meet therefore, this new demand in the surgical market, and to heal the bleeding wounds of his countrymen, 'a house with back concerns' was hired in Peter street, and by a summary process of mechanism, was converted into an anatomical theatre. The establishment was no sooner fitted up, than it was crowded by a motley audience of every possible shade of character. Apothecaries, old and young, spurning their lowly avocation bade an eternal adieu to the pestle and their native hamlets, and committed themselves to be ground at Mr. Kirby's mill. The class was numerous and soon assembled, but there was still wanted an appendage to the 'concern' to make it complete, for the pupils on going to London were required to produce certificates of attendance at some Hospital. An Hospital was therefore added, of dubious character, no doubt; but the form, and not the substance, it seems, was all that was demanded by the Examiners on the other side of the channel. There was then no 'Lancet' to set them right — to expose the evil tendencies of professional chicane — and to unravel the sophisticated webs of reviewers, whose accommodating creed consists in the convertibility of truth into falsehood. But to return — in this celebrated *La charitê* of Peter-street, there was but one bed, and we assure our readers that when we visited the place, there was no bottom in the same. When a case, however, presented itself, remediable by Steel, the scattered members of the bed were collected, and if the result of the operation happened to be favourable, it was made known in due course through the medium of the morning journals.

Such was the origin of this Institution, and of Mr. Kirby's fame — commencing in a favourable combination of circumstances, and carried to its present maturity by a singular acuteness — a property seldom found connected with the higher order of mental attributes, that are too often useful to all but their possessors.

Surrounded as Mr. Kirby is with a multitude of extraneous appendages, and yet so intimately blended with them all, so that it may well be said '*Mens agitat molem, et magno se corpore miscet*', how can we attempt to grapple with so complicated a subject, ignorant as we are of those arts he has made subservient to the extension of his professional celebrity? The graceful swing of his chaise, as it plays upon the obedient springs would learn to be communicated by his own more versatile movements — in the solemn rumbling of its wheels, imagination conjures up the awe-inspiring pathos of his oratory. And in the varnished stiffness and profusion of its embellishments, fancy cannot fail of finding a similitude for the gaudy tints of his rhetorical tulips. 'All', indeed, 'are but parts of one stupendous whole'. The very horses as they toss their heads on high, seem proud of their subjection to so stately a master, the light azure livery and silver lace of the mortal Phæton, holding the reins, are but the creation of his fertile invention; and the military shoulder knots of a blooming boy, perched like another Ariel upon the box behind, are emblematic of his picturesque taste. The entire equipage looks big with importance, and as it flouts your gaze in its rapid motion over the muttering pavements, you would think fortune herself was dragged into captivity at its wheels. In a city where merit and prosperity are considered as a cause and effect, such artifice is by no means unnecessary to insure success, nor should we censure the adoption, when confined within the bounds of moderation. But the practice is of such easy attainment, that it has been very generally abused, for since Mr. Kirby's success in this way has been known, his example has been followed by a host of imitators. We can scarcely pass a street that we do not meet numbers of those busy idlers, who to all but themselves appear overwhelmed with practice. One hurries away in a hired gig to No. O; another is all mud to the shoulders on horseback, after a *profitless* excursion to the Rock; and a third, an humble pedestrian, 'plods his weary way' through the crowd, to be seen in the vicinity of some door with a muffled rapper. — This precedent has doomed us to still greater afflictions, 'all quit their spheres and rush into the skies', we have lecturers on surgery whose operations were confined to the opening of a vein, and who retail 'Cooper's Dictionary', at stated prices and hours; in short, we have hospitals without patients, and patients without surgeons, — and professors in all the Ologies at the tender age of twenty-one! Thanks to Mr. Kirby for this race of beardless Esculapians. We sincerely hope 'they will increase and multiply', as the scriptural mandate enjoineth, and that they will beget didactive abortions to the end of the chapter. Few of them however will be able to rival their grand prototype, in being the founders of so profitable an establishment as Peter-street. Indeed we think it improbable that any individual however zealous in the cause of charity and science will ever come up to the unapproachable perfection at which Mr. Kirby has arrived. In every art there has been some extraordinary personage with whose name excellence is associated. In poetry we have but one Homer — a Demosthenes in oratory — a Walren in the Strand — and only one Kirby in the whole world. He has embodied himself with the public mind. He lives upon their lips, and has made himself, 'a local habitation' in their breath. — Wonder and mystery are the attributes of his name. The citizens look upon him with feelings of a doubtful nature, and the inhabitants in his neighbourhood are strongly impressed that his nights are spent in the exhumation of the dead, and accordingly take every precaution to secure their departed friends by depth of grave and quick rochelime, from his Mausolean depredations. The Irish have been long dubbed a superstitious race of beings, but we cannot now strip them of their fair fame; indeed there are stories told of Mr. Kirby, that would tend to prove the assertion and to place him far beyond Prince Hohenlhohe in the 'miraculous'. Has any person been *scalded to death* in the purlieus of the liberty? The unfortunate victim of hot water and whiskey was *restored to life* by some sanative application of Mr. Kirby. Has a gentleman's horse run away and *broke his master's neck*. Mr. Kirby was accidentally passing at the time and *set all to rights in an instant*. If a barrel of gun-powder explodes at the quarries of Dunleary and has sent five or six of the workmen on an aeronautic expedition; the melancholy accident is detailed next day in the Freeman or Saunders; the sly paragraph usually ending with, 'Mr. Kirby is in attendance, and

*entertains some hopes of their recovery*'. The ephemeral publicity
to be derived from newspaper notices, though very useful, was not
sufficient for Mr. Kirby. The fascination of authorism on a more
extensive scale had too many charms to be resisted, and yielding to
the temptation, he committed himself to the Press in a seven
shilling octavo of sixty or seventy pages. It contained many successful cases and an essy laudatory of the virtues of *Stramonium* in
various nervous affections. We had it in contemplation to celebrate
the 'Stramonium Redivivum', in a dirge over the other exploded
Narcotics, and had written as far as the following stanza:

> 'And what is opium but a name?
> A drowsy drug at best,
> A dose to dull the febrile flame,
> And lull the wretch to rest!'

When the Muse of Pharmacy interposing compelled us to desist
with the succeeding lines on Mr. Kirby's 'Killing Dulcinea'.

> 'Stramonium's still an emptier sound,
> Not worth a pinch of snuff!
> By all despised or only found,
> In Kirby's modest "puff." '

Yet this work of Mr. Kirby's met with the most unqualified
praise in the Medical Repository, no doubt a 'fellow feeling makes
us wondrous kind'. Frogs instinctively croak in concert. From
those outposts of his being, where, although absent, he may be said
to be present, if man live in his works, we shall pass to the consideration of him 'who bounds, connects, and equals all', in the capacity
of Lecturer. Of all professional recreations, to us an Introductory
Lecture has been at all times the most amusing. We have always
looked upon such an exhibition as a sort of barometric test, to estimate the extent of the speaker's powers. The subject being exclusively at his own option, will determine in some measure his judgment and resources. The execution admitting of the highest degree
of literary polish, may lead us to form some idea of his taste. And
in the delivery, by a species of lynx-eyed observations, fanciful,
perhaps, we imagine we can discover many things which may
escape the vision of the uninitiated in the art of sketching.
Burthened with such propensities it is no wonder if we should
indulge them by taking a walk to Peter Street, at the opening of the

winter campaign. There is at this period a kind of golden sympathy between pupils and professors. During the entire month of October, there are various reports afloat, and sundry preparations made to attract attention. The college depends upon the strength of its Museum, and Mr. Todd's *Nasiloquism*. Mr. Macartney of the University, to other physiological attractions, adds the sacrifice of a fat rabbit to demonstrate the gastric fluid. But *horribile dictu*, Mr. Kirby outstrips all competition by venturing upon the nine lives of a Cat! Well, then, we may suppose that the victim is bound neck and heels upon the altar, and to keep up the illusion, that the physiological high priest is consulting his oracles in the snug little cot behind the theatre, and that all without is impatient for his entrance. The opening of the door 'gives dreadful note of preparation', and in a moment the roof rocks with deafening huzzas. The dusty skeletons shake off their venerable coats, and seem to tremble into momentary animation, while the spirit of applause 'moving upon the waters' of antiseptic Inishowen, curls their surface into circling undulations. Nor can the devoted Grimalkin be all this time a silent spectator, but adding his melodious mews to the harmony already existing, leaves nothing to be desired, as Haggi Baba has it, by the lovers of discord. '*Ut primum placati animi et trepida ora queirunt*', or rendered into familiar English for the occasion,

> 'When noodle's heels had ceased the
> boards to batter,
> 'And doodle's tongue forgot its noisy
> clatter',

The Lecturer proceeds to the table, and dispatches poor puss! Having done so, he exhibits the gastric fluid, and relates many wonders of the all dissolving qualities of this fluid. His manner is an admirable comment on his mind. The sympathy between both is strikingly manifest. Every muscle seems in the most practised subjection to his will. Both mind and body are strained to the highest pitch, to produce effect. The tip-toe attitude and rapid gesture, indicate in a strong manner, the throes of ambition and struggles for popularity that are going on within. In his countenance resonant of brass, you can easily see that self possession and confidence with which he has fought his bustling way through the world, and scared death from the imagination of many a desponding invalid. He certainly possesses some requisites for speaking, and with the audience he usually addresses, he passes for an accomplished medical orator. A great deal of his success depended upon this method. Persons who have never asked themselves why they are pleased, and who have never analyzed the merits of any proposition are easily satisfied: they go to hear him for a certain purpose — to be amazed, — and do not wish to deprive themselves of the pleasure by the foolish labour of criticizing. It is no wonder, then, that his turgid declamation, set off by theatric fits and starts, has passed with such persons for eloquence. The subject, too, Physiology, is favourable to the deception. Full of mystery, and words of Grecian euphony, it is well adapted for Mr. Kirby's declamatory style. Tropes and figures jostle each other for precedence, and find in the corresponding vehemence of his action a faithful diagram, and an appropriate vehicle of conveyance in the affected intonations of his voice. He scorns the trammels of regular composition, and would think it a profanation were he to express the most simple idea without concealing its meaning, under a drapery of *sesqui pedalia verba*. There are two errors into either of which, speakers under Mr. Kirby's circumstances must fall; the one is dulness — the other, and by far the worst, is bombast. He that has never performed experiments must be content with detailing those of others, and however judiciously he may execute the task, his efforts can never possess that originality, which personal observation alone can bestow. Hence those puling, jejune effusions that are annually inflicted upon young dissectors, by teachers of anatomy in public and private theatres. If on the other hand the speaker, to avoid being dull, attempts to raise a fabric of his own upon the deductions of others, he runs a great risk of rivalling Mr. Kirby, whom the situation of a muscle, or the course of a nerve, leads into as pompous a description as if he had been treating the most important subject. This is not so much from the want of talent, as from a deficiency of material to work upon; for of the former article he has rather an abundant supply. But, having no foundation to build upon, the consequences we have just alluded to, are inevitable. Accordingly, he flounders away in the beaten track, 'paints the lily' of other men's creation, and 'gilds the refined gold' of their industry; and, like the bellows-blower who fancied himself a fine musician, he is quite in raptures with all he repeats, as if it were the legitimate offspring of his own brain. The fond Laodamia expiring in the embraces of a phantom, could not have looked more romantic or lanquishingly lovely than Mr. Kirby when the rosin-lightnings of his eyes softening into a celestial repose behind the downcast lids, he seems to contemplate in the distance some important object. — Oh! it was nothing but the shadow of his own greatness, the constant tenant of his imagination. Anon, he recovers from the self-admiring swoon, and labours to make good, in the minds of his audience, the grandeur of that being he communed with in his trance. Having regained his balance, once more upon the stilts, he stalks upon the very 'summits of declamation', leaving his audience to look up with amazement at his dizzy elevation. He next passes on to comply with that annual custom of advising pupils about what they should read. You would really think that Mr. Kirby, in his warmth of recommending classical studies, had actually caught fire at the sound, and that the beauties of the poets and orators of antiquity were as familiar to him as household words — '*nocturna versate manu, versate diurna*' was never more ably inculcated. John Hunter — the dignity of the medical profession — and an anathema upon all who would dare to practise the healing art solely for money, are the texts for many a sentence of spondaic longitude. Preaching in those cases is of little avail when not followed by example. To talk about doctors wearing big wigs, and gold-headed canes, and scarlet cloaks, and of Presidents sitting in five-and-twenty-guinea chairs, reveries which Mr. Kirby has sometimes indulged in, is worse than doing nothing — it is a gratuitous insult to the feelings of any person acquainted with the system of education in the schools of medicine and surgery in Ireland. Such vapouring and palaver come with questionable propriety from one who was the first to oppose an improvement in this neglected art, and who has been himself the prolific source of so much licensed empiricism. — How think you, Mr. Editor, would the Great Sir Astley* look, had he seen the Professor of a private school step out his carriage on his way to a levee at our castle, and in all the pomp and glitter of a court dress, diffuse his divine odours, and the flowers of his oratory over the putrifying mass of a

*Sir Astley Cooper of Guy's Hospital

dissecting-room? We fancy that the lips of the 'Surgical Colossus' would curl into a smile of contemptuous scorn at the ludicrous exhibition. But his wonder might be still more excited had he witnessed the facts upon which the following anecdote is founded: — Mr. Kirby being aware that the persons who composed his audience at one period were intended for military practice, and faithful in the discharge of his duties, he took advantage of every expedient to exemplify those cases they would have to treat. Gun-shot wounds were of course a favourite theme; as he happened not, however, to have much experience in this subject, except what he could learn from the misfortunes of an occasional duel, he hit upon a very ingenious alternative of making up for the deficiency. It was one of a strange description to be sure, but quite characteristic of the inventor. For the purpose of demonstrating the destructive effects of fire-arms upon the human frame, Bully's Acre† gave up its cleverest treasures for the performance of the experiment. The *subjects* being placed with military precision along the wall, the Lecturer entered with his pistol in his hand, and levelling the mortiferous weapon at the enemy, magnanimously discharged several rounds, each followed by repeated bursts of applause. As soon as the smoke and approbation subsided, then came the tug of war. The wounded were examined, arteries were taken up, bullets were extracted, bones were set, and every spectator fancied himself on the field of battle, and looked upon Mr. Kirby as a prodigy of genius and valour *for shooting dead men*. It is disputed, why Mr. Kirby has discontinued the *sham* battles. Some say that the return of peace has rendered his explosions unnecessary, but others with more truth affirm that the memorable pistols with which he was wont to do such execution upon the dead, were quietly delivered up by him to one of the living as he was returning on a moon-shiny night in his gig from the country. Oh! what a falling off was there! the hero of Peterloo disarmed by a foot-pad.

Many things more we had to say, but the longest day will have an end. Alas! that our light and page too, are subject to a similar fate. For had we at this moment the power of a Joshua, by a twirl of our pen, the taper should burn on still in the socket, and our paper lengthen as we wrote, until Mr. Kirby's portrait, difficult as it

†The Hospital Fields burial ground at Kilmainham.

might be to command its camelion head, would stand forth *relieved* in all the complexity of descriptive detail. But for that purpose, what sheet or mouldsix would suffice? With the expiring glimmer that flickers on our short space, we shall endeavour to say that a review of this gentleman's life, as a teacher, affords additional evidence of the imperfection of the plan of education at the School of Surgery in Ireland. There we see that the exertions of one man, attracted in the very teeth of a College, nearly as many pupils as the combined efforts of six professors, and two demonstrators, assisted by inducements and appendages. If one person then, can effect so much under the disadvantages of a faulty system, what might not be expected from the labours of so many, were they directed by the dictates of common sense? We will not, however, enter upon this important but neglected subject, until the rubbish of the old ruin is completely removed. Unpromising as the task may appear, we do not entirely despair, but like George Primrose, in his adverse rambles, begin to learn the 'knack of hoping,' and conclude with him, that as we are now at the bottom of the wheel, the next revolution may elevate, but cannot depress us to a lower state.

ERINENSIS
Dublin, May 15, 1824

# 6

# MR. CRAMPTON

*'A physician in a great city seems to be the mere plaything of fortune: his degree of reputation is for the most part totally casual; they that employ him know not his excellence; they that reject him know not his deficiency.'*

### Johnson's Life of Akenside.

THERE IS little doubt but the resumption of our place in *The Lancet* will be a subject of as deep concern to a portion of the professional body in Ireland as the suspension of our labours was one of congratulation. Week after week the trembling monopolists hurried over the pages of *The Lancet*, expecting their well-earned reward, but the Son of Erin was not there, and it was triumphantly asserted, that the wight who used to trifle so unceremoniously with professors' faces was no more. To this premature prognosis of our literary dissolution we must only reply, in the words of the philosophic poet, 'Nescia mens hominum fati, sortisque futuræ!' All is not lost that is in danger; for, lo! 'Richard is himself again', Renovated by the breezes of our dear native mountains, we shall endeavour to bring up, by 'forced marches', whatever was left undone during a summer of indolent repose. Even amidst those wilds, as we snuffed the fragrance of the 'heath and harebell dipped in dew', would our old acquaintances of the College intrude upon our solitude, and we almost longed for the day when the stage coach was to whirl us back to our city residence, mysterious as Blue

Beard's chamber, where we are now safely deposited, enveloped too in our former garb of anonymous obscurity, and reviewing, in the solemn vista of meditation, the subjects upon which our pencil shall be successively employed.

Could we give to our readers a plan of our intentions, and make them see at a glance the objects present to our mind, what a motley assemblage of men and things would they behold! Professors to be *painted*, practitioners to be *feed*, hospitals to be *described*, saints to be *salted*, books to be *reviewed*, and authors to be *chastised*. 'Quicquid agunt homines nostri est farrago libelli', shall be our motto. In short, the more minutely we inspect our subjects, the more numerous do they appear, and like the fleeting line bounding the horizon, that mocks every attempt at approach, they seem to shift their position according as we advance. We must, however, only do the best we can. The outlines of some already begin to swell into the similitude of the originals; the colours tempered and arranged upon the pallet, invite our willing hands, and though we should nightly 'outwatch the bear,' our lonely lamp shall not cease to burn until it lights us to the consummation of our designs. Should a strong and natural propensity to what is right ever give to our efforts a warmth of expression beyond what propriety would admit, we trust the candid, who in common with us feel that the accomplishment of their wishes must depend upon severe measures, will readily pardon the offence of setting off virtue at the expense of vice, and of indulging in the consolatory, some will say visionary, prospect of professional regeneration. Yet we know that society when corrupted, like stagnant water, contains within it the properties for restoring it to a healthy state; and is it, therefore, too much to assert of a system, which having arrived at the very acme of corruption, that it will one day or other be corroded by its own rottenness, and ultimately arise regenerated and purified from the dross in which it is sunk? No, surely not. The machine of Reform has received an impulse sufficiently powerful to perpetuate its motion until it turns up some substantial result. This no human power, however perverse its opposition, will be able to prevent.

A powerful effort has already been made (to which we may hereafter advert) to do away with that pernicious statute of the College — compulsory apprenticeship. It is, indeed, somewhat surprising, that when profit and popularity would be the consequences of concession, men so much alive to self-interest would not yield and enjoy both. Let them admit us but a few hours, each day, into the library and the museum, and it will go a great way to content us. Is this too much to request! Was ever Irishman so easily contented? Oh! but there is our old friend the Nasiloquist and his petty satellites, who would not for all the world suffer the Portland mosaics of the hall to be sullied by the unlearned footsteps of a pupil. Well done, Charley Hoe, if the Richmond formulary does not suffice to furnish a prescription to send thee and thy pests to rest, verily we know nothing of chemical decomposition. But we perceive we have been anticipating, and must not draw farther on the patience of our readers by deferring our narrative.

It was on one of those fine, clear, cool days that often close, in cheerful gleams of sunshine, the autumnal season, that we happened to be sauntering on the high road in the vicinity of the Dublin mountains, and enjoying the beautiful prospects which extended beneath us — the bay occasionally enlivened by the snow-white sheets of numerous pleasure boats, and as often saddened by the dusky sails of some collier, 'fetching coals to Newcastle', — Howth, like the huge Leviathan of the deep, rearing its rocky summits above the 'sleepless waves', and the city stretched out in ample circumference below us, seeming at this distance as if lulled in the sabbath of repose. Absorbed in the train of reflection which objects of such melancholy interest naturally inspired, we had nearly reached the limits of our walk, when suddenly the mingled sounds of hound and horn, in one loud and joyous concert, swelled on the breeze, and awoke us from our mid-day dream. A tallyho! in a major key of vociferation that would have done credit to Stentor himself, completed our excitation, and informed us that the immolation of poor reynard was momentarily expected. Ascending an adjoining eminence, the better to enjoy the rural sport, we beheld the full tide of the chace roll before us over hedge, row and brake. At some distance before the other votaries of Diana, there was one, who, from the cut of his courser and inimitable attitude in the saddle, appeared to us both calculated and inclined to be in at the death. The personage who had thus attracted our attention, was about six feet in height, slightly formed, elegantly proportioned, and elastic as corkwood; and if, instead of the gothic fabrics by which his graceful figure was distorted, he had been habited in flowing robes of 'Lincoln green', he might doubtless have passed for the model of James Fitzjames. A blue coat, with scarcely anything deserving the name of skirts; a pair of doe-skin breeches, that did every justice to the ingenious maker; top-boots; spurs of unsparing longitude; and a whip, called 'a blazer' in this country, completed the costume of this dandy Nimrod, which gave him no faint resemblance to a game cock, trimmed and heeled for the combat. His horse too, though as good a bit of flesh as ever felt steel, partook a good deal of the same grotesque aspect as his master; for his ears, reduced to one-third of their natural length, were sharp and short as the blades of a toilet scissors; his mane had suffered a similar mutilation, and his tail resembled nothing we had ever seen in the animal creation, except the caudal extremity of a rat that had been amputated in a trap. By the time we had taken the dimensions of this exquisite Centaur, the chace had come to a close, and all that remained of poor reynard was that for which he had been so brutally tortured — his *brush*, which now hung triumphantly dangling over Croppy's brows, placed there by the hands of the Surgeon-General, Mr. Crampton.

Having thus introduced our subject in the dignified character of an equestrian, we shall go back, *per saltum*, to consider him in the more humble capacity of a walking gentleman, at a time when he has little thought of being the hero of a memoir, as of driving four-in-hand through Merrion-square; not, indeed, without some apprehension, that our readers, after following us through the subsequent narrative, will fare pretty much like the hunting party just described, who having toiled the whole day in pursuit of the fox, had nothing for their labour in the evening but *a tail*.

Of the worthlessness of a splendid lineage, Mr. Crampton is a very distinguished illustration, as he proves, in his own person, that a man, without one drop of noble blood in his veins, may rise to the highest eminence in any profession. If the 'stemmata quid faciunt' of Juvenal be a good text, Mr. Crampton is an excellent comment; for of his immediate kindred, he is the most important himself; and of his ancestors, by far the most illustrious that we could hear of were Adam and Eve. From this venerable couple, he is descended in a direct line, and who can boast of a more ancient parentage? In later times, however, his family, suffering for the sins of their fathers, procured by their industry the necessaries, without being able to afford the luxuries, of life. 'Tis true his father was a professional man, a dentist, and the first bread which young Philip ever masticated was honourably earned by extracting teeth.

Having arrived at that age when the mind and body were fast hastening to maturity, he gave evident signs of a genius far above the level of drawing teeth or of polishing ivory. Such monotonous occupations were ill suited to the towering mind of the ambitious boy, whose kite, during the gales of October, was seen to soar beyond those of his companions, and whose *taw* was the terror of his playfellows' *shops*. At the distance of forty years (for Mr. Crampton is now turned of fifty) the reminiscences to be collected of boyhood are often imperfect; but, if report speak the truth, in conjugating of verbs and declining of nouns, he had no equal, and even that master-piece of pother and puzzle, the Greek grammar, became an easy prey to the force of his dawning intellect. These were prognostics of future greatness not to be overlooked by parental solicitude, and many an evening, when the infused Congou poured its balmy fragrance around, and the melodious simpering of the kettle harmonized the family fireside — when the tooth-key took its rest upon beds of softest lint, and dentifrices breathed from under their painted lids, did the happy parents of young Philip hold consultation upon the destinies of their son. But it would be to no purpose to rescue from oblivion the harmless gossip of parents about the talents and prospects of their striplings, for if there had been any truth in such prophecies, we ourselves would have been, ere this, only something short of a secretary of state, and instead of wielding a 'grey goose quill', we would be directing the energies of our country. To the good man himself, indeed, the choice of a profession for his son was a matter of little moment, being convinced, that into whatever sphere of society circumstances would whirl him, he would be unto that system as a centre and a sun. Mamma, however, having a turn for female theology, was anxious that her son should be brought up in the Church, for she often declared, that some time previous to his birth, she had dreams of ecclesiastical preferment, and that, on casting the *sortes* on the following morning in the breakfast cups, she saw a mitre fully developed in one of their bottoms. But time, the great disposer of all things and the genuine test of prophetic inspiration, soon settled the question; and neither the predictions or innocent sorcery of the devout lady had the slightest influence on the fate of her son, for he was shortly afterwards yoked in the wain of surgery, under the guidance, we are told, of Solomon Richards, whose tuition was just worth what it cost — *nothing*. The sober details of solitary dissection, and of midnight readings, as they present nothing either amusing or instructive, we shall pass over, and commence our narrative at another era in our hero's life.

After Mr. Crampton had obtained a licence to kill game at the Surgical Stamp Office, the army, that great refuge of professional indigence, afforded him a temporary asylum from the cheerless drudgery of rising to notice in a great city. The trifling stipend of an hospital mate, however, to a man of lofty pretensions and expensive habits, only prolongs existence to render it superlatively miserable, and, like a lamp ill supplied with oil, though the flame is still kept alive, it burns with a painful reluctance, only showing, without overcoming, the darkness by which it is surrounded.

It may, therefore, be easily conceived into what singular adventures a man of Mr. Crampton's magnificent mind and scanty means was driven during his professional vagrancy. His mighty soul 'swelled beyond the measure of his chains', and he sought the first or any means, that might offer to rescue him from the bonds of his narrow circumstances. He was then young, some would say handsome, and certainly accomplished in all the arts of fashionable life. In the field, and at the chace, he was the envy of his own sex. The ladies declared him the finest gentleman at the review; and it must be confessed, that in the ballroom, his heels did ample honour to his head; for in the graceful evolutions of the waltz, or the more lively movements of quadrille, there are few, even to this day, of living harlequins who could excel him. To a man possessed of so many mental and personal attractions, it is not at all wonderful that matrimony presented prospects of happier days, and that some fair damsel of fortune, just wandering on the confines of desperation, would rescue him from poverty, and consign him at once to independence and to bliss. But, to the eternal discredit of female discrimination be it recorded, that so great a combination of charms, recommended too in the seducing dress of a scarlet coat, was suffered, for many a year, to circulate the rounds of fêtes and follies unnoticed and unrequited by the conquest of a single heart.

It was in this melancholy plight that he arrived in Athlone, with a heavy heart and a light purse, while his boots, as we have been

told by one who saw them, gave unequivocal symptoms of their
master's decline, by gaping into sorrowful and unseemly chinks.
Still reposing, however, upon the supremacy of his charms, he
sought to keep up appearances by turning to advantage the intro-
ductions to notice which a respectable profession and a commission
in his Majesty's service always confer in new quarters. 'Ways and
Means' is a comedy of ephemeral utility, as the plot is soon
detected; and the lilly-handed, rosy-cheeked Mrs. Ganly Fallon, of
the Athlone restaurateur, after some unsuccessful appeals at the
mess-room, refused any longer to supply the hope-inspiring
contents of her cellar to our military ranger. But what of that? life
and death — pleasure and pain — are divided only by thin parti-
tions; and, the moment when our fate wears its darkest aspect, the
light of happiness may burst through the gloom. Nor is it wonderful (of such discordant elements is the world composed) that in
their rapid and clashing confusion, that some harmonious tones are
elicited, to which the heart of the way-worn pilgrim may beat in
sympathetic vibration. So it was with Mr. Crampton; his circumstances having arrived at that critical point when matters invariably
mend, female obduracy relented — he rose once more upon his
heels, and danced himself into the graces of an amiable and wealthy
young lady through the fascinating medium of an Irish jig. Thank
Heaven! the gloomy part of the narrative has now come to a close
— all henceforward shall be sunshine unobscured by a cloud.

To cut short a discourse which we fear is growing too luxuriant
under our hands, we will state generally, that he continued for
some time longer in the army — enjoyed a protracted honeymoon
at various head-quarters, and was under surgeon Stringer in Limerick, who now, strange to tell, is lost in the fame of his quondam
inferior. How fluctuating are the affairs of men! the wave that
sinks thousands only serves to roll some favoured minion of fortune upon the wished-for shore. Conceiving that travelling would
shortly become troublesome, he turned his thoughts upon the
capital, and determined on making it his future residence. Accordingly, he doffed the *insignia* of war, and devoted himself to the
peaceful labour of attending those who preferred dying upon the
'soft lap' of a feather-bed to expiring upon the field of battle.
Dawson-street was the place chosen for his abode, where he also
commenced teacher of surgery.

From small beginnings what great results have not followed? The Amazon, that threatens the ocean with overflowing, may be traced to an inconsiderable spring; and 'si magna componere parvis', the stable where horses chewed and grooms snored was the theatre where our embryo professor first unbound the energies of a mind which has since filled with wonder our little isle. Report attaches much importance to this course of *manger* lectures, but of what we have not heard we dare not speak. Be hushed, therefore, thou foul fiend of scepticism rebelling in our breast! It so happened, however, that a servant at one of the hotels in Dawson-street, whose voracity, it seems, exceeded his deglutitive powers, was nearly choked in attempting to swallow a piece of meat, which stuck in his throat. Mr. Crampton was called to his assistance — he operated, of course — the man fortunately recovered, and the surgeon was covered with glory. This, we believe, was his critical case, and his first introduction to public notice.

The marriage of his sister to Mr. Bushe, now Chief Justice of the King's Bench, tended very much to his advancement. So respectable a connexion could not fail of introducing him to the best society, and it was probably in this way he became acquainted with his great patron the Duke of Richmond. A peculiar flexibility of temper, the polished manners of a courtier, and other companionable qualities, had so endeared him to this Bacchanalian representative of Majesty, that he patented to Mr. Crampton the Surgeon Generalship, ere death had made the situation vacant. Mr. Stewart, his late predecessor, did not detain him long in sickening expectation, for he shortly after paid the debt of nature, and, contrary to every law of justice and of precedent, Mr. Crampton was appointed his successor. Mr. Owberry*, the gentleman to whom the situation should have devolved, in virtue of merit, service, and seniority, was offered some remuneration for his maltreatment, but, with a magnanimity worthy of record, he rejected the proferred boon, and retired in disguist into private life upon half-pay.

This new appointment gave Mr. Crampton additional importance, and it must be confessed that so great an advantage was improved upon with peculiar ingenuity. A splendid establishment

*Ralph Smith Obré

was fitted up, where lords and ladies, colonels and captains, and all
the titled vermin of Church and State, were served in a style little
short of oriental magnificence. Nothing could exceed the 'pomp
and circumstance' by which his festive board was constantly surrounded. The delicacy of the viands was only equalled by the costly
services of plate and china in which they were offered up to his
sumptuous guests. The extravagance thus expended in catering for
the capricious appetites of his luxurious visitors was soon and
amply refunded in munificent fees. Every new *fête* only extended
the circle of his acquaintance, and the fair dames, whom he led up
with so much elegance and skill through the dizzy mazes of the
dance, could not do less than have him to feel their pulse when con- ·
fined to the couch of sickness or of ennui. In fact, Mr. Crampton
became the fashionable doctor, and it was considered a heresy in
taste, as well as an error in judgment, to employ any other medical
attendant, until, like hope itself, he at length became 'a wreath for
each toil, a charm for every woe'.

Well, if we could only picture to our readers his matchless
approach to the sofa of a hypochondriac, or my lady in vapours —
there was 'music in his very foot as he came up the stairs', which
bespoke recovery, and told of happy days to come; and as he gracefully unfurled the perfumed 'India', you would think the goddess
Hygeia leaped from out the silken folds. Alas! the narrow limits of
description! words can convey no adequate idea of sound or
motion, and we must only leave it to our readers to imagine, with
what peculiar taste and delicacy he would put those queer questions
one would blush to indite; with what masterly command of voice
and of countenance he would listen to and compassionate the tale
of fictitious woe, until having extracted, by sympathetic artifice,
the secret cause of all her sorrow, he confidently assured his
desponding patient of a speedy restoration, which was half accomplished before he departed. But we must not intrude farther on
these tender scenes of domestic distress; our rude pencil would but
reduce them into the angular and graceless *contour* of the
caricature.

Circumstances are seldom wanted to those who have once
caught hold of the world to continue their grasp, for fortune is at
least so far consistent as never to abandon those upon whom she
deigns to smile. Lord Whitworth, at this period Viceroy of Ireland,

happened to be seized by one of those bowel complaints which Nature very often inflicts upon gluttons, as a chastisement for the violation of her laws. Mr. Crampton was of course called in. All remedies had been tried — they all failed, and the vital spark was hastening fast to extinction: when lo! the invincible hero of our story puts off his 'woollens', jumps into bed, and grapples with death face to face in the body of the moribund Duke. The caloric radiating from Mr. Crampton's warm heart re-animated his expiring patient, and just infused into his feeble arm sufficient strength to sign a draft of £500 on the Bank of Ireland, to be paid to Mr. Crampton as a trifling remuneration for his devoted attention. Surely this ingenious and magnanimous mode of treatment deserved no less a reward. In the whole routine of medical practice, we have never heard of any thing equal to this. Heroes, to be sure, have died for their country — lovers for their lasses, and friendship has had its force demonstrated by the attachment of a Damon and a Pythias; but avaunt, Romance! where shall we find, in thy world of wonders, love so disinterested and sincere — so profound, as this attempt to restore the dying by a combination of these powers, applied in the novel but elegant formula of an animal fomentation? The sublimity of this act could not be lost upon an admiring world; for who is there amongst us who would not have that man for a medical attendant who would thus lay aside the dignity of his profession with his garments, to soothe the pangs of disease, and to 'return sigh for sigh'?

In addition to the £500 the noble Lord, on his recovery, presented Mr. Crampton with a general's uniform, in which he shortly after appeared at the Castle of Dublin. Lord Norbury was one of the party, but so completely had the new apparel transformed his old acquaintance, that he asked a gentleman standing by him, who that was who wore the general's uniform? The gentleman observed, it was the Surgeon-General. 'Oh yes', replied the witty Lord, jocosely, who was never at a loss for a pun or a halter, 'I suppose that is the *General* of the *Lancers*.'

As we are on the subject of anecdote, we will detail another, particularly illustrative of Mr. Crampton's character. To ambitious minds only belongs the attribute of dissatisfaction with whatever they may have achieved. Alexander, as every person knows, having subdued one, is said to have sighed for the conquest of a second world; and Mr. Crampton, like the hero of old, having arrived at the limits of professional victory in his own, thirsted to extend his empire into another country. Intoxicated with success, and seduced by the partial representations of his noble friends on the other side the Channel, he resolved on transferring himself to a foreign clime; and if he failed in the attempt, it was surely, like Phaeton, in a great and glorious enterprise, which was neither more nor less than the detrusion of Sir Astley Cooper from the throne of English surgery. To support him in this unequal contest, he had, it is true, many and able friends, and ere he committed himself to the mercy of the waves, he was assured that the mantle of royalty itself was to compose a part of his manifold shield. On his arrival, and as soon after as an opportunity served, it is said, that the noble personage whom he snatched from the grave presented him to the King, remarking at the same time, that Mr. Crampton was the gentleman who had saved his life. Whether from ignorance of the etiquette to be observed or not in the royal presence, or perhaps from an over-anxiousness to please, Mr. Crampton, we are told, was not just the thing to suit his Majesty's taste; for with a *royal* smile, a thing of very dubious import, the King turned round, pointed to Sir Matthew Tierney, who was then present, and laconically replied, 'There is the gentleman who saved mine.' The patron and client thus abashed by the royal salute, Mr. Crampton immediately unfurled his sails, put to sea, and steered back once more to the '*Island of Saints*'.

Although we had been long acquainted with this gentleman's modes of practice, his great manual dexterity, and all that sort of thing, yet in consequence of never having seen him in the didactic capacity, we were at some loss how we should proceed to describe his person, under circumstances favourable to this design. Fortunately, however, a clinical course of lectures, delivering at the present moment in the Meath Hospital by Mr. Crampton, resolved this difficulty. Well then, away we went, 'with our martial cloak around us', on a very wet day in last November, to this institution, and having taken our seat amongst the expectant audience, we were led to suppose, from the apparatus on the table, that we were to have a dissertation on fractures. 'Blessed are they', says Swift, 'that expect nothing', a maxim which we invariably observe on these occasions. An anecdote of Napoleon, whom the lecturer call a *great man*, a pathetic episode of a clergyman and his wife, and the venerable simile (we mean from its great antiquity) of the watch and the clown, are all we can now conjure up from the recesses of our memory of this lecture. But what of the man himself, 'Sit facie, sura, quali fude, dente, capillo quali?' Why, he came in, as all fashionable men do, just half an hour late, with a port-folio under his arm, in which was deposited the manuscript of his lecture. After a hearty salutation on the part of the audience, and a polite acknowledgement, embodied in a bow, by the professor, he composed himself in his chair, just as he would at home in his own drawing-room. In doing all this, we confess we have rarely seen so much elegant mannerism combined with so much self-possession. The former so completely reconciled us to the latter, that we had nothing to regret from the total absence of modesty. Into such beautiful forms, indeed, has he wrought his *bronze*, and so highly polished is its surface, that with many observers it might pass for metal of more sterling value. It is, to be sure, the mere creation of art, such as we daily see turned out of the mould of military manners.

Whether our remarks of his costume on a former occasion, were the cause of a reformation in his dress, we will not pretend to say, but certain it is, he was habited in a plain, but elegant suit of black. No furs, no frogs, no flimsy fillagre of braid and bullion, were about him on this day; and we must declare it, as our opinion, that there was not so much as a *stays* in question. We never, indeed, saw him look better, nor more like one of his own species; for, on other occasions, he seemed to us half bear, half beaver, so completely had the pelts of these animals concealed his human form.

His features, by no means regular, and savouring a good deal of vulgarity, are, notwithstanding this drawback, particularly interesting and attractive. For this quality they are principally indebted to a pair of fine eyes, in which we think more of love than genius is manifest, and to a sweet smile eternally dwelling on his lips, that would liquify a heart of stone, and win the confidence of the most suspicious. Such are the manners and features of Mr. Crampton; pleasing without any apparent exertion, and dignified without being in the least degree repulsive. The delivery of his discourses, and their style, made an impression on us — by no means a favourable one. His voice is loud and flexible, but from the construction of his periods, invariably antithetical, the enunciation of them must be monotonously emphatic. The regular recurrence of sentences thus punctiliously divided into two members, and the inflexion of voice necessarily adopted in their delivery, gives a *see-saw* air to the whole, which very soon wearies an audience.

On the material or substance of these lectures, we cannot dilate. The speaker seemed to have no object in view, no advice to offer his pupils arising out of his own experience, nor any favourite theory to inculcate. His discourse, was a piece of fine patchwork, put together without any harmony of colour, or reference to utility. When one reflects on Mr. Crampton's great opportunities, and contrasts them with the little he has done to record the results, a singular contradiction arises, and a comparison with other men is the necessary consequence. We are told he possesses genius — granted. We know he has had extensive practice; but has he added, we ask, any thing to the stock of surgical information? Let his petty satellites of the Meath Institution, who swell into a fancied importance in his presence, but who degrade the human character by their slavish devotion, answer this question. Why then are we to be eternally *bored* by comparisons with Desault, Cooper, Abernethy, &c.? It is the essence — the very test of genius, to create, to discover, and to improve on what has been already made known. Now, if we are to judge of what Mr. Crampton has done in this way, we really tremble for his posthumous reputation. But let us not be mistaken in this point, or be understood as detracting from his great and extensive merits, for they are certainly of the very first order. All we mean to deny him is that great attribute which ever immortalizes the possessor, and forms the line of distinction between genius and mere talènt. There is as much difference between two men possessing these mental endowments as there is between the inventor of the steam-engine and the man that works it — between a Watt and one of his engineers.

We could easily account for the mistake into which Mr. Crampton's friends have fallen. He invariably performs the numerous experiments that are daily put forward in the world for well-known purposes, but which are very often nurtured in ignorance and propagated by credulity. While we profess ourselves the ardent admirers of rational experiment, we shall never countenance, by a concealment of our feelings, an innovation which would give one moment's pain to a fellow-creature, without a well grounded prospect of ameliorating his condition.

We happened to be present, some time back, at one of those scenes of scientific butchery at the Meath Hospital. The patient was a female: the complaint, if we recollect rightly, open scrofula of the knee-joint. A great concourse assembled to witness the operation; it was quite a *gala* day with the dissectors — a festival, seemingly, held in honour of the virtues of '*Steel*'. It was the first time, we believe, that the removal of the knee-joint was attempted here; we earnestly hope it will be the last. The operator, of course, accomplished his purpose with his usual dexterity. But could he have beheld, as we did, the contorted countenances of the spectators, the knife would have fallen from his hand, never to be resumed where it was not more imperiously indicated. To be present was indeed to be in torture. One man vented his feelings in a *wink*; a second in a *hem*; a third overcame his sympathies in a forced fit of laughter; a fourth put his fingers in his ears to shut out the wretch's screams; all, to be sure, admired, yet all disapproved; and before the performance was entirely finished, Colles cried out, in rather an audible tone, 'by J—s!*' — drew the door after him, and vanished. We say this poor creature, a long time after, endeavouring to drag her limb with her, by means of sundry *wooden* contrivances. How much more preferable would amputation have been in this case; a wooden leg, to a useless member kept from falling asunder by bandages and splints. And, forsooth, this is called cleverness! admirable surgery! Very well, let it be called by whatever name the sanguinary desperadoes of the profession choose, but we shall never be cheated out of our judgment, or fear to expose such practice when it falls under our observation.

We fancy we already hear some heroes of wit and brevity exclaim against our prosing and prolixity. Alas! for our own sake as well as theirs, we wish that we could treat them to something better. But we shall now only detain them while we inform them that Mr. Crampton was once, in practice, what his great rival

---

*'The plainer Dubliners amaze us
By their frequent use of Jaysus
Which makes us entertain the notion
It is not always from devotion.'

Oliver St. John Gogarty 1937.

Colles is at present — the attendant of every sick-bed in the metropolis. We will not pretend to say which of them makes most by his
profession, but we could easily tell who is oftenest consulted. Their
popularity and sphere of practice are of different kind; though
both were in a great measure indebted to circumstances for their
respective *quota* of patronage. Yet, with a trifling exception,
Mr. Colles may be said to be the architect of his reputation, and, as
it is to be presumed that he could not have raised so splendid a
fabric without sound materials for its support, it will be in proportion durable and lasting. The one, if we be permitted to allegorise,
was a plant of natural growth, reared up in open ground, braced by
the shower, and strengthened by the storm; the other a delicate
exotic, of morbid vegetation, fostered by factitious airs, and forced
into premature flower. The oak, though one of the last of the forest
to put on its 'summer robes', makes ample amends for its vernal
nudity by a long protracted verdure of shade, and resistance to the
inclemency of winter.

These observations extend only to their rise in life, and it is by no
means intended by the comparison to show in what their merits as
surgeons, or their talents as men, differ. Indeed a comparison
could not be well instituted between two men whose minds seem so
differently constituted. Each has his own peculiar powers and
excellencies, and it might be no easy matter, since both are so
highly endowed, to adjust the balance. Lines of distinction might
easily be drawn to point out in what respects they differ: but to
divide the palm of superiority would be too much for us, leaving
the invidiousness of such a task, as well as the uneasiness it might
cause, out of the question. We shall, therefore, add this item to the
long list of doubts and undecided matters, to which is generally
applied, 'Grammatici certant, et adhuc sub judice lis est'.

Our object in placing them beside each other, was not to
separate them by the *odium* of a comparison: for we wish them
united in sentiment, and successful in all their undertakings, as they
are liberal, enlightened, and friendly to the true interests of their
profession. It is indeed much to be regretted, that men whose co-
operation is required in the present neglected and degraded state of
the surgical profession, should be divided in opinion, and that any
hasty expressions, certainly unwarrantable, delivered in a public
theatre, should have driven the offended party to the summary

vindication of injury by *message*. Heaven knows, science has enough to contend with here, without impeding its progress on one side by abuse, and on the other by force of arms. We sincerely hope that, if any such differences should again arise, the assailants will abandon the pistol for the pen. To the mortal combats of this innocent weapon of defence we have no objection; let the parties *prime and load* as often as they please with 'paper bullets of the brain' — wound by a syllogism, or kill by a fact — against the smoke of a theory, or the flash of an invention, we will never protest — but in such matters as these, we confess we cannot abide the smell of gunpowder.

ERINENSIS
Dublin January 8, 1825.

# 7

# MR. JACOB

POSSESSED of local advantages superior to many of the capitals of Europe, the metropolis of Ireland is their inferior in literature, science, and the fine arts. It is enough for our present purpose, to state generally that such is the melancholy fact, without entering into a discussion upon cause and effect. Were we to trace these consequences to their origin, no sheet, of parliamentary dimensions, would suffice to contain the glowing narrative, nor the longest day bring us to its close: 'Ante diem clauso componet vesper olympo'. The shades of night and the yawning of our readers would press upon us much about the same time. Surrounded, however, by a singular combination of resources, the student residing in Dublin might, with the greatest facility, consult alternately the book of nature or of art: now turn over a leaf of Homer in his closet, and in the next half-hour examine stratifications, enthroned upon rocks of any formation he might choose. The mountains that almost overhang his dwelling, present the young geologist with the most ample illustrations of his favourite science: should he prefer a botanical excursion, the fields, extended before him, are covered with abundant varieties of common and indigenous plants: or if he be inclined for natural history, the coast not only allures him by its beauty, but tempts him to study the organic treasures with which it abounds. Yet how seldom do we find these advantages made available to intellectual improvement? How rarely do we see an embryo Linnæus ascend the mountain; traverse the mead; or wander by the 'sounding shore', accompanied by a pack of pupils in search of scientific game? These fertile sources of studious recreation, 'tis true, were once explored and hallowed by the footsteps of a Kirwan, but with him the practice and the place would seem to have lost their charms to please. If nature has done much for us, her labours are certainly not unpatronised by art; for Institutions we have, almost numberless; all splendidly endowed, and pompously labelled with gorgeous appellatives: an epithetic grandeur, a shadowy nonentity, a national cenotaph to science, is all we can boast of. We have a Royal Dublin Society, a Royal College of Surgeons, a Royal Irish Academy, a Royal College of Physicians — in short, we have every thing royal in name, but nothing majestic in nature. In all these establishments there are professors in every science, from horse-shoeing up to growing gooseberries on a large scale, inclusive. In our two botanical gardens, superior, perhaps, to any in the British dominions, we have two of these professors; yes, indeed we have two; one for advanced in the dotage of senility, the other as far gone in swaddling. The first, in the charming month of May, comes forth like one of the seven sleepers from winter quarters, dressed as gaily as Flora herself, and dispenses, through the hands of the 'ministering angels' of Glasnevin garden, a variety of vegetable productions to an admiring class of *he* and *she* 'basbleus', while the octo-genarian dandy himself is employed in pronouncing an oratorical panegyric on his brother professors, and the admirabilities of the Royal Dublin Societies; seldom pausing in his laudatory career, except on the appearance of some rare of beautiful flower, when, his eloquence yielding to his gallantry, he graciously bows to one of the *savants*, and says, with a venerable leer, '*pulcherrime detur*': the second, much about the same time, feeling, we suppose, the 'sweet experience' of the season, or perhaps, a 'visitation of grace', is sedulously occupied in strewing the philosophy hall of the University with 'green rushes', and constructing a new 'railway' to heaven, out of flowers and scraps of scripture. Happy people! we only know the variations of our climate by scientific announcements from every lamp-post, and even dreary November is not without its attractions, when professor Higgins, at the theatre of the Dublin Society, electrifies his 'fair audience' with a volley from his broad-plate battery, and in prelections, delivered in the genuine *patois* of Cunnemora, initiates his delicate auditory in the process of 'making water'; their suffused cheeks pitting into arch dimples at the idea of the unintentional *double entendres* of the abstracted author of the 'Atomic Theory'. Thus roll on the seasons, of which certain portions are regularly devoted to the study of some branch of knowledge, while we are still in the 'utter darkness' of ignorance; and now that spring is about to visit us in 'descending showers', we are invited to an intellectual banquet at Park-street, where a school of medicine and surgery has been just established under auspices the most favourable, and directors the most learned. The card of this Institution, put into our hands a few days back, reminded us strongly of a sign we once saw hung out over a village hotel, couched in the following terms, 'Good dry lodgings', while the elements, as if in mockery, rushed in and out the green turf that was thrown up to shield the traveller from the incursions of the storm. Nothing, however, could be more accurately allocated than the several duties to be performed, and the prices to be paid: the whole exhibiting an admirable parallel for the divisional compartments of the 'London Medical Repository': thus we have in the latter such a hoax as an 'Original department', followed up in a late number by a table of contents, and baptized by the author (what a joke!) 'A history of Absorption': in the former, we have such matters as anatomy, physiology, and surgery, honoured with the names of Wilmot, Cusack, and Jacob! And, oh! 'tell it not in Gath!' the practice of physic, 'per varios casus, per tot discrimina rerum', has at length found a cemetery in Dr. Graves: we don't mean a pun, but may nothing fatal be the consequence of this ominous union of names. The comparison, we assure you, Mr. Editor, is complete in all its parts, and as we have just now a few hours to spare, we shall devote them, in a further illustration, to the pages of *The Lancet,* that Julian star of medical periodicals, the reputation of which, like the fame of Marcellus, the young hope of Rome, has overspread the empire, and extends even to the centre of our own 'ultima Thule' of the western wave;

> 'Crescit, occulto velut arbor ævo,
> Fama Marcelli: micat inter omnes
> Julium sidus, velut inter ignes
> Luna minores.'

We know we are complimenting, at the risk of incurring your displeasure, but as Irishmen we claim the privilege of freely expressing our sentiments, though they should be somewhat out of place.

Having thus thrown off a debt of gratitude long due to a Journal that has been from the first moment of its existence unmeritedly assailed by every unmanly artifice that malignant ingenuity could devise, but which, notwithstanding, like the palms of Palestine, has flourished under oppression; or, like the hour-glass by old age, would be demolished, because its competitors discover, through its brilliancy, the rapid approach of their extinction, we shall proceed on our journey to Park-street. Well then, Monday (we forget the date) was fixed for the opening of the new school, and Mr. Wilmot was to have done the honours of the establishment; but somehow or other he fell sick, (was it a Royal gout?) and the proceedings were deferred in consequence, to that day-week. The complaint, whatever it was (we hope it was not a Lancet affection,) still continuing, it was determined, at all hazard, that the business of the institution should not be delayed, and on the day appointed the curtain rose, when loud applause hailed Mr. Jacob, as the Lilliputian hero of the Park-street boards. Tossed to and fro, like a ship in a gale, we ascended to the theatre, and soon found ourselves seated amidst a dense multitude, where we could easily perceive that there neither elbow-room nor liberty of conscience was to be expected; for on one side we were pressed upon by a fat, well-fed Esculapian, and on the other tormented by the perpetual fidgets of a corsetted dandy, glorifying in the anticipated suppression of the 'Popish Parliament'. Yielding to our fate, we settled ourselves, as well as circumstances would permit, for the short period which we had to endure this compound inconvenience of mental and corporeal intolerance. Our thoughts soon took a different direction from our adipose neighbour on the right, and our exquisite politician on the left, for looking round us on the assembled multitude, we asked ourselves what has brought us all here together to-day? Was it to *kill time*, to pass away an idle hour, to gaze and be gazed upon in the pillory or fashion — were these the ends for which this crowd had collected? No: we could not believe it; for though such silly motives might have actuated a few, we were more inclined to attribute what we beheld to a love of excellence, the insatiable thirst of novelty, the noble aspiration after perfection, inherent in human

nature: these were the objects proposed, these were the feelings that
excited the passions to be gratified, and which afforded a satisfactory resolution to our interrogatory. Let not the teachers of surgery
after this attempt to fling from themselves that odium with which
they have been branded, of creating, out of their own incompetency, the idleness and ignorance of their pupils, when an advertisement could thus bring together such a crowd, and all seeking for
information. No — we sate in the midst of a living demonstration,
an eloquent but silent refutation of the fallacy of such doctrine;
and as we glanced round upon this proud vindication of our principles, and of calumniated nature, we could well afford to smile upon
some persons present, whose looks, had they the power, would,
like the head of Medusa, have turned us into stone. Here then were
the materials attracted together by the instinctive desire of improvement, but where was the master-mind, to mould, to fashion, to
elaborate this mass of intellect into forms of excellence? where was
the Phidias, to clothe with beauty and life this rough unseemly
material, yet sound and susceptible of as high a polish as his own
beloved marble of the quarries of Pentilius? Of talent there is no
deficiency; of desire for improvement there was here satisfactory
testimony. Would that we could speak in the same tone of confidence that there was a corresponding portion of mind and of will in
those who undertake the instruction of youth, to maturate the
genius of our country. Often did it occur to us during the short
hour that we sate here, what an admirable opportunity did the
present circumstances afford to a man of genius to stamp his character by originality of conception in the art of teaching, and of
trampling down at once that foul hydra of the *old regime*. Were
such a being as our Promethean fancy formed at the moment, and
endued with imaginary life, to step forward and address that
assembly, how would every heart have responded to his voice; how
soon would the old have abandoned their prejudices, and the young
have adopted a system by which all their wishes might be gratified
— all their faculties developed into perfection with comparative
facility! But here there was no such being — all else was present; a
neat theatre, originals and imitations both in abundance; here lay a
fish that would have made a gourmand's teeth water; there a
copper-plate, almost making the shadow as real as the substance
itself; while between them rose skeletons in the naked majesty of

bare bones and pride of varnish; around was a numerous audience; but the soul, — the spirit that would have made this dumb trumpery eloquent, and those present feel unto persuasion, — this indispensable requisite was wanted, and all was consequently dull, monotonous, and uninteresting.

Impatient from a sense of certain disappointment, the moments passed slowly until a gentleman of *duodecimo* stature, so neatly habited, that the affectation of the *simplex munditiis* could not disguise the assumed indifference to toiletic arrangements and exterior appearance, stepped in by a side door and relieved us from suspense. He was harnassed in a pair of spectacles, so admirably fitted to the prominences and depressions of the orbitary processes, that one might have mistaken the whole optical apparatus as the natural production of the parts, or an expansion of the cornea spread out upon a delicate frame of silver wire. Over the springs of this beautiful piece of mechanism, that held the temples fast in 'close embrace', hung two luxuriant ringlets of auburn hair, like the tendrils of a vine, and writhing into beautiful contortions from the recent application of the 'actual cautery'. Had 'Crispissa' herself 'o'erlooked each *hair*' the tresses which we beheld could not have been more tastefully disposed. He advanced up to the table with a buoyant swing, and with such a smirk of self-complacency upon his countenance, just verging upon the laughing point, that we would have been pardoned at the moment, if we had taken him for a jolly disciple of Democritus, instead of a grave son of Esculapius. A momentary pause of amazement ensued, but the audience, as if sympathising with his feelings, gave vent to theirs in a loud burst of approbation. 'Ingeminant plausum Tyrii, Troesque sequentur', which hemistich we quote in obedience to Mr. Colles's mandate, that all surgeons should read the classics; and, to balance the account, shall translate it, to show our own skill in versification.

> 'Clap hands, clap hands, old mother
>     Stephens cries,
> And straight her sons with discord
>     rend the skies;
> While Richmond's corps of dandies
>     and of asses
> In depth of sound all rivalry surpasses.'

Emboldened by this cheering reception, the lecturer called up all his resolution, balanced a pencil horizontally between his index fingers, as if about to somerset through his hands — threw himself back into an oratorical position, and, as well as we could catch his words, expressed himself thus:

'Gentlemen, I believe you are all aware that it was *intended*, and Mr. Wilmot himself *intended* to have *performed* the duty which I find myself inadequate to *perform*; but Mr. Wilmot becoming *indisposed*, he was not *disposed* to *introduce* the *introductory lecture*, and the duty has consequently devolved upon me, *unprepared* as I am, but I have got these *preparations* to *give* the *lecture* a more popular form', or something in this impressive style, for our stenographic notes were imperfect; our evil genius, the restless dandy, having, at the very commencement, given our elbow a shove, which broke the point of our pencil, greatly indeed to our sorrow. Baffled in our attempt to lay before you the whole of this unique essay, which would have superseded all comment, we contented ourselves with listening in silence, and sketching in our note-book a likeness of the speaker, with the mutilated 'Coen'. On consulting this rough draught and our memory, we should be inclined to represent the man 'in our mind's eye' as an African born in the Queen's country, or an Hibernian Albino, wlhose features approximate the European standard from climate and circumstance. To begin above, the forehead is a massy fabric, indicative of nothing except superabundance of bone: in expression, the reverse of what one might suppose fancy's urn to be, as described by Gary, 'with thoughts that breathe, and words that burn'. We have already described (for eyes we could see none) the spectacles, which rest upon a nose hollowed seemingly for their accommodation. The facial ellipsis is nearly bisected by an orifice in which you look in vain for the 'coral teeth' and 'ruby lips' of the Minerva novelists. Yet around this medley of organs, individually, to be sure, not the most delicately finished, there breathes a halo of kindness; a conciliating effulgence of good nature, that compensates for the loss of the higher order of personal attractions, and a lady might with perfect consistency exclaim, 'what a dear charming little creature, what a good-humoured, kind-hearted, facetious gentleman is Surgeon Jacob.' We are sure his person will never stand in the way of his practice, any more than a want of abilities ought to be inferred from this description.

The subject chosen by Mr. Jacob was the locomotion of the various tribes of animals — of all, in fact, that creeps on earth, cleaves the yielding air, or gulps the finny deep. There was a time, he said, when comparative anatomy was considered more as an accomplishment than a matter of real utility; but, were we to judge the tree by its fruits, we should say, to the great scandal of Cuvier, that it was neither ornamental nor useful. He certainly seemed to have profited little by the study of animal motion, for every gesture of his was the antichrist of gracefulness. His action, however, was not the Tony-lumpkin awkwardness of an untutored *debutanté*; it was studiously inaccurate, and without restraint from the presence of an assembly; in a word, it was the product of bad taste and worse judgment. He principally trusted to his memory for what he had to say, but the treacherous jade betrayed him in almost every sentence. Nothing could be more amusing than the hide-and-seek game that he and the fickle lady that presides over the contents of the brain played together during the whole lecture; now he sought her in a sweet smile, as if to fill up the *hiatus* her inconstancy had made, but finding her inexorable, he applied to a slip of paper that lay on the table, but the manuscript memento, from the smallness of handwriting, generally disappointed. Through the whole of this ludicrous exhibition, it was a regular set-to between the speaker and his subject — now the one had the best of the battle — now the other recovered its superiority; for a long time they scuffled, scrambled, and mauled each other to their heart's content and the great soreness of our's, but we think the theme, in the end, had a complete victory. The great excellence, however, of this *spree* prelection consisted in the minute fidelity with which the speaker gave practical illustrations of animal locomotion. With the albatross, he seemed about to take wing and leave us all behind him; the penquien soon brought him down again to the very depths of the ocean; with the snail, his fingers crept along the wall, and now with the parrot he worked his way, *unguibus et dentibus*, through the dense umbrage of the forest; but we confess, when he came to illustrate the fantastic tricks of the monkey tribe, he looked the character to such perfection, that we could not help considering it, of all the characters he assumed, as his *forte*. After thus flying, diving, creeping, and jumping, and pulling and hauling the 'eel of science by the tail' for about three quarters of an hour, and letting her slip through his hands in the end, he concluded in a peroration without an end, as he commenced in an exordium that had no beginning.

It were much to be desired that those men, who undertake the instruction of youth in the most useful of all professions, 'with less of genius than God gives an ape', would at once persuade themselves, that lecturing is not synonymous with that significant dissyllable — humbug. No man has a right to convene an assembly without being prepared to meet them in a proper manner. Among the crowd we saw the several professors of the establishment. In longitude of neck and pensive attention, resembling a heron perched upon a rock, sat Dr. Graves, his finely acuminated nasal organ seeming as if employed in conducting to the 'judgment seat' every fragment of the helter-skelter improvisitation of his eloquent friend in the pit; above him, to the right was Dr. Apjohn, without one shade of analysis discoverable in his countenance, though we understand him to be the chemist of the firm; below, stood that man of books, the Domine Sampson of the College, Mr. Cusack, like a personification of abstraction, his eyes intently bent upon the boards, as if looking upon the book of fate, though we are sure his glances, for that time, into futurity were limited to the rewards and punishments of this life — the profits and losses of the account books of the Institution.

Our notice of Mr. Jacob's life was deferred to the close of this essay, because it was intended to have been but short. He is the son of a country physician, who, it appears, has been so well pleased with his own success in the profession, that he has given it, as a fortune, to no less than three of his sons. Like the cure of souls among the family of the Levi, the salvation of bodies is likely to become a hereditary property in the house of Jacob. The eldest, of whom we are now speaking, is yet a young man; his life must be therefore destitute of any public interest; on which account we must pass it over, for we have no wish for juvenile biography, or the enumeration of the adventures of the baby-house; besides, we have ever found mediocrity of intellect accompanied by a corresponding monotony in the details of life, while genius, by the restless exertions of its own powers, always presents something upon which the mind may dwell with emotions of pleasure of pain. As an author, Mr. Jacob is not wholly unknown. In some papers published in one of the periodicals, he lays claim to the discovery of an undiscovered something in the eye; but not a creature, we believe, gives credit to the assumption. We were ourselves present when he attempted to describe this 'mare's nest', but neither we, nor any of those around us, could see the imaginary creation. His greatest work, however, in the way of authorship, is a pamphlet written for the express purpose of proving the miracles of Hohenloe a bam! a work, surely of supererogation. It does, to be sure, great credit to his orthodoxy, but very little to his sense as a man, and less to his knowledge as a physician. It may tell well among the saints, by allaying their 'No Popery' tribulation, and so far answer the ends for which it was written. Who could become the pander — the cat's-paw of such vermin? — None but a Cantwell. Yes, we had almost forgot; he also claims the invention of an aneurism needle, an engraving of which appeared in a late number of Anderson's Quarterly Journal, and said to be the joint production of an London cutler and Mr. Kirby of Dublin. We certainly saw an engraving of an instrument somewhat similar to the one in question, and circulated by Mr. Jacob; but there is reason to suppose, from the silence on the subject, that the invention is neither the property of Jacob, Weiss, nor Kirby, but might probably be found in some old book of drawings long since consigned to the 'grave of the Capulets'. The modern invention too, in some fifty or sixty years hence, may be dug up out of some musty 'Repository' (The London for instance, if it be possible it can so long escape the snuff-shop), and foisted upon the world as a novelty. With this doubtful invention, we bid a long farewell to the school of Park-street; not, indeed, without some feelings of regret, for we will confess it, we did expect that good sense, industry, and a new order of teaching, would have compensated for brilliancy of genius and the higher order of professional attainments. In vain did we look around for some sign of better things — some feeble glimmer of the hitherto smothered light of reason in the scholastic usages of our art; in vain did we look out from the ark of hope for some manifestation of the subsidence of the waters of ignorance; but instead of finding this expected blessing hieroglyphicked in the proceedings of this Institution, we only saw in its darkness another addition of evils to the existing deluge that was overwhelmed so many beneath its desolating wave. Had we discovered in the enterprize any thing even savouring of common sense — any thing that could be

tortured into an omen of improvement on obsolete customs — had
we discovered a spark of intellect in the undertaking that promised,
in time, to explode the 'choke-damp' of the York-street Bœotia, we
should have been the first to hail the project it accents of praise; but
we did not: on the contrary, we saw no charter specifying the intentions of this institution — guaranteeing to the student a certain
value for his money — presenting a system of education that might
ensure to him a return for his labour — we saw no classes formed
— no examinations to be held — no premium to reward the exertions of honourable ambition. Good Heavens! were these men not
capable of getting up a prospectus worthy of a Joint Stock Company? Yet, of all the bad schools in Dublin, we think this will be the
best; and were we about to commence our profession again, we
should, perhaps, adopt this school as a choice of evils. It has not
come up, in any respect, to our idea of what such an institution
ought to be, and we have spoken accordingly. This we know will
subject us to the angry censure of some persons, we will interpret
our motives, as usual, *charitably*. But let these obliging creatures go
on, their railing will prove transient as it is harmless — evanescent
as the breath in which it is conveyed. At the conclusion of this
essay, it would be no place to weigh such trifles, 'light as air', in the
balance of discussion. When we consider the accumulation of
miseries arising to students out of the ignorance of those who usurp
the chair of surgical tuition — when we see the many young men
who are compelled to struggle with such absurd systems of education for years, we can no more suppress the utterance of our
feelings than the cord of the lyre can imprison its vibrations when
touched by the hand of the minstrel. Constituted as we are, our
opinion shall never harmonize with the present practices in this part
of the profession. Did we see things in the same light as those who
support them — did we believe that no good would result from the
adoption of our views, and the destruction of those customs to
which we are opposed, then might we be designated that malignant
being, that fiend, who could smile while he stabbed and gloried in
his victorious iniquity. The ball, as Johnson said, is not well sent
home when there is no rebound. We should doubt the efficacy of
our labours if they did not bring down on us the 'pelting of the
pitiless storm' of vituperation. All we say in return is, *encore*, gentlemen, *encore*; 'vent your thunders, let your lightnings play'. You

are only working in your vocations when thus exploding the vapours of a corrupt moral atmosphere. 'Tis now twelve, and we must to rest. May those gentlemen sleep as soundly after reading this as we shall presently. — So good night.

ERINENSIS
Dublin, March 12, 1825

# 8

# MR. MACARTNEY

WERE WE to apologize to you and your readers for every devia-
tion from the specific object of our pursuits, — the sketching of
Surgical Character in Ireland, — we can hardly think but the case
would be more productive of inconvenience than the disease. In the
present instance, however, we cannot send forth our licentious
aberrations without some qualifying accompaniment of penitential
regret, and though pretty much in the situation of the crafty
Italian, 'even in penance planning sins anew', like him too we hope,
by a candid acknowledgement of our offences, to be forgiven.
Before we come, therefore, to the pleasing duty of sketching the
distinguished individual whose name confers, at least, some importance on this portion of our labours, we solicit your indulgence to a
few observations on the Institution with which he happens to be
connected.

College recollections are a few of those retained longest, and
dwelt on by the mind with an intensity of pleasure seemingly
increasing with our years, as if this quality of our nature was meant
to recompense us for the loss of a supposed good now no longer
within the reach of enjoyment. So the story runs from sire to son,
for who has not been amused by the garrulity of old age, as it
borrows a temporary elevation of spirit during the recital of the oft-
told-tale of academical adventure? But perhaps it is

'Distance lends enchantment to the view,
'And robes the mountain in its azure hue' —

82

and that these bright links in the chain of memory, if more closely inspected, are only prized by binding us faster to the remaining remnant of life. The feeling, at all events, is general, and we have no inducement, at present, to dispute the expediency of those laws by which man is governed, though to us a college in a great city would seem a questionable source of the romantic, and the association of ideas produced by such an establishment, excites little worthy of retention. The rattling of dice and gurgling of bottles; the midnight brawl and afternoon delights of a debating club; all these, to be sure, have charms for congenial 'bloods', but they are pleasures which probably do not bear analysis, so we shall proceed without a word on their rationality.

In disserting upon the seat of our national literature, we shall not, like other keen-nosed antiquarians, debate the question of antideluvian learning in Ireland; neither shall we be tempted to take up the clue of history, and wind our devious way through the labyrinths of fable and fiction, to settle the Orecian or Phenician origin of letters in our country; nor shall we institute a comparison between the respective merits of the museum of the Royal Dublin Society and the *Eamania* (i.e. seat of fine arts) of Concovar Mac Nessa, however flattering the task might be to our national vanity. Were we, however, inclined for a sally of humorous imitation, we might take up the question in the same manner as Swift did, when he set about proving, that the Latin and Greek languages were derived from the English, and satisfactorily demonstrate to our readers, that the *Mur-Ollomhan,* founded at Java by that most generous patron of letters in his day, Ollom-Fodiah, was not only the model of the University of Dublin, but that it really excelled the Elizabethean institution in the cultivation of poetry, music, medicine, history, and legislation, for such, we are told, were the sciences taught by the grisly professors of the Bardic school. If, for instance, by any contrivance, human or divine, a 'gib' of modern 'alma mater' could be translated back into one of those Druidical seminaries, what would be his surprize on finding himself surrounded by circumstances having so striking a resemblance to those with which he had been lately conversant — an ard-filea (chief-bard) or provost, as haughty, and his cheeks as puffed up with proud flesh, as Dr. Kyle himself; gownsmen clad in the *cannathas* (a flowing robe), and their inspired heads surmounted with the *barred* (a conical cap), the very prototype of his own; the whole community governed by a series of laws called the *Il-Breachtha*, precisely the same as those now in use at the 'Virgin's' establishment, while each of the candidates, according to their talent, vocation, and standing, were rewarded by an *ollam*, (the degree of A.B. of those classic days of our ancestors.) Without further remark upon these curious coincidences of academical costume, and laws of ancient and modern Druidism, or deciding which was the most useful to mankind, we shall confine our observations to the past and present state of Trinity College; its abuses; literary and political character; school of physic; and, as connected with it, that hybridous anomaly, the College of Physicians.

Antecedent to the uxorious reign of the amiable Henry the Eighth, there were numerous colleges scattered over the country, and Bede informs us, that when a youth was absent from the Continent, it was usually understood that the baronial cub, the 'filius nobilis' of that day, was at college in Ireland. Things have taken a sad turn since, for instead of having pupils now from the Continent, our youth are seldom satisfied with a domestic education. But to return, the defeat of religious empire in these realms was followed by the abolition of monastic establishments, and, among the rest that suffered on this occasion, there was one, in the vicinity of Dublin, called All Saints, or All Hallows. Archdill, in his Monasticon, represents it as possessing considerable landed property, all which was delivered over, in holy keeping, to the corporation and citizens, at the annual rent of four pounds a year, a good bargain, doubtless, or money must have been then very scarce. During the remainder of the reign of Henry, the fertile fields of Hoggin Green (for so the abbey lands had been called) were appropriated to the private accommodation of the Lord Mayor's bullocks. On the accession of Elizabeth, various attempts had been made by Perrot, Chief Justice of Ireland, to form, or rather to remodel, the existing college, attached to the Cathedral of St. Patrick's, on Reformation principles; but Archbishop Loftus, not pleased with the loss of some perquisites arising out of the revenues of that establishment, opposed Sir John Perrot, and ultimately persuaded the Queen to grant her license for a new College, as he also did the worthy Burgesses of the Corporation, to give up the lands of All Hallows for the site. The pious work was commenced by rasing to the ground the old monastery, and on the 15th of March 1591, the first stone of Alma-Mater was laid by Thomas Smyth, Lord Mayor of Dublin. It had scarcely begun to disperse the gloom of Irish ignorance, when its labours had been nearly terminated by the insurrection of Ulster, headed by the celebrated chieftain O'Nial; the lands allotted for its support, out of the spoliated estates of the natives, being no longer productive to the treasury. The zeal of Loftus and Gardiner repaired the temporary loss, by allowing the fellows £46 in addition to their former stipend. The Queen too, moved by the prayers of the suffering community, granted them £200 more, from the next plunder committed by her myrmidons in Ireland. In after times it experienced the royal bounty, and James and Charles conferred new benefactions and new charters. Such is the origin of Trinity College, founded in rapine, conducted on the narrowest principles of bigotry, and, to this hour, a lasting monument of the political fallacy, that the religion of a people is to be ever subverted by the sword of persecution or penal enactments.

It is only of late that the growing influence of Catholicity in Ireland, and the extension of liberal principles in England, forced back the penal bolt that so long excluded the Roman Catholics from all participation in the benefits, derivable from a school drawing its chief support from the confiscations of their ancestral domains. No wonder the proscribed Catholic, as he walked its halls, that rose as if in triumph over his subjection, should burn with such feelings as we cannot describe, because we only know them by placing ourselves in his political condition.

After two hundred years that this college has existed, what treasures has it bequeathed to posterity? In vain you search its archives for one name that occupies a place in the public mind; its history is a mere blank — a pass-word of derision amongst the literary institutions of the world. True, some men of eminence, as Swift, Goldsmith, and Congreve, have passed through it, but they did so unnoticed, except by being illured, and they have taken care to record their contempt of its conductors in terms too pointed and sarcastic to be forgotten. The question has naturally arisen, — how are we to account for the almost total silence of its numerous professors? We confess, that while some sages maintain that poverty is the genuine source of inspiration, and while others think beef and claret are equally entitled to that distinction, it is no easy task to resolve the difficulty as it regards Trinity College, for we believe that the aggregate number of its fellows have experienced the influence of every degree on the dietetic scale. It is quite in vain, therefore, to look to a full or an empty stomach for an explanation of this question, for we believe the evil not to be at all of visceral origin. The fellows are very often needy adventurers from the classic soils of Munster or Connaught, who, having exhausted their Entick under the hedge, come up to town to drink deeper of the points and particles of Scrivelius or Eustathius in the garrets of the University. Having deposited their 'Path to Paradise', and religion, at home with the parish priest, and being taken with the bright prospects of a scholarship or fellowship, their whole time is devoted to the attainment of elementary knowledge — to finding out the husks of Parnassus. It is well known, that the prize is to be won, not by superiority of intellect, but by plodding perseverance; and the consequence of this pernicious practice is, that few persons submit to a drudgery as unprofitable as it is, in general, disgusting to a man of real genius. From this it follows, that men of second-rate mind are usually the candidates, and that having obtained the object of their ambition, there is generally a collapse equal to the former excitement, and that the remainder of their life is devoted to the employment of the *otium cum dignitate* afforded by an income of from two to four thousand a year. To these causes, tantamount perhaps to the explanation of the silence of the 'dumb sister', as it has been called, it might be added, that the duty of lecturing is discharged, indiscriminately, by all the fellows, while it is well known that a contrary usage has obtained for the Scotch University a preeminence, in this respect, over similar institutions. An attempt, however, has been just made, we perceive, to remove the stigma of literary supineness from this body, by the publication of a journal upon the plan of Brewster's and similar works, so that, after centuries of silence, Trinity College has been forced to commit an act of authorism, to allay public indignation. We confess that were we called to sit in judgment upon a work as transcendantly brilliant as the present is superlatively dull, and coming from this institution, we should be inclined to try the bantling of Momus and Memnon by the severest laws in the code of criticism. We have no taste for forced fruit, whether of terrene or of mental culture, and we can consider the present specimen but a bloated pompion, without the flavour or raciness of natural productions, and already floating down the stream of Lethe to oblivion. When we first heard that Alma Mater was pregnant, we did, in silence, contemplate an abortion, knowing that the sterile old dame was past the years of having a vigorous offspring. In mercy to the Thebans, who have been accessary to the birth of the Dublin Scientific Journal, we must inform them, that their plan of operations is erroneous, and that the execution is not much better. It is to no purpose that this journal reckons, amongst its contributors, a few men of the highest acquirements, such as Brinkley, in astronomy; the circulation of a merely scientific work, in a country like this, must be always extremely limited, while in other countries a sale cannot be at all expected, from being supplied with much better works and at shorter intervals. We doubt much whether the combined intellect of Dublin would support a tolerable periodical for twelve months; the elements of such a work as would ensure itself a safe sale, do not, we believe, exist in the country. Many of the best contributors of the English periodical press we know are Irish, but these writers would as soon commit their productions to the flames, as send them before the public under the damning auspices of a Dublin title-page; it would be so much labour lost. For any thing Trinity College will be able to achieve, we must, we fear, be content with importing literature of London manufacture, just as we do other fashionable commodities. Of the death of the journal that has excited these observations we are as certain as that we wish it a better fate.

So much for the literary state of our University, in the third century of its age, and in the *millenium* of its imbecility. We have been more emphatic in our censure, than we might otherwise have been, had we not been impressed, at an early period, by the lying statements which are daily put forward by some writers, an elaborate specimen of which trash may be found in Rees's Encyclopedia, where the author represents this college as a paragon of perfection, and modestly asserts, that it is much better for the public that the fellows should devote their time to instructing the pupils in the elementary parts of knowledge, and in superintending their morals, than in composing books for the aggrandisement of their own character. As to teaching the elementary parts of learning, even though the statement were as correct as it is notoriously false, we suppose any other schoolmaster would do the same just as well; and with respect to the morals of a university, in the common acceptation of that term, though no puritans ourselves, we should not have the least objection to see the man who could talk such folly placed a few hours in the pillory for his impudence. How any writer could venture, even in this 'age of bronze', to put such sentiments on paper is to as a mystery. It is not improbable but we may ramble into Alma-Mater some evening that we have leisure, and give a running commentary on the state of society within the holy walls of All Hallows. In the mean time we must proceed to the school of Physic in Ireland.

The school of Physic, as every person is aware who has consulted an Irish Almanack, is composed of six Professors, three of them appointed by the University, the other three by the College of Physicians, so that it is a joint concern between them; and for the greater accommodation of the pupils, the lectures are delivered in Sir Patrick Dun's Hospital and at the College, distance from each other about half a mile. At what time, exactly, this union took place we do not now recollect, but it were much to be wished that the partnership were dissolved, or that a more convenient coalescence could be effected. There is a grievous loss of time and shoe-leather in following these luminaries from place to place, hour after hour, and a 'rolling stone', they say, 'seldom gathers moss'. Between them they make sad business of it, and though they labour thus in common, yet each retains its own peculiar prerogative — the University, of making Bachelors and Doctors of Medicine; the College of Physicians, of making Fellows, Members, and Licentiates. Now we think that a university should have nothing at all to do with conferring medical degrees, for we know some of these same bachelors who are not fit to superintend a kennel of sick dogs. On the other hand, the College of Physicians, by what we suppose the law of involution, confer the most insignificant tile (a licence) in their vocabulary of honours upon those who have, in a great measure, the charge of the sick, and reserve the *summas honores medicinæ* for those who, in general, do nothing at all. To a mind unsophisticated by corporate ideas, which are usually of a very complex nature, it would appear, that the persons intrusted with the care of the sick, or engaged in the practical departments of their profession, are those whose experience should be most severely attested, and rewarded with the highest degree of sanction in the power of their Examiners to bestow. *Se diis aliter visum* — to those concerned it has appeared otherwise. We know that an exposure of such absurdities is a hopeless task, and that the personal interests of those individuals, in whose hands the remedy lies, will prove an overmatch for our remonstrances. So we abandon them for the present, with an intention of resuming our efforts in a future number.

When one has the charity (which is not always the case), to form a favourable opinion at first sight, he does not wish that his discrimination should be refuted by subsequent experience, or that the little philanthropy which he may happen to possess should be thrown away upon an unworthy object. It may be owing to this secret law of our nature that we still continue to cherish, with a sort of selfish pride, our original sentiments of the subject of this Memoir. We certainly were not niggardly in the estimate which we drew of his merits, nor had we any reason since to repent of a waste of benevolence, or of a want of judgment. The occasion from whence we date our recollections of him was too interesting to be soon forgotten. It was at an introductory Lecture, the best we had ever heard, in the theatre of the University of Dublin. The impression which the person of the speaker and the excellence of his address then made upon our mind has not been since obliterated. That spectator, indeed, might not pride himself much on his penetration who could not discover desert, or, at least, the usual concomitants of it, in a head so finely formed, and a cultivated intellect manifested in language so descriptive and energetic.

The gentleman of whom we are speaking is a very singular, if not an extraordinary personage; one upon whom the panegyrist might safely lavish a portion of his art, without any risk of satirising by a misapplication of praise; or the libeller, on the other hand, might exercise his vocation with almost equal success. His virtues and his foibles, his acquirements and deficiencies, are so obvious, that it would require little tact to place either in strong relief. They lie thick upon the surface, and are accessible to every hand. It would be no easy matter to decide whether his life or his lectures abound with most useful precepts; or whether his physiology is more valuable to the student, excellent as that may be, than the practical lesson of wisdom furnished by his unsuccessful career. A sort of biographical paradox, his history unites the extremes of scientific prudence and worldly neglect; of exalted merits, with the most incongruous accompaniments; of persevering industry, unrequited by its proper reward. Successful in every thing, except the great end for which most men submit to the labour of study, his conduct is correct, though daily censured by fanatical charity; with every qualification to be useful to mankind, his powers are neglected; abroad he is admired for those qualities which have rendered him an object of hatred at home; he is now an old man, professor to an University, recommended by a combination of circumstances to public notice, and, strange to say, the private practice of his profession does not produce him one hundred a-year.

The explanation of such an anomaly may appear difficult; but it is no such thing, and we shall give our reasons for thinking so. Mr Macartney was not formed by nature, or rather he did not fit himself, for the prosperous office of a liar, a pimp, a pander, or a sycophant. He could not rise into notice on the strength of a quadrille, or let his surgical dexterity be inferred from fingering a flageolet, or thrumbing on a guitar; he did not attach himself to a religious or a political faction, that he might physic the body by caressing the prejudices of the mind; he did not make the Bible (that book of woes to Ireland) a stepping stone to gain a Protestant Archbishop's ear, or reduce the influence of Catholic priests through the luxurious austerity of turbot and lobster sauce 'on days of abstinence'; he did not act the harlequin in the drawing-room, the 'Saint' in the church, the apostle of liberty at an aggregate meeting, and the minion of a despot at court; he was not a true believer before man, and an infidel with God; nothing of all this could he do; they were accomplishment far beyond the reach of an upright man. In an evil hour, however, he became connected with the College of Surgeons in London; worse yet, his talents made him formidable in office; more unfortunate still, he was appointed to a Professorship, though but a member of a despised school; and for all these crimes he has paid the penalty of being buried alive in the oblivious grave of defamation. The Royal College of Surgeons in Ireland, were the undertakers on the occasion, and it becomes our painful duty to bear mournful attestation to the fidelity with which they executed the ignominious task. Long may they enjoy the infamy of their victorious disgrace. Neither our time nor our inclination permits us to present our compliments on their success in a more elaborate shape.

The subject of this essay is now 'stricken with years', having passed the grand climacteric of life, but without any of those infirmities which generally accompany old age. He possesses, seemingly to the fullest extent all that the author of the oft-quoted *sana mens in corpore sano* could have desired in his most poetic aspirations, sanity of mind and soundness of body. Were we to attempt a description of his person, we should commence by tracing the outlines of a man of middle stature, his figure considerably inclining from the perpendicular, an effect arising from long habits of anatomical observation, rather than from any defect of nature, or the influence of years upon his frame. His head is decidedly one of the best we have seen, but loses much of its effect by being displaced from its proper position. It only wants altitude to complete its appearance. Without that towering altitude of forehead, where epic poems and other such matters are said to be nurtured by the phrenologists, his brows advance on the view with a majestic boldness that would seem to set all difficulty at defiance. His features, which are extremely regular in detail, are peculiarly expressive in the aggregate of intellectual energy, mingled too with a good deal of the severity of thought. Perhaps there is too much of the latter apparent not to suspect that other agents more powerful even than the love of study, or a passion for physiological discovery, had been working there; for there is an emanation of intense feeling which excites other sensations in the spectator than those of pleasure, particularly when subjected to the all-pervading glance of his eyes, which are full of fire, scrutiny, and animation, and as deeply set as those which we usually see in the ancient cameos of Greece. There is about his whole bust a classic elegance, a certain air of dignity, or marmorean repose, in the contemplation of which you are insensibly led to consider spirit in conjunction with its frail tenement of earth. It is this which warms the coldness of mere matter; animates the dull monotony of form; humanizes the physiognomy of man; elevates it above the passive indifference of the brute; that wins the affections, commands our respect, excites admiration, and converses through the silent language of sympathy.

We have rarely seen these remarks better exemplified than in the instance before us. His mind, though not sufficiently original or creative to be called by the name of genius, is, notwithstanding, of a very superior cast, and, as well marked, but not so regular as the portion of his person just described. We have no means of ascertaining whether he had any early predilection for his present pursuits, but that they must have been entwined with his strongest affections for a long time, the very food of his meditations, there can be no doubt, from his accumulated knowledge, and the ardour with which he cultivates them even at this day. There are men who have practised and taught their profession for many years, and are then just as little of the pathologist and the professor as the day they commenced their business. With such men, the practice of their art degenerates into routine; the didactic portion of it might be defined a mere mechanical enunciation of words, and a demonstration of certain parts, in the execution of which they feel not the slightest interest. Like so many machines, they go through the same revolutions today as they did yesterday, or if there be any difference, it is produced by external circumstances.

In such men, or rather in such *things*, there is no internal impulse; no stimulus to force them out of the old and beaten track. The communication of knowledge to their pupils, and the enlarging of the boundaries of science, which one would think ought to be the great end of their life, by a curious inversion of right and wrong, seems to be the least object of their labours. These remarks cannot be applied to the person of whom we are speaking; he possesses at least the merit of being in earnest in all he says and does. It is impossible you can sit down to hear him and fall asleep, or that you should wish that the hands of the timepiece moved somewhat quicker, or that you should become fidgetty, and relieve yourself by talking over the occurrences of the day to your companion; all which terrible visitations we have been compelled to endure under the infliction of Mr. Todd's eloquence. Mercurial himself, he is an antidote to *ennui* in others. A perfect exorcist of blue devils, they cannot tenant even the most congenial abode within the magic circle of his voice. His discourse is not a tissue of extracts selected, seemingly, for the purpose of rendering incongruity agreeable by the charms of the most powerful contrasts. He takes up any great question, places it in the proper points of view; argues and decides on its merits, like a man of general information and conscious of his powers. History, anecdote, and personal experience, are scattered in profusion, and artfully connected in a narrative which can never tire. His own strong convictions and earnestness of manner; his vast information and promptitude of application, gain him the confidence of his audience, and show them that he is not guessing at what is right or what is wrong. There is no pause, no indecision, no phrase-hunting, or lapses of the memory; his tongue enunciates as rapidly as his head conceives, and his manipulations of instruments and anatomical materials are equally correct and expeditious. He has a knack of discriminating between what is really important and what is not so. He does not talk gravely over a trifle, or make serious matters a jest. In a word, he is a perfect master of whatever subject he discusses; not a lecturer from books, or a Cooper's Dictionary professor, he furnishes the materials from his own mind; or if he borrows the tale ten thousand times told, it assumes a novel form under his plastic hands, and repetition becomes agreeable. There is an air of freshness, of discovery, or at least of renovation, about all he says, that makes the old almost as palatable as the new. These are very high recommendations to a public teacher, whose manner, if possible, should render the learning of his matter a pleasure to the student. We may live, perhaps, to afford specimens. The contrast between him and his contemporaries in Dublin is striking. We know not one who would bear comparison with him in physiology, or in general science. In comparative anatomy he stands alone.

The present would appear a proper place to consider his published compositions, but that they have already passed the ordeal of criticism in other journals. He has not written voluminously, but the few productions which have emanated from his pen bear testimony to his abilities in that line, and corroborate the opinions previously delivered. His principal essays are to be found in Rees's Encyclopedia, under the head of 'comparative anatomy', in which vast repository of heterogenous knowledge, he goes down to posterity, in conjunction with his congenial companion and fellow labourer Mr. Lawrence. These articles are composed in a plain, perspicuous, unambitious style; abound with judicious opinions, and manifest most extensive research. They give in a condensed form all the information known upon the respective subjects; and, as essays of reference, are well worthy of the perusal of students who have not leisure or means to consult more elaborate works. We should be better pleased, however, had he dipped deeper and oftener in ink, as the specimens which he has furnished rather

excite than satisfy public curiosity. So seldom does one find that
dusky element of good and evil employed to advantage, that he is
doubly disappointed when sparingly used by a master-hand. We
have heard him advance opinions and suggestions in his lectures,
which, with a little trouble, might be more successfully reduced to
the shape of a periodical essay, or even a book, than half the *one-
idea'd* cantos that daily issue from the Press.

But we have no right to dictate in matters purely personal, and
should rather be grateful for benefits conferred.

He has his share of eccentricities, and this may be one of the
number. Were we to rescue one half of them from oblivion, we
might gratify the curiosity of the idle, enhance the value of our
page no doubt to some, but without making that portion of character, with which we have to do, better understood. But old age is,
at best, a bad subject for the exercise of wit; it is its own shield
against even the harmless forms of ridicule, and wherever we find
the balance on the side of virtue, we shall ever be satisfied with
the account.

The principal features in his life being much the same that must
ever occur in that of a man of mind, and slender means, struggling
to rise above the level of his contemporaries and the tide of circumstances, we may well dispense with descending to particulars; not
but they would be found to raise him still higher in public estimation if brought to light. After a life of various incident and great
scientific exertion, it must be no small consolation to him to finish
his career in that place from whence, in the spring-tide of youth and
hope, he started into the turbulent scenes of the world — to rule in
that place where once he served — to succeed to that chair which
his master and predecessor in office had occupied. For how few is
even this reserved?

His professorship must be to him the more grateful, inasmuch as
he was elevated to it on the sole recommendation of his character as
a man of science, in opposition to the efforts of a number of candidates, seconded by strong interest and connexion. The contest at
the time was a theme of lively discussion, and would be worth a
period or two, had we space to record our recollections of the event
at proper length. The diplomatic qualifications of his opponents
were scarcely less objectionable than their intellectual incompetency, for had some of them succeeded, we presume the duties of

professor should be performed by proxy, as the want of doctorial initials were immediately removed, and brass plates blushed under the infamy of a St. Andrews degree. 'State surgery, how art thou fallen!' Operations, like charity, may, for a while, cover a multitude of sins, but, unlike that ever-during attribute, their reputation, without other merit to support it, soon fades away.

But to return — the punctuality with which Mr. Macartney insists upon the attendance of his pupils does much honour to his moral feeling. In fact, a certificate from any of the other Dublin Schools is rather a test of having paid a certain sum of money than of having received value for it, as attendance to the course forms no part of the stipulation.

His reputation has secured him a place in all the learned societies of his own, and of some in other countries. It was mooted, too, by some members of the Irish College of Surgeons, to confer on him an honorary degree, but the proposition was resisted by some influential members, on the grounds of his not having enlarged the boundaries of the art. When a man's feelings incline in a way which shall, for the present, be nameless, he is very apt to substitute a pretext for an objection, which, we fear, was the case in the present instance. It is more probable that the consequent admissibility of his pupils to an examination at York-street, under such circumstances, (a privilege which is denied at present, but we believe on illegal grounds), was the real cause of denying him a worthless title. The breach, we fear, between the parties is too wide to admit of a friendly approximation; we, at least, shall not prevent it, by dwelling on the injustice of the cause.

To him, the school of physic is indebted for whatever celebrity it possesses, for before his connezion with that establishment, it was comparatively unknown. Since that period, however, it has risen into considerable maturity, and the classes have considerably enlarged.

He attempted to establish a medical society for the discussion of professional subjects, but from the want of a corresponding feeling on the part of the members and the pupils, it has fallen into total neglect. Such is the apathy with which every attempt to kindle the torch of inquiry, and to increase the facility of acquiring information, is received in Ireland.

It is little to be wondered at, that their 'high mightinesses' of the Royal Dublin Society are, at the present moment, going-a-begging in English and Scotch newspapers for a chemist to succeed the late Mr. Higgins. What! not a Ure, a Thompson, a Hope, or any body at all to amuse the ladies in the theatre of that learned association? We hope the scientific poverty of the island and the society may not be typified in the election of Dr. Apjohn.

The preceding observations may help to give some idea of a man gifted by nature with a superior mind, of rare industry, great disinterestedness, but singularly unsuccessful, when considered in relation to his merits. His temper, moral feelings, and professional knowledge, have been the themes of unjustifiable calumniation. That disappointment may sour the disposition is easily believed; but we should prefer the honest irritability of such a man to the pliant sycophancy of a selfish speculator. The momentary animosity of the one seldom outlives the occasion which gives it birth — the malignity of the other never ceases but with the inability to accomplish its ends. Like other experimentalists, his name has been linked with the crime of cruelty, but the accusation is in itself so ridiculous that it requires no refutation. Of a similar nature is a charge circulated against him by certain fanatics, who seem, by a process of religious alchemy, to have converted charity into hatred, and Christian tolerance into persecution. Well may he reply in the words of Pope, 'All that disgraced my betters met in me'. Of the last item in the indictment, our own experience could furnish an ample refutation; but we should be doing him an act of injustice to notice seriously the scandal of an interested junto. That he did not devote that attention to the mere practice of surgery, to acquire great celebrity in that part of the art, is more to be regretted than censured. It was a fatal error, and should be a warning to all young men; for what avail the highest qualifications to the possessor, if only known to a few like himself? It is not the approbation of learned men or scientific bodies that will serve the young practitioner; he must make his merit known to the public, and that can only be done by successful cures and operations. He must make his worth obvious to their senses, and whatever medical man neglects to do so will live to repent it.

ERINENSIS
August 27, 1825

# 9

## DUBLIN HOSPITALS

*"Come draw the curtain, show the picture."*

*SHAKESPEARE*

IN A communication lately published in this Journal, a correspondent, whose praise, if it were usual with us to exchange compliments, we should willingly refund with interest, complains that we have not devoted sufficient attention to the Dublin Hospitals, and imputes our seeming neglect of these institutions to indolence. It may be readily supposed that such a charge must have proved to us an agreeable novelty, as it is the first time that a catalogue of our alleged offences has been enlivened by a public impeachment of a deficiency of exertion. Formerly, 'too much' was the fashionable accusation; 'too little' is now the word, so that in the fulness of time we may rationally expect that some new aspirant after originality will monopolize the 'cap and bells', by accusing 'Erinensis' with having said just enough! Our thanks, however, are due to this writer for his friendly memento, but he will permit us to correct a misconception of our motives, by assuring him seriously, that personal amusement, or the risibility of the public, though we should like to see them merry at the expense of folly, had as little to do in the composition of our observations on the Professors as indolence had in preventing us from paying our long promised respects to the surgeons of the Dublin Hospitals. To approach so formidable a body required some preparation, and, as our visit was intended to

97

be public, we preferred the evil of delay to an unworthy appearance before such august personages. Indeed we are aware that many of them have complained bitterly of our silence, and pined in secret for the honour of a notice in *The Lancet*. Our sensitive friend Tom Booney, for instance, has become hectic, we fear, through expectation; and Mr. Porter, the inspired editor of the 'Irish Farmer's Journal', (whom Nature certainly intended for the cultivation of cabbages, and the management of swine,) has begun to doubt of his own importance from our cruel neglect. We might quote a variety of amusing incidents, in which the pruriency of notoriety betrayed the disappointed feelings of these gentlemen in low murmurs of discontent. But really the amplitude of their talents, the unique excellence of their practice, and the picturesque diversity of their personal appearances, almost inspired us with a consciousness of our own incompetency to discharge the obligations incurred, by becoming the historian of these mighty arbiters of life and death. To all that attention which error in its most imposing aspect naturally excites in the human mind their title is indisputable, and our only merit, we fear, must consist in appreciating the magnitude, without doing justice to their claims on critical retribution. It is a matter of doubt with us, whether that prodigy of the age, Joe Burns*, 'who reigns o'er all the realms of nonesense absolute', would not suffer by comparison with his Irish contemporaries in pure, native, home-bred absurdities. But we are anticipating, and must conclude to commence.

Medicine and surgery are things of modern growth in Ireland. On looking over the eleemosynary records of that country, one would think that charity had been so too, or that the inhabitants were exempt from the ordinary lot of their species, for, until a period comparatively late, no public institutions were opened for the gratuitous treatment of disease. In walking through the wards of one of our modern gigantic magazines of lazars, curiosity naturally prompts the spectator to inquire how the paupers of Dublin, in the olden time, contrived to have their 'heads repaired' without the assistance of Mr. Palmer's trephine, or their calculi extracted without the use of the Dublin new 'landing net'. Such, however, must have been the case — they recovered of a fracture

*Surgeon to the Middlesex Hospital, London.

untortured by a saw, or perished of the stone without the aid of a surgical Walton. Happy patients! who thus lived and died, ere ingenuity had added another terror to the 'apparatus major', and the unnecessary interference of art obstructed the salutary efforts of nature, and sought to deprive her of the merit of recovering injuries of the head. This simple process of death and convalescence was incompatible with modern refinements, and no sooner had cultivation given birth to medicine and surgery in the metropolis, than Charity, smiling on the infant sciences, claimed them for her handmaids, and committed to their care the forlorn objects of her protection in an establishment first erected on the Inn's Quay, as late as the twenty-seventh year of the last century. The unavoidable procrastination of this alliance between physic and charity in Ireland has been amply compensated by the fertility of the union, for we have now every variety of hospital, from the wholesale house of recovery with three hundred beds, down to the pretty retail shop of health at a morning dispensary. It is no disgrace, however, to the country, that its early annals are unadorned by rich hospital endowments. Such institutions are the products of peace and prosperity, blessings which have only of late begun to smile upon Ireland. Whilst other countries were enjoying the advantages of equal laws, and the arts and sciences 'pursued the triumph, and partook the gale' of national affluence, Ireland, the Sicily of the British empire, had for her fair portion of its justice the blessings of penal statutes, and the fostering protection of some noble Verres, and the only medical establishment which the country possessed, an infamous College of Physicians, was either lost in the torpor of sloth, or if it showed any symptoms of animation, they were, like those of the serpent awakening from its sleep, to inflict the injury of oppression on the excluded native, and to carry into effect the orders issued at the imperial head quarters of St. James's. Charles, indeed, cast a charitable glance on Irish distress, but his chartered institutions in this country bore no resemblance, except in name, to what is at present understood by the word hospital; the first of these royal favours, the Oxmantown school, being a place appropriated for the exclusive education of the children of the lower orders of the Corporation of Dublin; the second, the Old Man's Asylum at Kilmainham, being a sort of military Elysium for the accommodation of the veteran heroes of the bayonet who faithfully assisted to keep their country enslaved. It is only surprising that the capital of a country so long the victim of all the disgraceful enactments of British legislation could present so numerous a collection of charitable institutions as Dublin can at the present hour. To the eternal honour, therefore, of Ireland be it recorded, that while statesmen and kings were restricting her commence, destroying her manufacturers, and gibbeting the cultivators of her soil, the maiden munificence of a Stephens*, the limited but generous benevolence of a Mercer, the melancholy humanity of a Swift, and the enlightened liberality of a Dunn†, wedding Charity to Science, to give each other mutual support, were ameliorating the condition of her people, and setting them an heroic example of philanthropy, which it should be their future pride to support and to imitate.

Having pointed out the causes which retarded the establishment of Hospitals in Ireland, and the means by which these obstructions to charity were subsequently overcome, we shall proceed to a notice of the last institution of this kind erected in Dublin. At the end of a dirty narrow lane, on the south side of the city, after having the jetty effulgence of Day and Martin superseded by a less splendid varnish of mud on your boots, if winter, or your clothes thoroughly saturated with dust, if summer, you arrive at a neat plat of ground, smiling with green like an Oasis in the desert, surrounded with a high wall, having two entrances guarded by gates of massy iron. Start not, reader, we are not about to introduce you to an enchanted castle, or to treat you to the story of a fair captive rescued from thraldom by the chivalry of Mr. Crampton, for in the centre of this enclosure stands, fresh from the trowel, the New Meath Hospital and County Dublin Infirmary. Passing through one of the aforesaid entrances, you proceed on a serpentine walk, admiring on your way the *tout ensemble* of the building, which is certainly prepossessing in its appearance, until you come to a pompous pile of steps, by which you ascend, and find yourself landed at once in an apartment which serves for the common purpose of a hall and a waiting room for entering patients, a portion of it being railed off for a surgery, where ulcers are dressed and minor

*Steevens
† Sir Patrick Dun.

operations performed. From this you enter a corridor dividing the
house through its whole length into two equal parts. On either side
of this passage, on the first floor, there are a variety of apartments,
amongst which a Board-room attracts the attention of the stranger
from an unnecessary splendour of decoration. One cannot help
reflecting, as he treads upon soft carpets, and looks upon other
appendages of cabinet luxury in a house of charity, that the money
so laid out is at least an injudicious expenditure, if not a fraud committed on the natural rights of the wretched. From this monthly
banqueting hall of the directors of the hospital, you turn to an
adjoining room, where you will be inclined to tarry a little longer to
observe the practice and study the physiognomy of the nosological
benchers assembled, behind a range of desks, in judgment on the
ravages of disease, with a crowd of pupils collected round each pre-
scriber, and all seemingly intent on treasuring up in their memories
the fortuitous combinations of calomel and jalap, salts and senna,
and that Irish *panacea* of treacle and water called *mistura pro tussi*.
In the aberration of your glances over this picturesque scene of
finery and rags — the bloom of health and deformity of disease,
your eye will, perchance, rest for a moment on the countenance of
a man seemingly pallid with thought, and perspiring wisdom at
every pore, while, to those who know him better, these foolish
symptoms of sapience, depicted in his face, appear but the prestiges
of constant deliberation on propriety, which a painful anxiety to
preserve only helps him in general to violate — this is Tom Booney.
Before, however, you have time to witness the various steps in the
complicated process of prescription, from 'what is the matter with
you?' to 'go to the apothecary', inclusive, and to observe the rapid
transits of the corresponding mental phenomena pass across the
disk of this gentleman's countenance, your ears will probably be
assailed by a violent objurgation, in which the slender *tenor* of
Mr. Hewson's voice and the screaming *soprano* of some old invete-
rate tea-drinker from the cellars of the liberty mingle into a hideous
concert, which generally terminates by sending the withered
amateur of Bohea to hell, with an asafœtid pill in her stomach to
cure her dyspepsia. Somewhat lower down, you may enjoy the
solemn farce of a lecture on ovarion dropsy, the patient recovering
in a few hours by parturition, from that wisest of all fools
Mr. Macnamara; or you may behold the novel spectacle of all the

diseases in Cullen's system summoned to surrender to the potency of mucilage by that Hibernian professor of surgery and agriculture Mr. Porter. Anon, the airy tread of Mr. Crampton is heard outside, and the pleasantries of this serio-comic exhibition are transferred up stairs, with dramatic celerity through the various wards of the house. Then, indeed, comes the tug of war, — masters and pupils jostling together on this ludicrous mission of health, to hear the fate of some difficult case decided, for it is the peculiar perogative of the 'Grand Lama' of an Hospital to exercise his magic powers, only, where some paltry reputation is to be gained. Here again the same process of prescribing, and snatching information at random, are repeated with increased confusion. Might not this lottery of knowledge be converted into some other scheme, in which the studious adventurer might obtain prizes with somewhat less of the uncertainty of chance? As the machine revolves at present the purchasers of tickets, like the faithless prototypes of the metaphor, generally find them blanks, and no wonder when the son of fortune presides at the wheel. Thus amused, for awhile, by the ever-varying novelties of this 'Comedy of Errors', your attention will probably be next attracted by a strange mixture of bibles and bottles, tracts and pill-boxes, piled up in formidable array on every table, and presenting a sort of miscellaneous battery of physic and divinity, for the overthrow of popery and disease. There is a ludicrous singularity in this union of the sacred and profane, a breadth of humour in this felicitous combination of a scriptural and medical pharmacopœia, which, if custom had not divested of its risible qualities, would make Heraclitus himself in his most tearful moments hold his sides with laughter. Only think, reader, of a bolus of jalap worked off with a chapter in St. Paul, or the effects of a dose of opium insured by the perusal of one of Mr. Jackson's soporific tracts! And we must add (by special permission) the hundredth Psalm chanted in unison with the chorus of the closes-tool. Oh! Joe Burns, hast thou any thing in store for us equal to this? The farce, however, does not terminate here, and, to enjoy its best scene, you should fall in at the fortunate moment, when Mrs. Geogehan, the evangelical haberdasher from the liberty, throwing aside her yard for the pastoral staff, and her case of threads and tapes for the cure of souls, glides into one of the wards, and with eyes flashing with the corruscations of the 'spirit', approaches the bedside of a moribund papist, and softly murmuring in his ear the tender expressions of damnation, eternal torments, &c. intreats him, by the hope of heaven and the terrors of hell, to abjure the errors of Rome for those of Lambeth, and, gently sliding her spiritualized fingers into a reticule, draws forth a little tract, holds up to the terrified sinner this two penny *magna charta* of his redemption, containing the conversion of some worker in wax or clipper of cloth in Plunket-street, and, to make sure work of it, sends home her inspired logic to the poor man's heart with a donation of a flannel vest or a calico shirt. Poor Pat 'knows what's what full bra'ly', and has not the least objection to accept the 'swaddling clothes', but, in his own way, declines the logic. Such is a specimen of the eccentric manner in which the evangelical harpies of Dublin prey upon the feelings of six-sevenths of the patients of our Hospitals. Women whom the madness of fanaticism has unsexed are in general the actors in these disgraceful outrages on decency, almost every Hospital in the city being patronized by some fair 'Marcellina', who tantalizes its inmates with tracts and belabours them with holy vituperation. We must add, and indeed with reluctance, that this vile system of intrusion on the religious principles of their patients, if not positively encouraged, is culpably tolerated by the medical officers of these institutions. Nay, the fire of religious animosity which burns in the breast of the master is sometimes observed to inflame the tender but susceptible feelings of the pupil. The following document, extracted from that museum of curiosities, the case-book of this institution, may serve as an example of this second-hand intolerance. 'Michael Ryan, ætat. 37, a soldier in his Majesty's 39th foot, while defending the barracks about 12 miles past Limerick, during the time of the disturbances, the rebels attacked the post at which he was sentinel, fired three shots at him, one of which took effect, having wounded him in the left hand, fracturing the forefinger and injuring the middle joint; he was in the regimental Hospital for some time, where the joint became anchylosed and the two upper portions of the finger so contracted as to be so situated as to be resting on the palm of the hand, therefore rendering the entire member perfectly useless; but such was a *mere digit* in the annals of those *murderous* and *rebellious* times — times in which no one but those of the *one party* could lay down in bed without the fear and trembling of being *butchered* before morning; neither was a man's property or means of living safe from the hands of those blood-stained marauders, for even this man was dismissed the service and was admitted into the Hospital 13 months after his misfortune, when amputation of the finger was his only relief and the only possible means of enabling him to earn his bread hereafter.' This is indeed a very *natural* species of composition, the *spurious* off-spring of passion, begot seemingly on some muse of easy virtue. We scarcely know which of its merits to admire most, the *illegiti-macy* of the puns, the *promiscuous* intercourse of the 'parts of speech', the truth of the assertions, or the excellence of morbid de-scription, and were we not aware to whom the whole matter was Alley-ed, we might be at some loss to discover the real parent of such an anomalous bantling. One can scarcely help smiling at the monkey-like ingenuity of the learned author of this compound of politics and surgery, in thus attempting to wound a portion of his fellow-students through the side of Hippocrates. Of such a silly document no notice would have been taken, if it did not help to explain the liberality of those gentlemen who superintend the concerns of this Hospital, and whose duty it ought to be to keep the sanctuary of charity and science unpolluted by party scurrility. Having enjoyed the picturesque, the statistical details of the house will not detain the spectator long. It is commodiously constructed, contains fifty beds, but seldom so many patients, and is attended by a number of pupils somewhat less. The wards were small, some would think too much so for thorough ventilation. The idea of an operating room, fitted up as a theatre, is good; but the view, from the injudicious arrangement of the seats, extremely bad. Every attention to cleanliness is observed; and, considering the squalid inmates of an Irish Hospital, the place has a look of health and cheerfulness. Clinical lectures are attempted, but, with the excep-tion of Mr. Crampton's, they are devoid of any interest. Here our praise must terminate. Morbid dissections are generally neglected, an omission the less pardonable in a city where prejudices against the post-mortem examinations of deceased relatives are rarely strong. The contempt manifested by some of the surgeons of this institution for their pupils is one of the most appalling absurdities which can well be witnessed. Yet it is quite natural that persons who pass for men of information, but possess it not, should, to maintain appearances, fence themselves round with an impenetrable barrier of ceremony, to guard against the intrusion of the curious. Ignorance, indeed, cannot afford to be communicative, or practice colloquial condescension with safety. Hence that sullen reserve and superciliousness to pupils, observable in Hospital Surgeons. And yet only touch on the string of their vanity, and mark with what freedom the praises of York-street and the anatomical superiority of Ireland will flow. Some practical anatomists, we possess, it is true, but what Irish name, after all our extensive opportunities, will go down to posterity united or identified with the science of anatomy? Yes, we must beg pardon, Harrison has written a book! Here, however, we must leave them for the present, in the tranquil enjoyment of their future fame and their national prejudices, while we proceed to notice an operation of lithotomy performed by Mr. Crampton in this institution.

This operation is seldom performed in Dublin at present; when it is, children are mostly the subjects; adults almost never. Whether it is that the disease is on the decline in the country, or that the increased number of better educated order of surgeons in the provinces, by performing the operation themselves, prevents the emigration of such patients to the capital as formerly, we are unable to decide — the latter opinion is probably correct. The case to which we allude has been rendered remarkable by an attempt to introduce a substitute for the common lithotomy forceps. The toy was, we believe, invented by a pupil of Mr. Crampton's, who seems to have a great taste for filing wire, and drilling holes in brass, having had some connexion with a watch-maker's shop. We scarcely can hope to give any idea of this childish product of Tunbridge-ware ingenuity. It appeared to us to be formed of a small oiled-silk purse, about an inch or so in depth and width, attached to a hoop of watch spring, or something of that kind, both ends of which passed up through a brass canula, forming the handle of this precious little plaything. It was expected, that by pushing this affair into the badder, the stone would instinctively fall into the silk purse, and that by pulling the ends of the elastic hoop, the stone would be nicely secured and safely ushered into light. Mr. Crampton accordingly adjusted himself before the patient, introduced a staff with much gracefulness, but made the incision, as we thought, a good deal too small. The new instrument was then handed to the operator; he forced it into the wound, which it completely filled, twisted it and turned it in every direction, but without any success. Another and another of these instruments (for there was a variety of them prepared for the occasion) were tried, and with similar effect. After tormenting the patient thus for fifteen minutes, the 'landing net' (as it was called by all those present, from its resemblance to that enemy of fish) was thrown aside for the old forceps, and the stone by its assistance, with much to do, was at length angled out. A great crowd attended to witness the failure of the 'net', amongst whom Mr. Macartney appeared to us twenty years younger than we ever saw him look before; and what was still more pleasing to us, Mr. Colles, as if convinced of the *opacity* of professors' heads, kept his own out of the spectators' view by crouching down on the floor, and never as much as relieved his feelings during this memorable operation by asseverating by any one of the three persons of the Holy Trinity.

ERINENSIS
Dublin November 26, 1825

# 10

## MR. CARMICHAEL

THERE ARE certain impressions which, though perhaps of little importance in themselves, the mind retains through every vicissitude with a singular tenacity. Such, in general, are those produced early in life by the observation of men pointed out to our notice for some personal peculiarities or intellectual endowments. Compared with what may well be called these proof impressions of the memory, struck off, as if, in the propitions excitement of the occasion that gave them birth, all subsequent recollections of the same objects are feeble and evanescent. Never did the learning of the Royal College of Surgeons in Ireland appear so awfully classical to my imagination since Mr. Hewson confronted me in a dialogue of Lucian, or Mr. Colles seem so sublimely physiological as when I first heard him hold forth on the freezing of a rabbit's ear. It may be owing to some influence of this kind, which original associations exercise over the mind, that I have chosen, almost instinctively, to describe the subject of this essay from a likeness taken at a very interesting crisis of my existence, and which, from the circumstances of the event, had bid defiance to all the casualties of obliviscence.

It is now some years ago since, walking in company with a friend into the Westmoreland Lock Hospital of Dublin, elate with all that consequence which an indenture just signed, and the anticipation of fame and fortune usually inspire in the breast of a surgeon's apprentice, our conversation turned upon the disease to which that once celebrated institution was dedicated, the professional characters who superintended its concerns, and the best means of converting its then numerous advantages to a profitable account. As eager to learn the particulars of an establishment, in which no small portion of my small capital had been vested, as my friend was willing to communicate the required information, we passed on through several apartments, observing as I went along, with qualmish curiosity, the frightful effects of the 'veneris monumenta nefandæ' that appeared on every side, but listening all the time was respectful attention, notwithstanding the delicate state of my stomach, to one of those parental admonitions which the experience of a senior pupil qualifies him to inflict on his younger acquaintance, about to commence the important duties of folding pledgets of lint and smearing old linen with various unguents. Entering another of these receptacles of female depravity, where every pallet exhibited some sad memorial of the truth of 'frailty, thy name is woman', my companion stopped, and pointing to a man at the end of the room, 'there', said he, 'is a gentleman who has lately published an excellent treatise on syphilis, from the perusal of which you will derive much useful instruction', accompanying the recommendation of the work with a high-wrought eulogium on the writer. Fixing my eyes on the revealed author with all that intensity of mute amazement excited by such a character as had been just described to me, in the youthful spectator, I endeavoured to discover in his countenance some manifestations of that superiority conceded to him by my admiring cicerone, but the only conclusion I could come to was, that he seemed a very strange-looking gentleman in black. He might, at the time, have been probably enforcing the truth of his favourite syphilitic doctrine — 'every sore has its peculiar secondary symptoms', — to a crowd of satellites, amongst whom he looked like an embryo thunder cloud, amidst its less dusky companions, gathering round the nucleus of the storm. Without being at all singled out as a subject of remark, or raised to the enviable dignity of the 'digito monstrari', Nature, in her unlimited powers of diversifying 'the human face divine', had bestowed on him quite a sufficiency of her attention in this respect to attract the gaze of one who had never even devoted an hour to the pages of Lavater. In so obvious a degree, indeed, was this the case, that had I met him amongst the gay illusions of the fancy ball, instead of the sad realities of a hospital, I might have mistaken his face for a mask, executed after a model of a North American Indian, in which the artist had essayed all his mimic powers to represent the bold, audacious bearing of the ruthless master of the tomahawk. The martial flexure of his nose — the determination seated on the closely-approximated lips — the halo of defiance encircling his ample brows — the mixture, shall I say, of mischief and design lurking in the corner of an eye half concealed by its length of lashes, which seemed to act as the conductors of this battery of mental expression — the oval disk of the countenance of an uniform tint, surrounded by a continuous fringe of dark hair and whiskers — formed a combination of features which awed me, I must confess, into a state of feeling bordering on fear. There was something so repulsive and intimidating about him, that I could not admit the truth of the panegyrics so lavishingly bestowed on him by my friend without painful reluctance; nor could I readily believe, that a man of so formidable an aspect could descend to trifle in soft dalliance even with the sanguinary Muse of Medicine, or that such muscularity of members as he exhibited, could be thrown away on the management of so insignificant a weapon as the pen. Hercules and the distaff scarcely presented an union of contradictions more incongruous than this gentleman toying with a feather, which, as Crayon well observes, would be more in character if placed in his head than held in his hand. This stiffness of manner appeared the very opposite to that flexibility of mind indicated in his compostions, while his look of haughty abstraction was at variance with the habits of minute observation testified in his works.

It is time, however, to acknowledge, that I was seldom more deceived, or my faith in Lavater brought to so low an ebb, as by a subsequent experience of the subject of the preceding remarks. Scared by the lion's skin, I should not have forgotten that it is sometimes worn by the most generous animals, as the tenderest fruits are often protected by the roughest rind. My pleasure was, therefore, equal to my surprize, when I afterwards discovered that his glances did not possess a petrifying quality; that mankind were not really suspended in contempt from the curvature of his nose; that he might actually open his clinched lips without stunning me by the thunders of his voice; and that the free exercise of his limbs was absolutely compatible with my safety; facts of which, at first, I entertained the most serious apprehensions; in short, all my fears, doubts, and dislikes were soon dissipated, as I am sure any prejudicial ideas that might have been excited by the foregoing innocuous attempts at description will be cancelled, by the name of Carmichael — a name which, to all those acquainted with the person whom it represents, is synonymous with many excellent qualities of the head and heart.

Duly impressed, however, at my first visit to the Lock, with the great importance of chancres, buboes, phagedenic ulcers, black washes, blue pills, Mr. Carmichael's physiognomy, and many other things equally appalling, I could not help bestowing a portion of my attention on the appearance of the society which filled this depôt of misery, for of all the spectacles I ever witnessed, this struck me as the most extraordinary. Whatever of visible effects the combined agency of passion and pain can produce on the human countenance, were here depicted in all the horror of reality and contrast. The reckless indifference of some — the heartbroken looks of others — the stedfast stare of confirmed guilt — the irresolute glances of virtue, still unsubdued — the composed resignation of penitence, the demoniacal abstraction of suicidal meditation — the healthless blush of hectic flashing across some pallid countenance, as if the vital current had rushed back to the bloodless cheeks of a corse — the white film mantling over some sunken eye, about to close for ever — the convulsive grasp of the hands, still clasped in the attitude of prayer, appeared in all the sad variety of woe on one side, while the hysteric laugh, the song of madness, and the exclamations of despair, resounded in my ear on the other, and without the slightest pretension to sentimentality, this unnatural medley of images, and strange confusion of sounds, realising more than the allegory of 'Sin and Death', affected me even to pain. Such scenes did the female department of the Lock occasionally present; and as I am on the moral picturesque of that institution, it may not be considered foreign to my objects to contrast its former with present state, as it has, since this period, undergone an entire revolution in its internal arrangements.

In no other country was there an establishment of greater extent devoted to the treatment of syphilis than the Dublin Lock. Three hundred beds were the amount of accommodation — the venereal disease and poverty the cheap prices of admission. The institution, at that time, was the great resort of the surgical pupils of Dublin — it is now without a single student in its wards; it was then the theatre of Mr. Carmichael's indefatigable industry, and of his numerous and able co-adjutors — it is now the deserted dominion of Mr. Henthorne, Tom Egan, and stupidity; it was then managed, at least, by men in their senses — it is needless to seek a better counterpoise for the antithesis than to say, it is now in the hands of the 'Saints'. As a charitable institution, half its objects have been sacrificed by the exclusion of males, who are now not permitted to profane the sanctity of a mercurial atmosphere by their presence, while the increased facility for receiving females holds out a sort of premium on prostitution. As a school of surgical instruction, all its advantages have been completely destroyed by excluding pupils, and reducing the number of surgeons from six to two, who certainly, at present, are not a 'host in themselves'. To be brief, it was once an establishment of great public utility — the source of health and information to thousands; it is now a sort of *haram* of penitent prostitutes, training up 'in the ways of the Lord', and of Paulus Emilius Singer. To Mr. Carmichael's experiments and excellent lectures, has succeeded an 'Avatar' of tracts, Bibles, and all the other unavailing agents of moral regeneration employed in modern times. The treatment of the patients received into this manufactory of Magdalens, is as fantastic as the opinions of their medical attendants are eccentric; every patient, on her admission, being put on a course of mercury and the Bible, and having spit her pint-a-day, and perused her diurnal portion of chapters, she has a choice of stitching 'plain or fancy work' in the Dorset Asylum, or go out to 'catch cold' once more in Sackville-street. Should she succeed in her mission after infection, she is indulged with a second admission; but should she break her vows of chastity a third time, her head is shaved in punishment of her obstinacy, and she is handed over to the 'powers of darkness' to pursue her avocations under the 'false pretences' of a wig, never again to be admitted into the sanctuary of the Lock. Thus by borrowed curls, and a new name, do these followers of their cyprian progenitors, defeat the 'wisdom of the wise', and get in and out of the hospital as often as they have a necessity.

To effectuate this ludicrous plan of arresting vice at its origin, one of the finest establishments of the kind in the empire has fallen a victim! There were certainly some moral abuses at one time in the institution, which demanded correction, for it became necessary, in consequence of an open communiciation between the male and female wards, to keep Venus and Cupid at arm's length by placing military sentinels in the passages, but it was soon found that these true disciples of Mars, like him, were caught too in the Vulcanian net (was Mr. Crampton's sublime invention of the 'net' founded on this mythological fable?) with some noseless beauty, redolent of œzena and blue pill. A classical barrier of brick and mortar was next interposed, as a substitute for the frail defence of flesh, and the lovers of the Lock left to murmur their assignations through a partition without a chink. Yet this perfect state of separation would not satisfy the suspicions of the Saints, who were, it seems, determined to rule without a rival in this grand *refugium peccatorum*, which they have now entirely in their possession. Leaving them then, for the present, in the undisturbed enjoyment of the ruin of a fine establishment, a theme of a more agreeable nature throws its refreshing shadow between us and these tinkers of the broken china-ware of female virtue, who have succeeded in propagating a vice just in proportion as they have lessened the risks attendant on its commission. So much for the moral effects of a hospital theocracy.

If it be true, as it has been somewhere asserted, that the life of an author is best studied in his works, Ireland has as yet produced no man connected with the profession of surgery, upon whom such an experiment might be made with so much propriety as on Mr. Carmichael, whose history is intimately entwined with his books. In their ingenuity, adaptation to profitable purposes, and aptitude of subject to catch the *aura popularis*, may be detected, some at least of the causes of his advancement in the profession. All, however, who write upon cancer, scrofola, syphilis, and other subjects of the same class, are not subject to the imputation of acting on the well known gullibility of the public, nor can it be supposed that Mr. Carmichael could have done so. I mean merely to state a fact without the involution of a motive. He has not, however, escaped such suspicions; nor, indeed, is this at all to be wondered at, since the daily multiplication of medical books has universally given rise to an opinion, that their authors are solely influenced by selfish views. On this head the public is not much in error, for not perhaps so much as one volume of sterling merit, or one, to use the language of the green room, which 'will keep the stage', appears amongst the some hundreds that annually issue from the press. This rapid production of books is obviously the result of an established law in the medical profession, that no man ever yet has made a first rate improvement, or discovery in the art, who has not been rewarded by the public. So certain of operation is this principle, that even its abuses have produced successful results, as the fortunes accumulated by various pretenders to superior knowledge sufficiently demonstrate. The facility of making such experiments of imposition, has tempted thousands, and will tempt as many more to the trial, for the compiling of a book is not after all a matter of such great difficulty. What operation, for instance, plan of treatment, or even principle in the practice of surgery, which might not be speciously altered or entirely superseded by a man of cleverness and tact? Then in medicine every person knows that the same effects may often be produced by the most opposite means; that to the diversity of these means there is scarcely a limitation; and that so long as this book-making susceptibility of the science continues, so long shall we be overrun by tomes on the bind, perhaps, of a slip of wire, or the fortuitous results of a drug. In this *index indicatorius* of medical literature have some of Mr. Carmichael's works been included, and certainly his first essay on cancer, from the boldness of its pretension, had rather a suspicious appearance of coming into the world with the 'original sin' of a book-making parent on its back. The secret of 'guilty or not guilty', must to be sure rest with Mr. Carmichael, but it is more probable that he was sincere in his professions of the efficacy of iron in the cure of cancer, or intended his treatise to be considered as an allegory, after the manner of the rust of the Telephean sword. It is at all events a production of singular speciousness, and if Mr. Carmichael did not succeed in making good the discovery of a specific, his profits were not in the least affected by the failure, as every old dowager afflicted with cancer, in her flight to the doctors of London and Paris, stopped on the way to pay tribute to the Baron Storck of Dublin. The leading propositions put forward in this very elaborate performance are, the vitality of cancer as an animal fungus, and its destruction by various preparations of iron. Both these propositions are supported throughout in the first style of hypothesis and ingenuity. By the assistance of analogy, simile, and supposition, the architect has succeeded in the construction of a fairy labyrinth, in the beautiful intricacies of which reason loses its way, and, like virtue in the temple of pleasure, is almost deprived of the powers of self-extrication. It would be superfluous to enter on a formal refutation of doctrines which have refuted themselves, or to canvass the efficacy of a medicine which time has deprived of its salutary properties — things which their author, at present, only regards with a smile. Nothing, indeed, is easier, in competent hands, than to raise one of those filigree works of the imagination, by a happy selection of materials and a judicious disposition of the parts. The bolder and more daring the design, the greater the chance of success, it being a curious anomaly in our nature to believe that pretension is synonymous with desert; as when a giant tells us in a placard that he is full eight feet in height, we immediately strike a standard of our own, by taking off an inch or two from the wonder, and give him credit for being at all events a very tall man. So with the doctor who professes to cure the 'incurable', we make a little allowance for exaggeration, and swallow the bait, though we suspect the hook. Nothing can be farther from my intention, than to insinuate that Mr. Carmichael had in view these frailties of our nature in the composition of his work, which I am rather inclined to attribute to a fertile imagination, and an ardent desire to benefit mankind, than to motives which actuate only the vilest quacks.

Having established a sort of property *in fee* in the breasts of his fair countrywomen by his treatise on Cancer, Mr. Carmichael next converted the nursery, that doctorial potage, into a very lucrative freehold, by the publication of an essay on Scrofula, dedicated in 'high heroic prose' to Mr. Abernethy, with whom he contends the discovery of the chylopoietic chimera. Giving Mr. Carmichael full credit for his assertions, it is somewhat strange that so vast a secret should have so long remained confined in the privacy of his own breast, and that so long a period as four years should have been permitted to elapse between the publication of his claims, and the full establishment of Mr. Abernethy's, without any attempt being made to vindicate a priority of right to the miracles of the blue pill. It is possible that heaven might have revealed to him this grand *arcanum* before it was dreamed of by the Chancery hero of defeat, but it must be confessed, that it is not according to the disinterested ways of doctors, to deprive the world of the advantages of discoveries by suppression, when their promulgation leads to fame and emolument. In the execution of the work itself, there are many points connected with the origin, progress, and objects of the celebrated doctrine which Mr. Carmichael advocates, that might be made subservient to interesting observation, but within the limits of five pages, scarcely sufficient for that purpose alone, such a task cannot be attempted.

We next come to his work upon Syphilis, upon which his reputation as a medical writer mainly depends. Without entering minutely, for the reasons just stated, into the merits of this publication, it cannot be denied that it has influenced the treatment of syphilis not only in the country where it was composed, but in others also, by checking the indiscriminate use of mercury, and by directing the professional mind to the variety of sores which had been previously confounded with syphilis. Though there are many positions advanced in this work, which admit of great latitude for doubt and speculation, yet if Mr. Carmichael had conferred no other benefit on society than this work, he would well deserve their gratitude. Besides these works, he has given to the public an essay on mercury, with numerous other detached pieces published in the Journals, and all written with a degree of literary ability and rhetorical tact, which seldom falls to the lot of medical authors. Something, and only a little, remains to be said of the *man*, now that we have done with the *author*, in obedience to the Paul Pryism of the age, so curious in this respect. To those persons, however, who have been amused for the last quarter by descriptions of Dr. Parr's wig, his shoe buckles and *bon mots*, Mr. Carmichael offers little to gratify a propensity for gossip. He is a man of very plain manners, unpretending address, unostentatious habits, and on every subject of liberal opinions. As a surgical operator, his bold use of the knife would be awful to a spectator unacquainted with his perfect knowledge of what he was doing; and as a lecturer, though I have heard him in that capacity, my recollections on the subject are too indistinct to be reduced to language. He is one of the few surgeons of Dublin, whose success has grown out of the fertility of his own mind, unwatered by a rill of lordly patronage. His fame is therefore not the polluted exhalation of a job, or his fortune the fruit of the forcing-frame. Neither bishop, priest, nor parson, nor any other secondary minister of Providence on earth, had any thing, that I know of, to do with placing him, as he is at present, on a level with the highest in the profession in Dublin. By self-exertion solely, he has worked his way to eminence and independence — the highest praise that can be bestowed on a professional man in Ireland, where so many efforts are made to deprive merit of its rewards. One drawback must be made upon this unqualified approbation. He has not taken that place in the College Cabinet, which his talents and, above all, his honesty, qualify him to fill. Why stand by in silence, while Mr. Todd and his creatures are voting away the establishment to destruction? Does he experience no self-abasement at the prospect of seeing such a man as *grinder* Harrison appointed to a professorship at the retirement of his brother-in-law Mr. Colles, who has it in contemplation to inflict this farewell disgrace on the College, when he can pack a court base enough to succumb to his dictation? Does he think the existence of a law unrepealed on the statute book of the Corporation, by which law such an abuse could by possibility be committed by any individual, is compatible with the duties which he owes to himself and society? Does he feel no qualms of conscience, no indignation rise within him, at seeing two hundred pounds given to such a man as Mr. Henthorne, under pretence of buying plate for him, while the registered pupils, whose money is thus squandered away, are not allowed as much as a book to read? If he do not feel the gorge of honest contempt swell his breast at witnessing such corruption, and come forward to resist it with energy, then, indeed, the estimate just delivered of his character has been conceived in ignorance, and executed by a partial hand.

ERINENSIS
Dublin March 4, 1826

P.S.   I have to acknowledge the receipt of a 'Sketch of Mr. Harrison', forwarded to me a long time back by the Editor of *The Lancet*, and to return the writer my sincere thanks for the perusal of that document, which shall be made use of at a proper time.

ERINENSIS

**Dr. Steevens' Hospital.**

FOUNDED A.D. 1720.

# 11

## STEVENS' HOSPITAL*

THE LIFFEY flows from the west into the capital of Ireland, through a valley of great beauty. I shall detain the reader for a moment on the margin of this pleasant ravine. The declivities forming its sides terminate at the base in a rich sward, about a thousand paces in width, and spread out above into what may be relatively called two table-lands, comprising the Phœnix Park on one side, and a champaign country on the other, extending as far as the range of adjacent mountains, whose rude asperity gradually softens down into this luxuriant plain. Standing upon the verge of this chasm, a prospect of extreme magnificence opens to your view. Immediately beneath, spanned by the majestic arch of Island bridge, the river rolls through a serpentine channel, fringed with a copse of scattered hawthorns and other shrubs. On the opposite bank rises the venerable pile of the Old Man's Hospital, with its avenue of stately elms, the whole seemingly muffled in the mantle of time, and participating in the senility of its superannuated inhabitants. To the right, continuous masses of wood crown the heights along the course of the river, while to the left, the domes, spires, and all that pinnacled perspective which a great city discloses when viewed from an elevation, pierce the heavens with an endless

*Dr. Steevens' Hospital

variety of surface. In the rear of this splendid panorama of nature and art, groups of trees tastefully arranged through the park by Chesterfield, open into innumerable vistas, through which the Viceregal Lodge, the residences of the Secretaries of the Irish government, and other public buildings, may be discovered, half veiled in a profusion of shade. While lost in the mute admiration which a scene of such grandeur is calculated to excite, your attention, perhaps, may be arrested by a murky edifice, whose narrow windows, contiguity to the river, and otherwise industrious aspect, might, at first sight, mark it out as the probable abode of steam engines and spinning-jennies. Should your curiosity, however, induce you to cross the Rialto of Dublin, in order to explore more minutely the nature of this dusky mansion, you will be not a little surprised on a nearer approach, neither to hear a furnace nor a fly-shuttle resound within its walls. On the contrary, an air of unusual solemnity breathes around the place; the tall chimnies puff out their smoke in silent convolutions; the hum of the city, though just at hand, is scarcely heard in the distance; and nought, save the occasional rattle of an Irish jaunting car, or the heavy tramp of troopers on the military road, disturb the stillness of the valley. The suspicions which an economy of glass, and the absence of white-

Dr. Steevens' Hospital, the Quadrangle.

wash, had previously awakened of the presence of manufactory of cotton or cast-iron, will being to subside at a closer approximation, and if a drop of doctorial blood circulates in your veins, you will begin to think that the dingy structure is well situated for a temple of Æsculapius. The conjectures thus excited of the intention of the building, will be further strengthened by the protrusion of some haggard head from one of the windows, surmounted by a night cap, on which the alkalies and sunbeams would seem to have lost all influence, and ornamented below with a crop of grisly beard, disclaiming all connection between the once-united handicrafts of shaving and surgery. Apprized of the real character of the institution by this appropriate emblem of nosology, reducing the table of contents to Mason Good's 'Study of Medicine', into a hideous personification, you arrive at a gateway on which the following unostentatious inscription on a marble tablet informs you of the names of the founders of the magnificent establishment which you behold:

> 'RICARDUS STEVENS, M.D. *dotavit*
> *Griselda soror ejus œdificavit.*'

Breathing a heart-felt benediction on the memory of the rivals in benevolence, you cast your eye along the steep roof, out of which a small capola ascends, containing a clock, and finished at top by a vane, which, from its site, one might be led to suppose was intended to ridicule the mutability of medicine. Passing the arched entrance, you find yourself in the court of a quadrangular building, upwards of a hundred feet square, the enclosed area being divided by walks into four grass plats, and having a small pyramid in the centre, the pivot on which the whole concern would seem to turn. It is impossible to look around, and not to be struck with the superiority of our ancestors' ideas of hospital architecture over the boasted notions of modern times on the same subject. To the naked, four-storied, dandy-looking edifices of the present day, out of which a convalescent can scarcely venture his head, without being frost-bitten by the cold, or deluged with rain, the snug sheltered piazza carried round the interior fronts of this building, presents a most comfortable contrast. Imagination instantly peoples such a colonade with sunny invalids, wooden legs, bandaged arms, and all the other *insignia* of mutilated humanity. Being sure, however, by this time, that the building is a hollow-square, two stories in height, with an attic in the long roof, a piazza constructed by a series of arches, supported on insulated pilasters, having a corridor between them, and the curtain wall of about twelve feet; that, in fact, the whole concern has a good old-fashioned look of comfort and solidity: convinced of all this, should one of Mr. Cusack's twenty-eight apprentices be your cicerone, he will next conduct you to the library, containing an useful collection of works accessible to the students, then to the Museum, a filthy niche, covered over with pipe clay, and variegated with red injection; he will afterwards introduce you into the wards, expatiate on their extent, cleanliness, and convenience, all which is certainly true; insist on the advantages of having distinct surgical, medical, venereal, cancer, and ophthalmic wards; hitch in a compliment or two to his master, and having thus shown you the 'Lions' of the establishment, conclude by asking you to a dinner of execrable beef steaks, with a washdown of whisky-punch, and with this mess of carbonized cowskins putrifying in your stomach, treat you to a 'set-too' with the 'gloves' *a la* Dan Donnelly — an amusement in which the young gentlemen residing in the hospital were no mean proficients in my time. After an evening spent in this edifying manner between the gloves and the glasses, you cannot fail to perceive that the surgeons of the institution have taken advantage of the super-abundance of house room, and converted a part of it into dormitories for their pupils, each of whom, according to seniority, is entitled to a residence in the hospital for a certain time, generally two years. During this period, the resident pupils possess as many opportunities of acquiring a knowledge of their profession, as any similar institution in the united empire presents. Hence the value of a surgeoncy to this hospital; for though there is no emolument of any importance attached directly to the situation, the patronage which it creates, and the number of pupils which it secures, are sources of certain wealth to the possessor. The considerable revenues derived in this indirect manner by patients and apprentices, are not sufficient to satisfy the insatiable avarice of the surgeons to this hospital, who exact an exorbitant annual fee for admission from the visiting pupils.

Amongst all the anomalies, indeed, which have disgraced the profession in Ireland, there is not one can be put in competition with this practice. It is a restriction on the attainment of knowledge, an unnecessary tax upon the student, and a vile impost on poverty and disease — deprived, too, of all justification by being alienated from those objects, on whom, if collected at all, it should be scrupulously expended. Is Mr. Colles not ashamed to oil his carriage wheels with this purulent income? Does Mr. Crampton feel no apprehension of suffocation from imbibing the claret of the Meath? Does Mr. Piele experience no twitches of chastising gout in his tight legs, swathed in Richmond gaiters? Or Mr. Palmer no humiliation in paying his landlady in French-street with the small change of Mercer's? Fie! fie! Gentlemen, your 'offence is rank, and smells to heaven'. By what authority these fines on scientific pursuits are imposed, is not very evident. Does the will of Dr. Stevens, or the Act of Parliament which empowers the Governors to manage his bequest, go so far as to entitle these gentlemen to invest the surgeons with an unlimited power to levy such exactions? I believe neither to be the case, and must conclude, that the conduct of the surgeons in this instance is not only disgraceful, but also illegal; they might just as well stop a pupil on the road, and take so much money out of his pocket, or out of the funds of the institution. There is not a man who pollutes his fingers with this peculation, who does not well know that the practice is unjustifiable. It is not, indeed, one of the least urgent arguments for the destruction of the London heptarchy of corruptionists, that they have encouraged, by their odious enactments, this simony of the property of the poor. Were the certificates of our minor hospitals admitted, as they should be, at the Court on the other side the channel, the serpent's head would soon be crushed here. The influence of bad government is seldom local in its operation. Like the fictitious Upas of Java, it diffuses its poison to an incredible distance from the source, and it cannot be denied that the spirit of monopoly in London has been the parent of hospital exaction in Dublin. The foundation, however, of this system, seems at length to be sapped, and the train laid, which must eventually produce its explosion. It is impossible, indeed, that any medical or surgical college, as at present constituted in these countries, can long withstand the tornado of popular odium gathering in the scientific horizon, with a Lawrence and a Free Press to guide its omnipotence.

Already the flag of reform flies from the walls of the Irish College, — nay, I would say, the very 'cap of liberty', but that Sir Peter Courtenay might not sleep soundly under so awful a sign.

Great things are doing, but I must draw breath before the recital is commenced. In the meantime men are beginning to think for themselves, and to act with becoming independence. Disenthralled from the leading strings of authority, the junior members of the profession are no longer depressed by the nightmare of official names. A better spirit seems to animate their intentions, and more prudent principles to direct their energies. They appear to have learned of late what they should long since have known, that, equality of rights, suffrages, and advantages, is preferable to a state of things in which the few are elevated, by artificial distinctions, over the majority. In them the power resides — they have only to will the deed, and it is done. For what, after all, does a young man, by his subserviency, gain from a senior optimist? Courtesy, compliments, and a dinner. 'Many are called, but few are chosen', might be assumed as the motto of these veteran professors of, 'whatever is, is best', and should warn the youthful expectant of the literal profanity with which they adhere to the text. Submission to authority may be carried to a guilty excess, and respect for experience made to stifle the dictates of conscious rectitude. It is a truth, of which there have been but too many melancholy proofs, that grey hairs are not always accompanied by generosity of feeling, nor years enriched by commensurate acquisitions of wisdom. At least in these degenerate times, old age as often produces an 'Overreach' as a Solomon. He that has nothing to boast of in the council, but the days he has numbered; who has no other arguments to second his advice, but the trammels of custom, and the dogmas of his will, should betake himself to some more fitting scene of action, where he may indulge his desires without injuring society. To hear an old Sir Oracle, a '*laudator temporis acti*', hold forth on the horrors of change, you might suppose that reason only ripened as the body declined, or that the extinction of the senses was necessary to the perfection of the mind. Of all the cants of this canting age, the cant of danger from innovation is the most indefensible and hostile to the progress of improvement. It is the pitiful scream which the sloths who batten on corruption raise, on all occasions, to scare away the intrusions of the enemies to both. Amongst the venerable personages who support error on the strength of such arguments, some juvenile delinquents may also be found. If you analyse a scheme or a job, you are sure to discover one of them, like a *caput mortuum*, at the bottom. Speaking of jobbing and heads reminds me of Mr. Porter. Poor gentleman! he would transplant the filthy politics of the Guild of Merchants into the College — sow the seeds of an oligarchy in a republic of letters — convert the purlieus of York-street into a conservatory of *Dutch* flower-roots — and mount the cameleopard of Mr. Pearson with a statue of King William. The poor gentleman! when passing this way again, I may be tempted to 'drop in' on the labours of the political horticulturist; at present I must emerge from a digression induced by the nature of passing events.

Though this hospital is capable of containing three hundred beds, the income is unequal to the support of more than about half that number of patients. This is the more to be regretted, as, notwithstanding the numerous charitable establishments in Dublin, one-half the sick poor remain unaccommodated. The government of the Institution is not so happily constituted as could be wished, and leads to consequences which could never have been contemplated by the founder. It is vested in the hands of men whose connexion with the church, the bench, and with the higher circles of society, leaves them little leisure for the performance of eleemosynary duties. The necessities of the poor seldom transcend the lofty barrier that divides them from the aristocracy, nor are the hands of the affluent always the most scrupulous in doling out the scanty, but sacred treasures of charity. Whatever economy the rich may be blest with, they generally appropriate for domestic use — in the distribution of public money they forget the arithmetic of frugality, and act the spendthrift without expense. A lord chancellor (with reverence be it spoken) may not be the most profound judge of the washing of blankets, nor the palate of an archbishop, accustomed to the complex savour of turtle and malakatanni, be capable of deciding on the merits of the simpler juices of beeves' heads. Out of the 23 nominal governors, only five or six take any interest in the management of the institution. Neglect of servants, extravagant salaries, and a superfluity of house officers, are but too often the necessary result of the indifference of hospital guardians. The professional attendance, though conducted in conformity with the design of the testator, is not more happily arranged. It has not kept pace with the recent wants and circumstances of the establishment. The increased number of pupils and patients would seem to demand a less niggardly supply of medical attention. There are seven officers of this class — two visiting, two assistant, and one resident surgeon, with a visiting and an assisting physician. The surgical business is principally conducted by the assistant and resident surgeon. Besides the hospital department, a dispensary is attached, where externe patients receive medicine and advice on stated days in the week. About a hundred pupils generally attend; apprentices only are permitted to dress or to perform minor operations. The clinical system of instruction as practised in foreign hospitals has never been attempted here — an error which the facility of accomplishment makes still more apparent.

Such, however, is Stevens' Hospital in situation, architecture, and internal policy; some notice is due to the memory of its benevolent founder. Of the private history of this individual little, I believe, remains, nor is there any written account. From the histories of Dublin, of which there are many, all we can collect is, that he was a practitioner in medicine in the city, having an estated property to the amount of six hundred pounds a year, which, at his death, he bequeathed to his sister during his life, and afterwards to be laid out on the erection of a hospital. Preferring the relief of the poor to 'a youth of folly, an old age of cards', this amiable lady immediately commenced the accomplishment of her brother's wishes in 1720, on a scale of magnificence worthy of ampler means, reserving for herself but one hundred and fifty pounds a year, with apartments in the new establishment. In trusting to national generosity for the completion of her extensive designs she was not entirely disappointed. Amongst the many who contributed from time to time, during the infancy of the institution, was Mrs. Johnson, better known by the poetical appellation of Stella, and her unfortunate attachment to Swift. At her death she willed a thousand pounds for the endowment of a chaplaincy, and thus, along with some other additions since made to the same fund, the spiritual comfort of the establishment has been secured. Of late, Government has advanced considerable sums, and still pays the annual sum of five hundred pounds to the establishment — not the least useful item surely in the Irish Estimates. The whole revenue of the house, including this grant, amounts to about three thousand a year. As a lasting monument of private benevolence, this hospital is an honour to the founder and to the country that gave him birth.

Of the manner in which operations are conducted here I shall give a short specimen. Matters of this description have latterly attracted much notice, and it is now quite the rage to attend such exhibitions at Stevens'. Mr. Cusack is the acknowledged 'Magnus Apollo' of this department, over which, it must be confessed, he sheds a sort of murky illumination. To do him justice, however, he spares neither pains nor expense in providing materials for these bloody saturnalia of our art. The method of securing a constant supply of such cases for weekly consumption constitutes a science in itself. To Mr. Cusack we are indebted, and I take this opportunity of complimenting him on his tact, for reducing this practice to a regular system. Before this time it was usual for the surgeons to wait until God sent patients, or the exigency of disease compelled them to seek relief, but this gentleman, anticipating the natural course of events, meets the reluctant victim on the road and hastens him on to the knife. He seems to possess an instinctive faculty of discovering latent disease, and an ambition of acting journeyman to Nature in remedying her defects and deformities. There is no garret too high, or cellar too low, to conceal a tumour or a calculus from his lynx-eyed research. The country and the city are as closely drawn as a fox-cover; and if game be started, its passage to the metropolis is liberally paid on a stage-coach. As yet, however, I have not heard that he has paid a pension, like some of his contemporaries, to his patients as a recompense for surgical mutilation. But let us suppose, for the sake of brevity, that a case is secured. The first step towards the operation, when a crowd is expected, is to issue tickets in order to insure a select assembly, a device of which Mr. Cusack is the inventor. Before I proceed farther I must describe the *locale* of this motley spectacle. The architect of the hospital, it appears, did not consider that an exhibition-room was necessary to his plan, as he provided no theatre for that purpose; one, however, has been lately added: it is of a pentagonal shape, capable of containing about a hundred and fifty persons, and looks like an exostosis on the western exterior front of the building. From the first floor corridor of the hospital two passages lead to this place, one for the spectators, the other for the operators, which bears a strong resemblance to the *proscenium* of a puppet-show, a drapery of faded green being suspended from an arch, and intended, I presume, for a screech-damper, by the ingenious con-

triver. A small stove, a water-tank, and a chair, seemingly coeval
with the institution, constitute the rest of the furniture of this
apartment. From daily opportunities of enriching my portfolio
with sketches of the *memorabilia* of Stevens', I shall select a recent
operation as the subject of my pencil. It was on Saint Patrick's day.
Tickets to a large amount were distributed to a grateful multitude,
one of which bits of paste-board I had the honour of receiving at
the hands of Mr. Cusack himself, little suspecting that he was opening the gates of Troy to the Grecian horse. The Sinon of the drama,
as some might call me, I took my seat amongst the crowd, and after
waiting some time, a nurse of vast circumference, and combining in
her appearance all the attributes which should distinguish a
priestess of Hygeia, flowed down the steps to make the necessary
arrangements. To this plethoric personification of the hospital
dietary succeeded the serio-comic contrast of Mr. Cusack's face,
evidently in a state of civil war with his feelings. A burst of
applause from the benches composed this struggle of the passions,
and a leer of assumed satisfaction mantled over his countenance.
You could still, however, perceive the anxiety of anticipated difficulty exciting the muscles of expression into a revolt against the
tyranny of affected indifference. The miscellaneous assortment of
his features, each being an antithesis to its neighbour, favoured the
full development of this contention between voluntary and involun-
tary motion. He was presently relieved from this physiognomical
dilemma by the entry of Mr. Colles, with a sort of nautical waddle,
his hands thrust up to his elbows in his breeches pockets, a bunch
of shamrock dangling in his hat, and a gibe full fledged playing
round his lips, ready to take wing with the first opportunity. Mr.
Piele and Mr. Wilmot completed the joint stock company for the
operation, which was immediately commenced by the party on a
female, having a tumour situated in front of the ear. Though the
knife was held by Mr. Cusack, like Joe-Burns, the by-standers
seemed to have divided the labours of the operation, a practice
which, though often intended well, is both unfavourable to the
reputation of an operator, and excessively disagreeable to the
spectators. There was nothing further worthy of remark in the case.

   Mr. Cusack's operating has been the theme of much discussion
in the professional *coteries* in Dublin of late, and he is certainly
entitled to much praise for many bold and successfully under-

takings in that branch of surgery. Without a mechanical turn of mind, his motions appear stiff and confined, and though you can readily discover the tact of a practised hand in whatever he attempts, it seems to be more the effect of a mere knowledge of anatomy than of natural taste. His operations want that happy amalgamation of qualities in which science scarcely restrains the movements of the instrument, and the hesitation of caution is artfully concealed by a vigilant presence of mind. Just as he had concluded the present operation, and the class was about to retire, he stepped forward, and with a wink of inexpressible comicality informed them, that there would be more fun instantly. The young gentlemen took the hint, composed themselves for the second course, and another tumour, situated under the breast of a female, was served up, and removed by Mr. Wilmot, whose late elevation to the vacant Professorship entitles him to a full-length portrait in the pages of *The Lancet* by

ERINENSIS
Dublin, May 6, 1826

# 12

## MERCER'S HOSPITAL

AT THE junction of four streets, in a central and densely popu-
lated part of Dublin, there stands a building of a very singular
appearance, to which a Mrs. Mercer, some eighty years ago,
bequeathed her name and fortune. I know not well how to describe
the plan of a structure which, in one language of architecture,
might be called shapeless, and to which no combination of lines
known to me bears any resemblance, except, indeed, one of the
'five irregular bodies' might aspire to that distinction. If it were
square, round, or elliptical, I might then have some chance of being
understood; but instead of being bounded by four right angles, as
most Christian dwellings are in these days, so, Euclid be my
witness! no less, I am convinced, than eight or ten wrong ones
distort the 'chance created form' of this Babel-tower of Surgery.
To convey, therefore, any notion of so strange an assemblage of
stones I entirely despair, and have only to entreat the reader to
consider its exterior aspect as something picturesque, Chinese,
Arabesque, a compound of the three, any thing, in short, he
pleases, provided it be different from every thing he has ever seen
before in the way of masonry, while I attempt to enumerate its
more tangible peculiarities.

First, then, there are four stories, and two fronts, one pro-
truding in cut stone, the other receding to some distance behind, as

if shy of its humble pebble-dashing, while four gables, I believe, tapered out into long chimnies, crown the brows of this monstrous creation. Descending from these lofty outrages on taste, to others of a more lowly station, we find economy and convenience once more violated by a terrace, which renders this mansion of broken legs accessible to those persons only who possess the perfect use of their limbs. For what other purpose than as a type of the difficulty of attaining the benefits of charity, this architectural stratagem of admission was erected, I could never learn, except it might have been the intention of the builder to imitate the hall-doors on the round towers of Ireland, never less than fifteen or twenty feet from the ground, and which induced Swift to remark, in his inimitable irony, that they were built for the sole end of puzzling future anti-quarians. At the base, and in front, as the anatomists express it, of this '*Scalæ Gemoniæ*', rises a fountain, the daily incidents occur-ring round which might have furnished the 'Dean' with the mate-rials of another 'City Pastoral'. At all hours may here be seen the Galateas of the adjacent lanes and alleys replenishing their pitchers with the bubbling spring, or stripped to an altitude above the knee of very questionable propriety, trampling the stains out of their tattered garments in tubs of foaming suds, while the water, thus saturated with the pollutions of the city, flows in gentle ripples over the pavement, and, with the co-operation of the sun, manufac-turers an odour which takes the passenger by the nose in a most ruffianly manner. If a guess might be hazarded on so abstruse a point, mayhap this exhalation tends to lessen the salubrity of the Hospital; but not being deeply read in pneumatics I will not posi-tively affirm that the 'Governors' of the establishment are culpable in permitting this problematic nuisance to continue in sympathetic operation. But to pass over the other adjuncts of this grotesque edifice, which had excited by curiosity so much, I was resolved to explore the interior, and soon found means to accomplish my object in a succession of visits. I perceived, on the first of these occasions, that the composite style of the exterior had been preserved with the most consistent fidelity in the internal subdivi-sions of the institution, which seemed to have danced into their places to the music of 'Wolf's Glen'. Entering a hall of ample dimensions, I turned to the right, and found myself in an apart-ment, fitted up with becoming frugality, for the accommodation of the 'Board', and examination of patients. It is worth pausing in this venerable niche, in order to review its timeworn contents, every article of which is stamped with the 'wear and tear' of very long service indeed. Amongst these faithful fixtures, a chimney-piece attracts the homage of the spectator, as a fine specimen of the style of ornamenting fireplaces in the 'olden time', by a massy frame-work of wood, exhibiting in its tracery every possible combination of the ovalo, astragal, and abattus, which moulding planes could execute. On either side of this splendid altar of the 'Lares' and 'Penates', stood two presses, in which Mrs. Mercer, I guess, might once have stowed her high-heeled shoes and long-bodied gowns, but in which now, probably, repose the 'archives' of the institution, shortly, I understand, to be edited by Mr. Aunlech, the geneologist. A deal table, curtailed of its legitimate height by the moths, covered by a cloth which was once green, and indented by many shining depressions from repeated frictions of free-stone, stretched its enfeebled frame along the centre of the room. A set of chairs, disdaining the luxury of hair-cloth and chopped hay (Bride's alley forgive me!) completed the furniture of this interesting chamber, except two portraits, in which scarcely a vestige of 'the human face divine' could be discovered through the opaque varnish of years, and here and there 'letting in new light through chinks that time had made'. The carpentery work corresponded in fashion and colour with these elegant cabinet chattels, and save the doubt inspired by its investment in the rust of antiquity, might be put down from its ochry hue as the genuine growth of 'Shilelah'. The walls too, I suspect, were once painted, but gradual decomposition has either restored the ingredients of the mass to a separate independence of lustre, or a compound of such a prismatic diver-sity of tints has been produced, that it is not safe to assert which may be the prevailing shade at present. A ceiling, which might still retain some traces of butter-milk and whiting, if the sable frescos of at least twenty generations of flies had not sadly obscured the pig-ment, with the assistance of a religious light streaming in through glass frosted over with dense incrustations of dust, formed an appropriate firmament to this little world of wonders.

After indulging in the ludicrous associations excited by those objects, I almost repented the folly of a malicious fancy, when I became better acquainted with their history, and learned, that some at least of these defects were the consequences of accident rather than design, but which, as a faithful painter, I am bound to copy without flattering the subject of my pen. Wherever the cause of humanity is advocated, whether under the shelter of architectural pomp, or the humbler roof of limited benevolence, the intention consecrates the means, and we should perhaps more properly say, in the name of the afflicted, 'God bless the giver'. In converting her residence into a refuge for the diseased, the generous foundress (one of those phenomena of her sex who surprise as much by the rarity of their appearance as by the actual splendour of their virtues) could have no presentiment of the extent to which her example was to operate on congenial minds, nor exercise any control over the appearance which their liberality was to assume. Her bequest may therefore be looked upon as a nucleus, round which the tears of human compassion, collecting in successive drops, at length crystallized into these irregular forms. From containing originally but nine beds, it now boasts of fifty, and was for a long time one of the principal Surgical Hospitals of our metropolis. Its connexion with some eminent practitioners, who flourished in the infancy of the art in Ireland, and with the College in its greener days, invested it with a temporary importance, which has declined with the removal of their causes, so that the morning tide of disease which once rolled to its door for relief, has since receded and left its hall a deserted spectacle of some twenty or thirty cases for treatment and selection. This duty, I soon observed, was performed consistently with Irish ideas of regularity, that it, generally an hour after the appointed time; or should the bowl circulate freely on the preceding evening, the mass of disease in waiting was left for that day to spontaneous convalescence, notwithstanding the restorative influence of 'Thwaite's double soda' on squeamish stomachs and throbbing temples. Making the necessary allowance for these intrusions of Morpheus on the rights of the sun, I was fortunate enough, however, to fall in when the process of artificial cure was in progress, and it was a goodly sight on these occasions, while sitting under the shade of the aforesaid altar of the 'household gods', to contemplate the rising generation of surgeons, and their professional elders, assembled in the miscellaneous avocations of talking politics and polemics, and now and then diverging into the field of medicine by way of varying the conversation. A man-like-master sort of feeling seemed to pervade the members of this little family circle, and to produce a social loquacity that sometimes rose into the dignity of actual declamation. Whatever difference might have existed between their scientific attainments I know not, but to all appearance that halo of respect, which knowledge ever draws around the profession, offered in this instance no opposition to the familiar incursions of the pupil on the converse of the master. Though an advocate for freedom of intercourse between persons placed in these relations to each other, I could not help regretting that the dignity of office was not supported by such an ascendency of intellect as might prevent their communion from degenerating into a licentious equality. — Amongst the foremost of these juvenile disputants with their superiors, were two young gentlemen of very opposite principles and appearances indeed, and whom I understood to be the senior pupils of the establishment. The logical sublety and argumentative tact displayed by them on one of those themes of discussion which keep Ireland in a state of perpetual excitement, rivetted my attention on the speakers. They certainly looked the characters which they respectively supported with an authentic identity of expression, not to be excelled even by dramatic artifice. The one, an advocate of 'Ascendancy', was blessed with the complacent plumpness of feature characteristic of the professors of that prosperous creed; the symmetry of his elegant form was admirably developed by the auxiliaries of the most fashionable apparel; his dark hair mantled into curls of 'dreadful beauty' over cheeks glowing with the rose, while his fine brown eyes sparkled as if with an instinctive consciousness of promotion to the next snug place in the gift of his 'friends'; so that making some allowance for disparity of size, he appeared not unlike a Cupid, or an Adonis, turned into a politician, and decked in the habiliments of a modern dandy. To this smiling disciple of Hobbs and Burlemaque, a portion of his college course to which he seemed to have paid particular attention, stood opposed the champion of 'Toleration', with deeply chiseled features of Roman configuration; a care-worn cast of countenance, as if it had been ground to an edge on the wheel of everlasting thought, and imbibed its sallow hue from the pale light of the lamp; lank hair, tossed into revolutionary disorder across a forehead spurning the indignity of disfranchisement, and altogether present-

ing such an assemblage of qualities as imagination might bestow on
the shade of Milesius mourning over his persecuted race. While
these youthful representatives of their country's 'rights' and
'wrongs', with all the argument on one side and the prospect of a
very substantial substitute on the other, illuminated their syllogisms
by the collision of their emulous glances, farewell to all ideas of
Hippocrates and John Bell. Every other consideration was merged
in the attraction of the dialogue, and the pen of prescription itself
was seen to stop in its hurried manifestoes against coughs and
colics, as if fascinated by the passing charms of political dispute.
Though the contest was conducted with the utmost good temper, I
could not but lament the existence of a state of things which would
thus diffuse its poison into all ranks of society, and divert the
thoughts of even the young from more useful pursuits.

The echoes of the combat, however, had scarcely died away,
when the hilarity of the scene was again revived by one of those
ludicrous exhibitions that sometimes occur in a Dublin Hospital
during the examination of that singular compound of cunning and
simplicity, the Irish intellect. I copy the circumstances from
recollection, and claim indulgence for the errors of a memory more
sensitive perhaps than tenacious of its impressions. On the consulting 'tripod' sat, at the time a diminutive personage of a very
curious aspect. His dress of gaudy tint had evidently seen some
service, and manifested as little familiarity with the brush as his
matted locks, plumed with the down of the pillow, did with the
application of the rack-comb. His countenance was tinged with
such an intensely chlorotic hue, had contracted into such a medalic
pettiness of circumference, that it might have been mistaken for a
bass-relief sculptered on a gall-stone. His eye stared through a halo
of misty light, as rayless as the moon through an autumnal haze,
and his beard, which was black, and of more than one day's
growth, stood out from his chin in grisly luxuriance, as if imploring
the assistance of some charitable barber. His lips were kept by
compression alone, from expanding into a perpetual yawn; and his
whole features partook of that dreamy expression which the face
assumes when the senses, half awakened by the morning-beam,
struggle to shake off the lethargy of sleep. I was startled, I confess,
by such an apparition, and almost believed that the genius of the
'Sheriff's Prison' had come to play the doctor in mockery of my

notions of the dignity of that character. The wandering of my fancy was soon recalled to reality, by the entrance of a gigantic hawker of fish; her mouth, in the effort to say something, spasmodically thrown open like the jaws of a gasping cod. Are you costive? exclaims the little Pæon, in a husky baritone, as if aroused by her formidable appearance: 'Och! your honour! in troth I don't well know what is't that ails me,' the hem of the respondent's nether garment touching the boards in a profound courtesy: 'How many motions, then, have you in the day, Ma'am?' with increased emphasis, and all eyes now turned to the rencontre: 'An that's beyant countin, honey, for am'nt I runnin up and down the town de live long day wid dat ould basket dere on my head.' 'Why you confounded old witch, I want to know how often do you go to stool?' 'Jist as often as I can, jewel, and dat's not very often, ony now and den at a jintleman's hall door or de likes, whilst shellin de pays or opinin de oysthurs.' 'Curse your peas and oysters! tell me how often are your bowels open?' 'Little enow, docthur dear, bud aboud a couple a hundred or dere aways, since de riz de price of de Carlingfords on de creturs, God help huz'. 'Out of my sight, yourself and your infernal oysters, I'm talking about opening your bowels'. 'God's blud-anouns, what's this for! Arrah! patience, a rich-ma-chree, an don't be angry wid a poor cretur of my sort, for sure if it's dem you'd be talking aboud, it's just tree days to-morrow since de war opined, wid de blessing of God'.

The gravity of philosophy itself could scarcely resist the influence of the spectacle, and I added my mite of laughter to the general chorus, while the enraged Pæon was dismissing the confounded nymph of Ringsend, with a pill or a mixture, quite regardless of the 'Key-Letters' of Paris. While this storm of pleasantry was at its height, it was curious to observe how the sound of merriment subsided into the silence of respect for talent and dignity, in the approach of that master-spirit of the scene, the late president of the College, Alexander Reid, I had almost said 'Alexander the Great'; for saving the difference between holding empire over the satraps of a hospital, and the princes of the earth, I perceived that the plenitude of his sovereignty in his own sphere was as perfect as that of his imperial namesake. But omitting a comparison of the 'Autocrat' of Mercer's with the 'hero of the Granicus', I was struck by his demeanour and appearance, and inquired into his history. I learned with some surprise, that a man of his stoical deportment was at one time a 'first rate swell'; set the fashion to half the professional 'bloods' on town; could bound over any church-yard-wall in a case of surprise; and pommel half a dozen of 'charleys' to his own suit in a resurrection spree. But of the elastic limb, light heart, and fashionable addictions, the rheumatism and official cares have left us but the shell, if I may say so, in which these juvenile attributes once effervesced. At present a stick supports his painful steps; his manner of address, to one unacquainted with him, might seem to border more on the condescension of misanthropy than the mere reserve of polite civility; and his dress might now be described as negligently elegant, if the Gordian convolutions of muslin into which his neck-cloth folds across his breast did not betray some lingering devotion to the goddess of *bon ton*. His features, in a state of quiescence, were peculiar rather than expressive of the predominancy of any particular faculty of the mind; but when excited by thought, a grim dissociation of the lips unveiling a liberal surface of ivory, a stern fixedness of look, and an inspired rigidity of attitude, communicated to his delivery of a prognosis the character of a Sardonic revelation. Though holding his appointment, I believe, for many years, he is still a young man; and the peculiar advantages which he possessed, seem to have been cultivated with success. His observations on disease were highly indicative of an ingenious mind. In cases of doubt, no hesitation of acknowledging that nothing was to be known; in obvious matters, no catering to self importance by mystifying the plain truth; in difficulties, no delusion; in certainties, information alone. He seemed in such instances above the paltry artifice of being accounted clever on the chances of a guess. A patient investigator of nature, he is a competent pilot to the inexperienced, and I was gratified by observing, that when advice was sought with becoming zeal, it was invariably imparted with good will, and he was consequently a favourite with every student capable of appreciating so liberal a guide. His general conversation, from being enriched with much of the matter-of-fact acquisitions of experience, and having an agreeable favour of books along with the style in which he spoke, led me to suppose that the materials of instruction not only float in his mind, but that he also possesses the power of reducing them to an available form. To the qualities of an accomplished surgeon, he adds, in a superlative degree, the knowledge exclusively claimed by the physician; and in the management of that multifarious burthen on the memory, the 'Materia Medica', I have rarely seen him surpassed by any professor of his own art. Neither are the moral principles of the man exceeded by the attainments of the surgeon. His strict adherence, indeed, to the letter of propriety, struck me as throwing a shade of the 'Heautontimorumenos' into his conduct, which, with every respect for the cause, will sometimes force a smile from the spectator, as it did from me on this occasion. For while passing through the wards some person vociferated 'whiskey', another cried 'tobacco', (luxuries indulged in by the inmates of hospitals to the great risk no doubt of the fire-engines being brought into requisition,) with the intention of bringing the subject under his notice. The perfume of the latter drug threw his sensorium into a convulsion, and he really looked as if the flames had already made some progress in the devastation of the edifice, while he enunciated 'Mr. Booth', with a syllabic emphasis truly awful. The meekest of God's apothecaries, after a pause entered with the face of a truant and a passive humility of expression, as if not unaccustomed to similar calls, and forcibly reminded me of Goldsmith's schoolboy as he turned in dumb compassion towards the querist, yet somewhat anxious to trace 'The day's disasters in his morning face'. The nurse was next summoned, and a Mrs. Somebody made her bow. Of the alarming seriousness that followed, during an investigation in which I momentarily expected the stick would have inforced the logic of passion, I could not hope to give any idea, unless I could print the faces of the parties, and set their tones to music; while the humour of the scene was considerably enhanced by observing the unruly wag, who had given the false alarm, thrust a fuming cigar into his pocket.

Such, however, was the gentleman whose glances as he passed the 'Board Room', stilled the noisy worship of Comus, and called all hands to work. His merits, indeed, may have been magnified by the medium through which they were seen, as light acquires additional brightness from being viewed in the dark; but virtue, like the diamond, is increased in value by its scarcity: and in this instance I may well be excused for rating his worth at a famine price.

I had now an opportunity of seeing another of these personages who wield the scalpel of Mercer's. He advanced towards us in double quick time, as if on some important errand, his thumbs impacted into the arm-holes of his vest, and his brows corrugated into an habitual frown. The pitted cicatrizations of his visage indicated an era in the history of beauty anterior to the discovery of Jenner, and the aristocratic inflation of his air would lead one to believe that the days of 'Feudalism' had not yet expired. He nodded to some indentured vassal, as if conferring a boon, buried his head between his shoulders in a shrug, and, with the clutched satisfaction of the feline race, purred something about the pedigree of the new Member for Dublin in a guttural compound of the English, Irish, and Scotch accents. Though short of stature, he seemed to stand very high in his own opinion; and understanding that he had taken to give 'Lessons in Elocution', I thought I might as well witness the expansion of his mind as I had the turgescence of his person. I therefore followed on to the scene of action in a back-house of the hospital, where, before a table covered with scarlet cloth, he commenced reading some surgical 'pic-nickery' on urinary complaints, produced, as he observed, by affections of the mind, such as grief, fear, and *tetanus* and proceeded at such a rapid pace that I was not at all surprised, when at the conclusion he remarked, with a sweep of the head, (the *atlas* making many a full revolution on the *dentata*,) 'that indeed he had not yet acquired the tact of knowing how much matter would suffice for an hour's perusal, but he hoped that would be sufficient for that day'.

So thought I too, Mr. Ainleek, as I mused on the metastasis of tetanus to the mind, a discovery that surprised me, not less than perhaps the transition of the scene from a lecture room to Morrison's hotel, may startle the reader. But so it is, that a very sensible custom prevails in this hospital, compelling every young gentleman on being bound an apprentice to one of the surgeons, to entertain his fellow students at one of the metropolitan taverns, with a splendid breakfast, or in case of non-compliance with this salutary usage, to undergo the penalty of every variety of the 'practical joke'; such as stealing his hat, improving the tint of his cloth with lint and spermaceti; and of being pasquinaded in all manner of ways that playful malevolence can suggest.

I was much pleased with the idea of beginning the toils of the profession in so rational a manner, and the courtesy of invitation (for none are admitted of right to these banquets but apprentices) being extended to me, I proceeded in company with my young host on one of these occasions to witness his social inauguration in the joint rites of Esculapius and Apicius. It was a most solemn and imposing spectacle. Only conceive about thirty empty stomachs whetted by the expectancy of a sumptuous repast to a late hour of the day, and then imagine a table such only as Morrison could supply, covered over with rosy slices of Wicklow ham reposing on beds of parsley, cold fowl of most tempting plumpness, and frosted over with crystals of picromel, steaks, the genuine incarnation of the shamrock, flanked by mountains of sallelun, but, *defleuent vires*, I must leave you to guess the fearful conflict of knives, forks, and mastication that instantly ensued, having all the sublimity of a battle, without the danger. I had here the pleasure of seeing some others of the medical officers of Mercer's in their proper places, as they should have been on so important a festival. Amongst these there was one with regular features of Grecian outline, but without the animation of that school of beauty, and for whom my fancy, ridiculously perhaps, found a comparison in the metamorphure of a '*Venus*' into the other sex. The rounded contour of his form, and the feminine delicacy of his manner, peculiarly fitted him for the duties of an obstetrician; and I learned, with some self-gratulation on the correctness of my views, that Mr. Michael Daniel had consecrated his talents, in conformity with the indications of his person, to the service of Lucina. But the person who had attracted the greatest share of my attention, was an old man, who I understood to be Dr. Hill, and physician to the establishment. By accident he was dressed in the fashion; his coat, to the cut of which he has inviolably adhered for sixty years, presenting then as great a space between the hip buttons, as the most 'exquisite' of his neighbours. He talked of the Greek and Arabian lights of medicine, of Rhazes and Avicenna, and the rest of the Fudge-family, and on entering the room, I thought that one of the figures of Hogarth's 'Examination at Surgeon's Hall' had descended from the wall, to converse with us on the topics of his day. He seemed to enjoy the repast with much zest, and it was truly consolatory to his junior friends, with the prospect of old age still before them, to behold successive cargoes of every thing on the board descend into the hold of an octogenerian vessel that had sailed in safety across the quicksands of all the climacterics, and whose timbers still promised to withstand the assaults of many another gale.

Highly edified by the festivity of the scene, I gave God thanks, beckoned the waiter, and pledging the 'memory of Mary Mercer' in a libation of 'Nantz', departed in silence to my home.

I purposely omitted an exposition of the economy, domestic and professional, of this Hospital on a former occasion. The facts connected with that subject, I perceived, on estimating their importance, would, when leavened by the zest of observation, have expanded far beyond the limited capacity of this Journal, which must necessarily condense a variety of matter in each impression to keep pace with the exuberant growth of medical intelligence. Besides, it did not exactly harmonise with my views of rhetorical propriety, to mix up descriptions of moral and physiognomical architecture with the councils of a board-room, or the proceedings of an operating theatre. In addition to my literary scruples on this head, there were some other points of general interest, such as Hospital Elections in Ireland, which I conceived could not be more appropriately introduced, than in a notice of an institution presenting so many illustrations of their abuse. To attain, therefore, if possible, these several objects, I deemed it the more eligible course, for once, to divorce the *utile* from the *dulce*, and at the hazard of a classical denunciation, to make each a theme of separate consideration; but of explanation enough.

The government of this Hospital is quite a curiosity in its line, being a sort of hermaphrodite dynasty, composed of both sexes, or, if you will, of gentlemen in petticoats and ladies in pantaloons; the latter, I presume, claiming a right to one-half of the sceptre by virtue of the female origin of the establishment. They accordingly meet to debate, in weekly committees, the comparative detersiveness of white and black soap, of free-stone and the rubbing-brush; while their coadjutors content themselves with exercising their parental functions on some extraordinary emergencies only, such as the appointment or dismissal of a porter. The superintendence of the floors and the laundry, however, form but a small item in the catalogue of the ladies' concerns, compared with their spiritual labours; of it would seem as if they entertained some notion of colonising the 'New Jerusalem' with a cargo of converted Papists from Mercer's, so deep an interest do they manifest in the reformation of its inmates. To accomplish this amiable intention, they supply the wards with the most approved tracts, and other small inspirations of the tea-table, and procure hebdomadal lectures on the 'Pilgrim's Progress' and 'Holy Writ', by the John Bunyans and Crispins of Goat's-alley. Lest these ordinary stimulants of 'grace' should not succeed, their operation is occasionally quickened by the administration of controversial works of the most rancorous description, smuggled into the appartments in the orthodox recesses of a reticule or the *sanctum sanctorum* of some Lucy M'Swadlum's muff. The only result which can be discovered to flow from all these pious artifices, is to enliven the sick chamber by religious disputation, and of course to add, in some degree, to the tortures of disease by the excitation of the *odium theologicum* in the minds of its wretched victims; and this, forsooth, is to imitate the practical benevolence of the 'Sœurs de la Charite' of France! to run about, like so many fanatical Thäises, desolating the human heart with the torch of religious discord!

While the female portion of the conclave thus transcend the sphere to which nature and decency ought to confine them, a part of the medical officers err in an opposite, and much more culpable manner. By one of those overt acts of treason against the interests of medicine, for which the English statute book is so remarkable, the election of physicians and surgeons to the establishment has been vested in their own hands. The charter, or act of incorporation, requires the appointment and attendance of six surgeons and two physicians to this institution. The law, as to number, is at present fulfilled to the letter, but its spirit is grossly violated; for of the eight whose labours were required, no more than five perform their professional duties. For several years, neither Doctor Hill nor Mr. L'Estrange, the one a physician the other nominally a surgeon to this Hospital, has penned a prescription in its wards. In the whole range of hospital abuse in Ireland, I know of no parallel for this shameless job. To be sure their absence may not be detrimental to the welfare of the charity, and disease may vanish though they stay away, but to save appearances, one would think, their presence might be necessary. No, not even this homage to decency is observed; for I am informed, that except on a board-day, these gentlemen never enter the wards of the Hospital. Are they not ashamed to hold situations which their infirmity or their convenience does not permit them to fill? Will they too retain the reins of power like their quondam associate in years, and neglect the duty until an apoplexy snatches them from their hands? What have they to expect from a connexion with such an establishment? Whatever advantages might have accrued to them from such an office must have been long since attained. They have arrived at that period of life when professional reputation, whatever it might have been, retrogrades rather than advances; when the seeds of fame, sown in the labours of youth, have ripened into full maturity; when the exertions of the past must stand for the future; when, if they have not turned early advantages to profitable account, it is now too late to make amends for the want of prudence and industry. If time has deprived them of the sensibility to perceive the delicacy of the ground on which they stand, or to feel the odium of public opinion, I would appeal to their virtue to avert that obloquy which their conduct is so well calculated to excite, and ask them, is it becoming the dignity of old age to trifle thus with the sacred interests of charity? They should recollect, that while they have nothing emolumentary to gain, much of what should be more dear to them than any pecuniary consideration, may be lost by the retention of a mere honorary title, and that a few years must render that resignation thankless and inevitable, which, if voluntarily performed, would have secured them a lasting tribute of respect. Their perverse adhesion to office, they may rest assured, has not been adverted to in a spirit of wanton personality; for if there were on picture of human weakness which my pencil would disdain to embellish, it would be that of old age ingloriously clinging to corruption, while death was dissolving the feeble grasp. From the example of his predecessors, Dr. Lendrick, who has been lately appointed physician to this Hospital, may learn an useful lesson. He may not, perhaps, be aware, that the motives which led to his election originated in the vile presumption, that he would have adopted the line of policy pursued by Drs. Hill and Bayton; or that another person, Dr. Grattan it is said, was the gentleman intended for nomination, until his late rupture with the College of Physicians, stigmatized him with the name of an honest man in the eyes of Messrs. L'Estrange, Macklin, and Auchinleck, and one 'not to be trusted' with the secrets of a surgical borough. Could these gentlemen have selected another person, on whose subserviency to their base designs of converting the Hospital into a hereditary depot for the professional aggrandisement of their 'nati metorum, et qui nascentur ab illis'.

Dr. Lendrick may be certain that he would not have been chosen physician to Mercer's. He ought, surely, to appreciate the compliment which has been paid him, and if an opportunity should arise for the exercise of his elective functions, prove to these secret libellers of his character, that they have mistaken their man. But of the system which has been carried on in this Hospital, I shall give one or two examples, after having stated, as I proposed, the modes of electing officers in the Irish metropolis.

There are four bodies in Dublin, in whom the power of appointing to medical situations resides: the Local Government, the Corporation, the Governors of public charities, and in the Surgeons and Physicians of some of these establishments, as in Mercer's and other hospitals. Each of these modes of appointment is liable to great, and as experience has shown on numerous occasions, to manifold, objections. When it so happen, for instance, that some broken down lord or earl is sent from England, for the double purpose of representing Majesty and recruiting a fortune, to Ireland, the offices in the gift of the Lord Lieutenant are regularly sold to the highest bidder, and it may be presumed, that at these, as at every other sort of sale, the pounds, shillings, and pence of a dunce are just as acceptable to his 'Lordship', as if they were paid down by a Hunter or a Bichat. The state surgeoncy is one of those situations which has been trafficked over and over again; but as the better sense of courts has latterly dispensed with the merriment of royal jesters, it is to be hoped, that the same attention to economy and propriety will remove the absurdity of a state surgeon, and save the country the expense of three or four hundred a year. The Corporation are not only vendors of patent places, but generously permit their customers to sell out life-interests to secondary purchasers. Conveyances or assignments of situations in their gift, are as notoriously transacted as those of any other species of property. That a Lord Lieutenant, or a Corporation, should dispose of their favours at the highest price, is what can be readily conceived; but that the governors of a hospital should imitate their mercenary example, is a little puzzling, it must be confessed. The thing, however, has been put beyond all doubt, by an occurrence still fresh in the recollection of every medical man in Ireland, from the great interest which it excited at the time. The circumstances of the case were simply these: By the death of Mr. Dease, a vacancy occurred in Jervis-street Hospital. As usual on such occasions, the rush of candidates to occupy his place, might be illustrated by a comparison with the fury of the elements to fill up a vacuum. Money they could not directly offer for the office, but the expedient of making governors to elect themselves, answered every purpose quite as well. 'I will expend a hundred on the speculation', exclaims one; 'I will give two', cries another; 'I will treble the sum', rejoins a third; 'ten times the sum, or it will be mine', adds a fourth; and to it these honourable competitors set. The governors of the hospital, delighted at the prospect of increasing their capital by the donations of their ambitious suitors, encouraged their pretensions, and on the day appointed for the election, the doors of the establishment were thrown open for this singular exhibition. The two great opponents in the contest appeared early on the ground, each having his pocket freighted with a cargo 'Nathaniel Lowes'; while their mutual friends from the adjoining counting-houses stood ready to be dubbed governors, as the exigencies of the case might require. For a long time the combat seemed doubtful, and governors to the amount of one, two, three, four, five, and six hundred pounds were made, when just as the clock clicked three, Mr. M'Dowel was seen to move down the quays, ejaculating, in a sort of delirious jabber, 'cæstus artemque repono', while Mr. O'Reilly, his antagonist, was proclaimed the conqueror, at an equal expense, of this unprincipled exhibition.

The next form of election, is that which experience has found to be the most obnoxious of all, namely, by the Surgeons and Physicians, or what has been called the Medical Board of a hospital. It is in this species of the elective system that we generally find fathers retiring in favour of their sons, uncles predestinating their little nephews to office before they cut their teeth; and friends 'doing a kind turn' for each other, by adding another worth neophyte, or 'sound member', as Dr. Harty has it, to the little confraternity of jobbers. An instance of this kind lately occurred in this Hospital. There were two vacancies at the time, and two assistants were appointed, Messrs. Jagort and Daniel, who it was presumed, would have been nominated as surgeons to the institution as a matter of course, at the expiration of their noviciate of two years. In the mean time a new candidate started up in the person of Mr. Palmer, on the interest of Mr. l'Estrange, to whom he had been, I understand, matrimonially connected. Of the three candidates, public report represented Mr. Jagort as best entitled, both by seniority and qualifications, to fill one of the situations. As the day of election approached, he waited on Mr. Macklin to solicit his vote, when the following characteristic dialogue is said to have taken place. 'Hark ye! Mr. Jagort, you know I have a son learning the profession. Now, before I make you a promise of my support in this business, you must pledge me your word, that whenever my son is a candidate for a surgeoncy in the hospital, you will vote for him'. A qualified consent was given to the proposal, but not sufficiently strong, it appears, to warrant Mr. Macklin in calculating with certainty on the attainment of his object. He accordingly transferred his affections to a more congenial candidate, and Mr. Palmer was consequently returned for a seat in the conclave, through the united and corrupt influence of Messrs. l'Estrange, Macklin, Auchinleck, Hill, and Boyton, Mr. Reid being left in an honourable, but solitary minority. Things remained so until Mr. Macklin the younger was *ground* into a surgeon, when his father, without any vacancy in the hospital at the time, would have him nominated what he modestly termed a supernumerary to the establishment. The proposition was made in due form to the electors; but nothing could exceed the astonishment on the occasion. They were immediately seized by a paroxysm of conscientious alarm for the honour of the borough, and all declared that it was quite inconsistent with the usage of the house, to elect more than six surgeons. Mr. Palmer in particular, on being applied to for his sanction of the measure, was obstreperous on the side of propriety, and after sundry endeavours to summon up resolution to break through the ties of gratitude for past favours, replied, 'I protest, Sir, I cannot think of infringing on the laws of the institution in this affair; and unless you think proper to make a vacancy for your son by your own resignation, I cannot, though I am extremely sorry for it, consent to have him appointed'; while the state surgeon, throwing into his countenance a look of sarcastic pity, turned on his heel, and muttered in a tone of melancholy disappointment, *'Et tu Brute'*.

Enough, however, of the workings of these vicious systems of medical election has been produced for the present to weary the reader, and to prove their erroneousness. It would be no difficult undertaking to follow up the exposure by a preventive remedy; but such a task would as yet be premature. When the errors of this, as well as of every other system by which medicine has been disgraced, and its progress retarded in these countries, shall have been sufficiently discussed, the public may be better able to appreciate the advantages of an alteration, and more willing to receive suggestions for a thorough reformation of the economy of the healing art.

ERINENSIS
Dublin, October 21, 1826

MERCER'S HOSPITAL IN 1735.

Mercer's Hospital, Dublin

Founded in 1734, rebuilt in 1754, reconstructed and enlarged in
later years.

A small two-storied building in its grounds, styled the Surgeons' Theatre was the original home of the Royal College of
Surgeons in Ireland, 1789–1810.

## 13

# LETTERS FROM EMINENT CHARACTERS
# WITH COMMENTS ETC

LORD Byron very justly observed, that no man could speak long and agreeably of himself. It is a theme of which an audience soon tires, and with which readers soon become disgusted. We are generally too poor in merit to bear with placidity the recollection of our own littleness, evoked from the quiet recesses of our self-love, by the crowing of some egotistical chanticleer. The praise even of a Shakespeare, if sung by himself, might for this reason be as offensive as the melancholy vapouring of James Copland, when, slipping off the harness of criticism, he (James Copland) appeals to us in the royal plurality of a WE, about his hectic repository. Yet it must be admitted that occasions may arise, when a recapitulation of services may not necessarily imply the guilt of vanity, and men may state the effects of their exertions on the public mind, without infringing on the nicest distinctions of propriety. But fear not, gentle reader; it is not intended by this condemnation of a vice, to conclude in the usual manner by its commission, for no such thing has been contemplated as to throw dust in thy eyes of "sparkling blue", which are now watching with the intensity of a basilisk's vision for the turn which this perhaps suspicious exordium may take. On the contrary, my impartiality compels me to publish at a great sacrifice of personal feeling, the following communications, containing, as you shall presently see, any other sentiments than those of respect for my labours; but I must first let you into the secret of the reception of this packet of abuse.

Walking a few days back into the alphabet department of the General Post Office, Dublin, to inquire after some letters expected through that channel, I observed a large parcel on one of the shelves, superscribed with that word which gives me an ephemeral existence in the minds of my countrymen, and looking like a poor soul in limbo, waiting the happy hour of deliverance. Without appearing to have taken any notice, I demanded if there were any commands addressed 'Erinensis', when the man of letters replied in rather a tone of surprise, 'Why, sir, yes, some dozen or so'. 'Post-paid, I presume?' having some misgivings as to the prudence of encountering the expense of such a consignment of paper at the present rates of postage; 'To a letter, sir', said the minister of Mercury, handing out the precious bundle, with which I hastened to my shadowy dwelling. Smash went wax and wafers; but, Lord, how shall I describe the contents! A very Pandora's box, without a hope in the bottom! From this collection of complimentary favours, I shall take a few specimens at random; and now for the lottery! Spirit of Bish, guide my hand, and give righteousness to my operations! Ah! Aby, I knew thou wert ever a lucky fellow, and thou hast won the start!

                                         Stephen's Green, Oct. 10, 1826.

Sir, — Though I heartily despise any anonymous attacks on my character, I cannot omit this opportunity of informing you, that I consider you a disgrace to human nature and your country. Your talents are as mean as your malignity is intense; and had not disappointment whetted the obtuseness of your intellect, the world would never have been troubled by the writhings of your desperation. If my merits had been less prominent, they had probably escaped your censure; but the public will appreciate the justice of remarks, provoked solely by my envied prosperity. While my fellow citizens are content with my abilities, and their fees enable me to ride in my coach, I may well afford to smile at the sarcasms of jealous scribblers who go on foot. Instead of proving my practice erroneous, you assail my person; and, without show-ing cause, condemn my College politics in the aggregate. All sensible men will agree with me, that the purity of academic elections must ever be in proportion to the paucity of votes, and that efficient professors can be secured by that excellent system of franchise, the boroughs, which makes England the 'envy of surrounding nations'. The demand of a library for the students was but another example of your ignorance of medical education, as every person must be aware, that a multiplicity of books distracts, instead of enriching the youth-ful mind, unprepared for their perusal, as a multitude of viands impair digestion, instead of giving strength to the system. To your complaints about the Museum, I would oppose much the same arguments, and leave it to common sense to decide between you and me, whether a mere tyro could possibly unravel the mysteries of a collection of morbid anatomy, unassisted by an explanatory catalogue in print, which would be a wanton expenditure of the funds of the College. In your flimsy account of my hospital, in which you have shown a better acquaintance with rhetoric than surgery, you taunt me with a taxation of knowledge, and support your impertinent objections by a parable with the French charities; whereas, in one of my lectures I shall demonstrate that the inferiority of French to English surgery may be traced entirely to the gratuitous opportunities of instruction afforded by these institutions. Had Baron Larry, for instance, the sagacity to charge pupils twenty guineas a-year for the use of a hospital, think you he would have been such a goose as not to know a cancer, or the treatment of aneurism at his late visit to Stevens'! In maintaining these opinions, Sir, I but express the sentiments of that respectable portion of my College, who prefer rising to eminence by years, rather than by any foolish pretensions to merit; and though you have succeeded in raising a clamour amongst a few radicals and disaffected persons, I rely on the fidelity of Auchinleck, Porter, and my other fast friends, who only wait the word of command to obey, to support my ascendancy in the corporation. I must in conclusion tell you, as I have lately in the 'Committees', and those opposed to my designs, that unless they accede to my wishes, and elect Mr. Harrison on the next occasion, I shall leave the College without one who can be called a professor in the hour of its distress.

Yours, in contempt,
A. Colles

As I hope for heaven, Abraham, thou art a clever fellow, fit to write up a page in Blackwood, or John Bull, any day! No! not for worlds would I have suppressed thy irresistible specimen of the cut-and-thrust point of a draper, united to the reasoning powers of a filmer. How I regret that arguments so convincing, and wit so pungent, can be fully estimated in the precincts of York Street only, and that I have not time to explain their operation on the minds of those creatures, (don't blush, M. Auchinleck,) who crouched like so many spaniels at thy beck, in the late Committees of the College, while hastening to draw another prize. Cusack! thou man of many apprentices! right welcome thou art to thy successful haul — so here you go:

Stevens' Hospital, Oct. 6.

Sir, — Being but a plain sort of man, and neither having a taste for fashionable accomplishments, nor the formation of my physiognomy at my own disposal, I think it peculiarly hard that my graceless movements, and the expression of my features, should be made a matter of serious accusation. I promise you; if, I should ever take a posture-master to reform my gesture, or happen to have my countenance remodelled, I shall consult your judgment in a choice of artists; but as this is a matter of some difficulty, even in the present improved state of personal decoration, 'to put a new head on old shoulders', I am of opinion, that for our mutual peace of mind, it would be just as well to let me wear the old one, without any future molestation. To your criticisms on my manner of operating, I have but one reply: that I study safety rather than effect; and never having dissected before a looking-glass like my friend the Surgeon-General, my management of the scalpel will, of course, bear no comparison with the elegant incisions of that Hortensius of surgery. Though I am quite unable to comprehend the means by which you obtain your information, I am free to confess that I have expended some pound-notes occasionally, on supplying the theatre with cases for exhibition; at the same time that I think one less censorious than you, in drawing an estimate of my character, might have given my professional cunning the credit of an act of charity. As you also seem inclined to include me amongst the opponents to innovation, and as I am on the subject of explanation, I may as well admit, that, like many others, I always vote with the majority; first, because it saves one the trouble of thinking; and, in the next place, serves my interest, to keep things as they are; for if that plan of education, with which you and *The Lancet* have been threatening us, were once to come into fashion, farewell to any more pupils, and a thousand a year; to loose which, between ourselves, would be no joke. And now with respect to issuing tickets on 'state days', to exclude strangers: my only object was, I assure you, to secure a facility of observation for those who had purchased a claim to the advantages of the hospital. I never, believe me, intended to shut out 'Erinensis' by this device; and to prove the contrary, I hereby invite you to attend *propria persona*, at the next operation, and to partake, after the business is over, of a *snack*, of which I beg leave to assure you, a 'cold shoulder' will constitute no part.

Sincerely yours,
H. Cusack

Thank you! Domine; a plenary indulgence of three months violation of the graces, and as many more of voting with the majority, shall reward thy good humoured epistle. Better always acknowledge the truth, than defend errors by depraved sophistication. But, mind me, don't deal more in that inhospitable usage of 'invitation cards'; not that I have any interest myself in the suppression of the practice, for I am at your 'shoulder' every morning in the year; but there are a great many clever young fellows, who can as little afford twenty pounds, as yourself could some time ago, and who wish to be present on these occasions. There are, besides, a good many strangers, North and South Britons, amongst us just at present, and to hand them over to the mercy of a porter, is, to say the best of it, perfectly un-Irish. 'Pray you avoid it' — you know I could talk to you in a very different tone, but that your civility demands a return, so — '*cave ne titubes, mandata que frangas*'.

'*Bella, horrida bella*!' What's this, sealed with a diagram of the 'Battle of the Boyne?' Mr. Porter must surely be at the bottom of this — *alter et idem*.

Kildare Place, Oct. 15.

Sir, — While you imagine you are injuring me by your scurrility, I feel great pleasure in informing you that you have been rendering me an essential service. Since you had the good fortune to point out my political principles to public notice, I've had the honour of paring my Lord Manners' corns twice, and of prescribing physic three times for Lady Mary Saurin's lap-dog. In addition to the attainment of the patronage of such distinguished personages, I have also been retained at a handsome salary as water-closet inspector to the 'Beef-steak Club'. For these favours I thank you, and invite your future hostility as the most useful tribute which your hatred can pay to my loyal principles. The better to secure your profitable enmity, I beg leave to assure you that I must persist in believing the good old system of a few staunch protestants (Mr. Porter, I presume, means Orangemen) putting in their pockets the rights and emoluments of a whole profession, is the only form of government under which a corporation can flourish, and that the affairs of our College can never prosper, until a 'perpetual dictator' is appointed; every trace of damned republicanism be eradicated from its constitution; and every cut-throat papist be excluded from its walls. ('Bite, viper, bite.')

H. Porter

Bravo! Porter and king William for ever! I am, indeed, most happy to learn, that I have been the unconscious means of doing you some service, knowing how much it was wanted; and I anticipate, from the insertion of your present favour, your immediate preferment to the attendance of the bipeds and quadrupeds of the household of my Lord Archbishop Magus. But, hark ye! should you attend any other loyal poodles, pray be so good as to send me an account of their cases, and I promise to commence with them a series of essays on canine pathology. Your arguments I of course consider quite unanswerable, and advise you by all means to adhere to them, as the surest means of rising to eminence in Ireland. Good bye! I'm just now in a hurry for another revolution of the wheel.

Bless me! a *billet doux* on embossed paper, soft and white as new fallen snow on Maria's own bosom, which doubtless was meant to be emblematically transfixed by this arrow, seemingly transferred so perfect from Cupid's quiver to this wax, rosy as her lips; and oh! the perfume! 'all Arabia', or — the angel's breath. Mungo, (my dusky valet,) a scissors — it were a profanation to destroy so beautiful a specimen of the 'Art of Love' — I shall cut it out and place it amongst my choicest intaglios — 'tis done; but can it be that any one has taken me for a 'Venus', or a 'Madame Vestris?' impossible — and yet, why these *insignia* of the 'tender passion?' — Innonstre — as I live, 'tis Crampton's! and I shall read it out:

Merion Square, Oct. 16.

Madam, — Allow me to assure you that I consider it one of the happiest events of my life, to have been the humble instrument of restoring you to convalescence, as I am informed by your grateful favour of this morning. To administer health to any suffering fellow creature, is one of the most agreeable reflections to which the practice of our art can give rise; but how much this pleasure is enhanced, when so amiable a being as yourself is the object, it is not for one so poor in words as I am to express. In the course of the day I shall send a mixture, made up with my own hands, which, if the sincerest desire for your happiness could avail, would possess all the virtues ascribed to the 'immortalizing elixir' of Paracelsus. That it may charm away every lingering trace of disease, and communicate a portion of that esteem which I feel for your person, is the first wish of,

Madam,
Your devoted and ardent admirer,
P. Crampton.

Heighho! hands off, Mr. Crampton, if you please; 'Erinensis' is neither a lady, sick, nor in love, but stands more in need, at present, of an Œdipus, than a sentimental doctor, to help him to a solution of your enigmatical mixture of affection and physic. *Eureka*, I have guessed it; the mistake of a superscription explains the mystery, and the letter intended for me, — oh! cruel chance, — has by this time reached poor Maria. How I pity her feelings during the perusal of, perhaps, a challenge to single combat, instead of gratulations on her recovery; but there's no help for spilt milk, as we say in Ireland, and the wound inflicted is surely in good hands; — so to business.

'Angels and ministers of grace defend me!' what have we here? black seal, cross bones, hour glass, a scythe, and the Bible, all the emblems of sorrow and sanctity! Mungo, have any of our friends died or turned saints lately? We shall see farther — Eh! noun-substantives of six syllables, and epithets of ten, rivetted together by words of one, the whole forming a concatentation of 'longs and shorts', like an iambic verse, or one of the chains of Menai bridge! — one of Mr. Kirby's lecturers on anthropology, for a ducat? 'tis but a letter:

Harcourt Street, Oct. 20.

Sir, — I have been informed (for I would not condescend to peruse the virulent vehicle of your lucubrations) through an authentic source, that you have been endeavouring to obscurate the resplendency of my professional renown, by the caliginous emanations of your spleen. But, Sir, *exegi monumentum*, which, *ære perennius* as my Lord well observes in his immortal work on architecture, not all the power of your inflated declamations, shall be ever able to overturn. Who, Sir, (and I rejoice in these interrogations,) first elevated the metropolis of Juverna, as Ireland was called by Bede in his antiquities published at Amsterdam in the tenth century, to be the first anatomical school in the world? Who discovered, explained the operation, and brought into notoriety, the virtues of the datura stramonium, that plant of the mono-gynia order of vegetables, according to the natural system of Linnæus and of Joussen, which has bestowed such multi-tudinous blessings on the human race? Who, Sir, composed that mighty manual of anatomy, whose approach has been annually announced by myriads of placards at the vestibule of that celebrated temple of dissection in Peter-street, and which, owing to its vast magnitude and importance, will take many more years to commit it to the press? But, Sir, of the greatness of this world, and its evanescent glories, I have had enough; and, like Solomon in his wisdom, having buried in forgetfulness the object of all my sublunary affections, I have taken unto me a new spouse, to be the comfort of my old age, and the angel's name is — Truth. I therefore turn to warn thee, young man, of the evil ways, for thou art sitting in the shadow of death, and knowest not the hour nor the minute when the Almighty, in the whirlwind of his tempestuous wrath, may*****

Oh, no, not yet Mr. Kirby, if you please; 'sufficient for the day is the evil thereof', and I have no fancy to be reminded of disagreeable journeys in this world or the next. If chanting psalms after dinner has supplanted the social feelings once excited by Moore's melodies and champagne, visit not me, I beseech thee, with the gloomy inspirations of water and sacred song. Of the accuracy of your classical quotations, history, botany, &c. &c., I was pretty well aware; but pardon me if I were not prepared to hail thee, the bridegroom of Bethesda. But man is frail, and we should be indulgent to each other's foibles. Amen.

Only five read yet, and but half a page remaining! I must merely take a review of my remaining correspondents. Palmer, bad spelling — Auchinleck, threat of assassination — Harrison, remonstrance on the loss of the professorship — Sir Peter Courteney, something about roasting Erinensis on a gridiron — a Rejected Candidate! a hard case, no doubt, but it may be worth inspecting what the criminal has to say, why sentence of death should not have been pronounced against him:

Circular Road, Nov. 3, 1826.

Sir, — I make no secret of my rejection, because in my case I do not consider it disreputable, from the manner in which examinations are at present conducted by the Court of the Royal College of Surgeons in Ireland. The number of pupils lately rejected there, has excited a general suspicion that matters are not all right in that quarter, and masters have publicly declared that their apprentices have been denied 'letters testimonial', through prejudices entertained against themselves. Now, as you are present on these occasions, and must be intimately acquainted with the manner of examining candidates, the profession, and more particularly the pupils, expect your opinion on this very important subject.

Yours, &c.
A Rejected Candidate.

In compliance with this request, I beg leave to announce, while 'on my legs', that the Court of Examiners of the Royal College of Surgeons shall form the subject of the next Sketch.

ERINENSIS
Dublin, November 25, 1826

# 14

## MR. WILMOT

I REGRET the necessity of having to approach the subject of this paper through the portals of a tomb which claims no passing tribute of public approbation; and should, consequently, prefer any other course to one in which silence might be considered disrespect to the dead, if the plumes of the hearse did not point to an important moral on the way. It would seem to be with scientific bodies as with empires, the death of an individual often discloses their weakness or their strength, either of which will be manifested in proportion as folly or wisdom predominates in their respective constitutions. In a well regulated state, where competition exercises its salutary influence, and promotion is the unerring reward of desert, the inconvenience experienced by the fall of official personages is of short duration; the nursery which produced them, in all probability, will soon supply their place; and the last accents of sorrow which mingle over their grave, may be the prelude to the orison of gratulation with which some worthy successor is hailed to their seat. In communities, on the contrary, whose vitiated ordinances have paralysed emulation, where the sunshine of patronage is dispensed through the chilling medium of monopoly, there is some danger that the dwindled and degenerate crop of intellect, reared in such an atmosphere, may ultimately produce a famine of worth. A pertinent illustration of this kind occurred in the Royal College of Surgeons in Ireland, at the demise of the late Mr. Todd. The system which had chosen him for its centre had so vastly improved in those tactics, to which his own elevation was attributable during his short dictatorship, that it was with great difficulty his surviving adherents could procure an inheritor of his principles, with a sufficiency of other requisites, to fill the anatomical throne of York Street. Exertion had been so completely neutralised, and the ambition of the profession so successfully prostrated during his administration, that not a voice was heard to contend the highest honours to which genius could aspire. Mr. Carmichael contemplating, at the time, the founding of a new academy at the Richmond, and naturally imagining it more dignified and independent to lead in an orchestra of his own, than to play second fiddle to Mr. Colles in the theatre of Stephen's Green, very properly declined a canvass which his odious liberality, had he made the attempt, would have rendered a measure of more than doubtful success. Mr. Crampton, on the other hand, preferring the hunter's horn to the trump of fame, the clatter of the chase to the clink of boot-heels, and the saddle to the professor's chair, looked down from his elevation with contempt on the drudgery of didactic philosophy, and determined that the remainder of his life should be *legibus solutum*, free as the air of his favourite mountains. Mr. Kirby, on whom the eyes of the public were next turned, prudently withstood their challenging gaze without entering the lists, supposing that his laurels might wither if transplanted into a foreign soil; besides that, he had been meditating for some time the enjoyment of the *otium cum dignitate*, and the gout, in one of the shady glens of Wicklow, and had just turned over a new leaf in the book of 'Genesis', in the cultivation of which, it is to be hoped, he has made some progress. Mr. Harrison alone performing the part of the fox in the fable, threw a longing look on the vacant chair; but the 'grapes were sour', and facile as circumstances now made the capture of the prize, it was still immeasurably beyond the reach of his pigmy grasp. He alone destined not to succeed, pined in secret for the degraded office, unless report for once spoke the truth, and that Messrs. Porter and Auchinlech entertained some notion of becoming candidates; but the story must have been intended as a sarcasm on the better sense of this *par nobile fratrum* in science and politics. In this general slumber of the passions, or hybernation of Irish intellect, as if frozen into repose by the cold and heartless influence of College institutes, the sound of the die, which turned up a new professor in the cabinet, at length awoke the multitude, and rubbing their eyes with astonishment, beheld Fortune, as if to give another instance of the fickle dispensation of her favours, silently lowering the diadem on the brows of Mr. Samuel Wilmot, a gentleman of great private worth, much practical knowledge, but whose fame had not yet transcended the bounds of the Circular Road, except, perhaps, in the direction of Stevens' Hospital. Though residing in Dublin, and arrived beyond the middle term of life, his character had never been impressed by the stamp of publicity. His name was quite unconnected with books, extraordinary operations, and every other badge of distinction, by which the modern harlequins of the profession may be recognised in the crowd. Nothing could be more unexpected, than that a man of his retiring habits and extreme modesty, should have conceived an idea of abdicating the comfortable sovereignty of his Swiss car, for the laborious avocations of the lecture room; — of talking for an hour without intermission, whose powers of speech had previously been seldom extended beyond the Parliamentary standard of eloquence in saying 'Yes' or 'No', in a case of consultation. It was, therefore, with considerable surprise that it was heard a few years back, that he had embarked his taciturnity and his purse in a speculation of teaching in conjunction with Messrs. Cusack and Jacob, at the Park-street Academy. Where the lectures were to proceed from, or how they were to be elaborated by so unpromising a machine, were questions more readily asked than answered; for it was almost impossible to imagine how the more delicate processes of cogitation could be conducted within a cranium compressed by so much adipose substance; or how fingers, in such a state of obesity, could brook the fatigue of leading the pen through its wearisome evolutions. In doubt, like many others, of the compatibility of intellectual vigour with corpulence, I confess I felt anxious in the result of the experiment which was about to be tried, and accordingly hastened to the scene of action, with a fervent hope of witnessing another instance added to those of Johnson and Gibbon, of the triumph of the spirit over the flesh, a phenomenon exclusively evinced amongst the dignitaries of the church. In a short time the object of my curiosity entered, his lower extremities moving in melancholy cadence of a minuet, his arms hanging in lethargic perpendicularity from his shoulders, and his head as motionless on the trunk, as the apex of Sugarloaf mountain on its adamantine base. Not a muscle seemed to indicate vitality, or a feature to feel the mental impulse through their dense investment of fat, which was rendered still more conspicuous, by being squeezed into a shapeless rotundity by a sort of military undress, giving to the wearer the appearance of one of those half-pay lieutenants of fifty, whom rest and good quarters have pampered into a caricature on the heroic proportions of the hour-glass waist of our modern 'men of war'. Without any great stretch of fancy, you might suppose him to have come to perform the part of a somnabulist, and almost suppress your respiration, lest it might disturb his helpless tendency to sleep. With the exception of the eye, which has that cast of suspicious timidity, of fearful vigilance peculiar to hypochondriacs, none other of the senses manifested any signs of expergifaction. At length, however, he did commence, but with such an infantile delicacy of voice; and faultering utterance, that one look exhausted your whole stock of commiseration. The exhibition instantly excited that painful species of sympathy which humanity feels for its kindred in cases of embarrassment, and you are half inclined to be angry with the temerity of an attempt to wield the passions, or command the attention of an audience, by such inadequate means. But his passive humility and look of imploration completely disarm your critical hostility, and you would as soon snatch a reed from a drowning man as entertain a harsh thought against him; and I should wish myself, that truth might for once be compromised in description, for the sake of feeling. At first you would suppose that his discourse was the product of extemporaneous inspiration — the efforts of a mind rich in the recollections of reading and observation, but unable to manage its own wealth — to reduce the chaos of facts, arguments, and theories with which it laboured into shape. In the course of a few minutes you will discover your mistake, and perceive that the speaker has not only reflected most profoundly on his subject, but that, with every appearance to the contrary, he has really distilled his meditations through the pen, though he left the receiver of the product at home, trusting to his memory to give some idea of its qualities. The endeavour to recover the sentential arrangement of the composition only adds to his confusion, out of which it has been said he was not unfrequently helped by one of the pupils turning prompter on the occasion. The practice, if generally introduced into our theatres, would certainly be a great improvement, and might be justified by the high precedent of the Roman

Forum, when a *tibicen*, I believe, or flute-player, by the modulation of his instrument, always kept the orator in tune. Much time
would thus be saved from consulting slips of paper, many unseemly
pauses prevented, and a signal act of mercy rendered to the English
language, which suffers such serious mutilations in the hands of
maiden lecturers. From the fitful manner in which Mr. Wilmot's
discourses were delivered, it was difficult to fix the value of the
matter; but it may probably be fairly set down of average quality.
In those specimens in which I heard him on unsettled points of
surgery, his views did not seem to have transcended the known
boundaries of the question — not to have penetrated farther than
his predecessors, the *terra incognita* of the dispute — to have
remained, in short, satisfied with a mere negative or affirmative
adjudication of the difference at issue. Of the routine information
on any given subject, and the capability of its application in practice, he appeared sufficiently possessed; but to the spirit of pathological enterprise, to that philosophical discontent excited by the
inadequateness of therapeutic agency to the exigencies of disease,
he seemed a total stranger.

In the other department of his duties as professor, it is not
surprising that a man, not much in the habit of dissection, should
be guilty of anonymous anatomy in his lectures upon that subject,
and he might now and then be heard descanting very learnedly on
'this artery which accompanies that nerve over the muscles which
you see here', &c., from which descriptions much knowledge may
of course be derived. In one of the requisites of a teacher, and not
one of the least important, the power of communicating his ideas
and of vividly impressing them on the minds of an audience, he is
obviously defective; his other qualifications may be tolerated, but
can never command admiration. When we contrast the place with
the performance, the office with the man, the disproportion is too
obvious to escape the notice of the most superficial observer. The
private whom we admire in the ranks, if elevated to a command
would sink rather than rise in our estimation from the apparent
discrepancy between his fitness and the responsibility of his new
commission. It is therefore in the capacity of lecturer to a national
establishment, as the representative of the present, and the instruc-
tor of the future surgeons of Ireland, that Mr. Wilmot fails of
giving satisfaction, and not as a private practitioner or hospital

surgeon, for in either of these characters he has perhaps no superior in Dublin. This distinction may be the more necessary on the present occasion, as observations of a similar import made upon other individuals have been ingeniously tortured into constructions which were never dreamed of by the writer. Without the slightest reference, therefore, to the merits of this gentleman, the writer must persevere in thinking that it is an inauspicious omen to see the highest offices filled, the most confidential stewardships disposed of in the republic of science without a concussion of intellect — a collision of the faculties by which the lightnings of genius might be elicited from its oftentimes clouded abode. Such, however, must ever be the case in all societies whose laws discourage competition, by placing the fate of merit in the power of a few, for it need scarcely be observed, that a scheme of favouritism may be more readily perpetrated by a dozen than by twice that number, and so on in proportion. Under such circumstances, few will take the trouble to contend for superiority where merit is at the mercy of a junto, where selection means congeniality of principles; and judgment is but another name for elective predestination. The evil does not terminate here, (though the disadvantage of inefficient teachers is sufficiently great,) it extends its malignant influence throughout the whole body — represses the energy of the pupil as well as of his master — and thus contaminates the professional embryo in his first moments of scientific existence:

'For who would virtue of herself regard,
Or wed without the portion of reward?'

Where there is no object there can be no preparation, no more than there can be imitation without a model; for human nature can rationally aim only at what is attainable by human means. Whatever is placed beyond its reach by a contingency over which it can exercise no control, excites no expectation, and of course the means of securing success are neglected, to the manifest injury of the public and the advancement of the science. It may, therefore, be of greater importance than the acts of the York-street legislators would as yet evince, that those prizes in the lottery of life, though few, should be generally understood as the invariable bounty of excellence; that all obstacles to ambition, which are but too numerous without the adventitious aid of cabal, should, as much as possible, be diminished, and that the humblest may hope to obtain the reward, if his strength carries him to the goal; as it is only be extending the circle of competition, procuring the highest standards of instruction and example, and scrupulously dispensing patronage, that science can be diffused, emulation excited, the profession raised to its destined elevation, and when lecturers are removed from their mortal toils and wept for their virtues, that worthy successors may be found amongst the living; as the rose, plucked at eve from the healthy stem, will be followed by another, as fresh and fragrant, ere the returning sun go down.

ERINENSIS
Dublin January 13, 1827

# 15

# MR. HARRISON

THE Royal College of Surgeons in Ireland, during the year which is about to loose itself in the great cycle of eternity, has simultaneously undergone a moral and physical revolution. No less than three new names have been added, in that short period, to the catalogue of its professors; while the structure itself has expanded, as if for the reception of this important addition to its former members, into twice its original dimensions, with an incalculable increment to its beauty and accommodation. Among these alterations the succession of Mr. Macnamara (with those merits I may one day or other make the public acquainted,) to Mr. Hewson, in the chair of surgical pharmacy, and the conversion of that anomalous fraction of the duties of the chemist and naturalist into a full course of materia medica, have turned out obvious improvements. Mr. Macnamara being attended during the last season by a numerous class, a novelty in that department of education in the college, and the certain criterion of the utility of the science, and the efficacy of the teacher. By the unanimous consent of the college, Mr. Jacob, whose portrait already adorns the pages of *The Lancet*, has been transferred from Park Street to Stephen's Green; and Mr. Harrison, the more immediate object of consideration, has at length, in conjunction with him, obtained the long-sought consummation of his hopes, a professorship of anatomy. Mr. Colles and Mr. Wilmot confine themselves in future to surgery, and much is, and may be reasonably, expected from their exclusive attention to a branch of the art in which both excel. These movements of our surgical establishment are so far progressive with the improvements of the age;

and as such are the indisputable objects of approbation, more particularly at an era when its elder contemporaries behold its rapid advances, immoveable as the index of the dial which only marks, without participating in, the motions of time. Constituted as it is at present, and with all its energies brought into full operation, it would present the most comprehensive and efficient school of professional instruction in this, I might indeed say in these, countries; and with the addition of a national hospital, there is no reason why it should not demand, and why the power should not be granted, of conferring medical as well as surgical degrees, since they will not be conceded by the legitimate source.

Various circumstances conspired to effectuate these innovations. A considerable sum having accumulated in the college treasury, (which the popular constitution of the body fortunately preserved from private embezzlement,) it was judiciously decreed to the enlargement of the plan, and the correction of the defects in the architecture, of the original building. The appropriation of such a public fund to such a national end, is at least indicative of the healthy state of the fiscal arrangements and liberal spirit of the institution; and deserves a passing tribute of approbation, as an honourable exception to the usage of other corporate exchequers, whose incomes, flowing in a full stream, are visible for awhile, but suddenly disappear by a secret absorption, like certain rivers which at once vanish from the traveller's sight in the sands of the desert. To no other purpose could property collected in the name of science be more properly devoted than to the decoration of its shrines, and increasing the facilities of its cultivation. Stone has been the universal medium on which the moral spirit of all civilised ages has impressed the image of its own majesty, and sought, by such lasting records, to perpetuate those feelings in which they originated. The progress of every country to improvement has ever been associated with public works; and the gradual rise of the arts may be traced on the map of history by the number and splendour of the temples dedicated to their cultivation. From engraving moral sentences on tablets along the highways of Attica for the instruction of its inhabitants, Athens, in a more prosperous hour and munificent spirit, taught the classic portico to rise amid the gardens of the academy, for the reception of her literature and philosophers; and until the temple of Apollo rose at the command of

Rome, she had but few sons worthy of occupying its niches with their busts or productions. Such monuments, next to the creations of the mind, are the best testimonies of a nation's devotion to science, while they supply inexhaustible fuel for its lamp; for, there are few so indifferent even to external objects, as to look on the accumulated labours of the human mind in the recesses of a library, or to behold the records of industry collected in a museum, without sympathising with the spirit of the scene, and feeling some twitches of emulative emotion. For the excitement and indulgence of such aspirations such structures ever have been erected, a truth which cannot be too forcibly impressed on the founders of that which has called for this tribute to their exertions; for if it be intended only as a more magnificent sepulchre of the labours of the illustrious dead, accessible on state days through the key of some official verger, instead of being a memorial of their wisdom, the pyramids of Egypt are not a more obvious evidence of the vanity and folly of its kings, than will be this pile, a monument of the unmeaning prodigality of its possessors.

The spirit of improvement, which directed the expenditure of the funds in the manner described, also suggested, or rather approved, the proposition of the education committee for the appointment of two additional professors of anatomy and physiology. It was observed that the number of private schools lately called into existence, by the increasing reputation of Dublin, as a place of professional study, and the talents displayed by many of their proprietors, threatened to thin the benches of the theatres in Stephen's Green. It was, besides, perceived that the years and avocations of Mr. Colles, and his colleague, incapacitated them in some measure for the performance of the duties of the anatomical chair. Mr. Colles, indeed, seemed rather inclined to favour than to discourage the rumour of his anatomical infirmities; and, like those monarchs, whose early fame supports them in the inactivity of age, appeared, for some time back, more solicitous about establishing the succession in his own family, than in forwarding the interests of the commonwealth. The report favouring the accomplishment of his design, he embraced the opportunity of effecting his object; but though well prepared for the enterprise, he found it somewhat more difficult in the execution than he expected. A fact thundered on the public ear by the twelve thousand peals of *The Lancet*, cannot long remain a secret, or fail of making an impression; and it was consequently well known, through this awful medium of publicity, that Mr. Colles long entertained the paternal notion of making Mr. Harrison a *locum tenens* during the professional minority of his own son, who, I believe, is not yet released from the bondage of an apprenticeship. The influence of public discussion, if not triumphant, was at least sufficiently felt to throw the college into an attitude of opposition against the incumbrance of a dynasty; and if the system of election had been of a more popular form, and a candidate of even equal qualifications with Mr. Harrison had appeared, the result of a contest would have been far different. Mr. Ellis, however, a young gentleman of great scientific attainments, was the only individual, except a Mr. Hargrave, who presented himself on the occasion. Having received a 'circular' intimation of the approaching election, and relying on the specious forms observed, and the oaths taken, by the electors, he offered himself as a candidate, quite unprepared by any of those mystic ceremonies of sycophancy, politely designated a 'canvass'. Though he swallowed the bait, he suspected the hook; but instead of replying, as he did, to the electors, by stating that the testimonials and representations of candidates were no tests of their competency, and that he was willing to submit to the *experimentum crucis* of an examination, as the only means of settling the question, he should have protested against being a party, even by implication, in the proceedings of a tribunal unfairly constituted. He should have known better than to sanction the measures of the court, even by a conditional acknowledgement of its right of decision; or to give the semblance of a fair competition to an election unjust in principle, and in effect long since determined at Mr. Colles's fire-side. But the result of the experiment may teach him and others, that half measures, without serving those who adopt them, only provoke further aggressions on the birthright of talent; and that compromising with a violation of principle, is, in general, as useless to the stipulator, as the faithless charm of the magician to the mariner against the storms of the eastern seas.

While the usual forms of election were preserved on the hustings, Mr. Colles had already the command of the poll-book behind the scenes; and to all who had the slightest insight into the dispensation of place, and the talents of the successful candidate for its attainment, the event of the contest could not be doubtful, for Mr. Harrison, to his high professional qualifications, unites the useful accomplishments of the man of the world in an eminent degree. He is one of those elastic, persevering votaries of fortune, whom no coolness or procrastination of the goddess can repulse from her worship. Let her fly him, or frown upon him, his sprightly physiognomy neither evinces a shade of despondency, nor his devotion one moment's intermission. Just at a time when she seems least inclined to favour his proposals, his constitutional buoyancy of spirit flows over in an effervescence of hilarity; his gay countenance brightens into a more coaxing smirk; his pace quickens into a more lively jauntiness of movement; his eloquence ripples in a more playful and brisker current, until she sinks into his arms, overcome by the patience of his suit and the obstinacy of his caresses. The assiduity with which he pursues his object knows no relaxation, or his measures to secure it any other bounds than the limits of his invention, which happens to be fertile in diplomatic resources. He glances through futurity, comprehends the contingencies of an event, still slumbering unseen by others in the womb of time, with the rapidity of his own twinkling eye, while his pliability of character bending to circumstances which it cannot resist, meets opposition at all points, and disarms it of half its hostility. His sagacity in these respects is the more admirable and effective, from being concealed from public view by a mannerism bordering on levity, and a complaissance approaching servility. A frankness of address conceals all appearance of artifice, and no pupil bowed into admiration, or spell-bound by the accents of condescension, could ever suppose that these manifestations of personal attention, led to the vulgar profits of a private dissection in a public school, or to an evening *grind* in the study at Stephen's Green. These talents, which have so powerfully aided his progress in life, seem to have developed themselves at an early period, and to complete their versatility, to have even assumed a sentimental cast; for love, that springboard of promotion, was the salient point from which he bounded into a professor's chair. I believe it is by no means uncommon with pupils of a handsome person and aspiring turn of mind, such as Mr. Harrison must have been in the days of his indentures, to divide their thoughts between their master's library and his drawing room — to relieve the monotonous pursuits of pathology, by indulging in the agreeable reverie of securing professional patronage by a matrimonial alliance. The practice and its advantages did not escape the ken of the future professor, for during his apprenticeship to Mr. Colles, his suavity of manner and good-humoured features laid the foundation of his success in the affections of that gentleman's sister, who was pleased to lead him by the royal road of marriage to immediate notoriety. His qualifications for teaching were instantaneously discovered by the light of the nuptial torch, and as soon brought into operation by an appointment in the dissecting rooms of the College. In the capacity of demonstrator, he has continued for a series of years to the present crisis in his affairs, when, after a long course of coquetting with his hopes, the College have terminated their pets much in the manner of Julia with Don Juan:—

> 'A little still she strove, and much repented,
> And whispering, "I will ne'er consent" —
> consent'.

His numerous friends, I have no doubt, will be grateful for having those professional excellencies pointed out, which, like those useful talents already described, his modesty may have concealed from their indiscriminate admiration; for Mr. Harrison has had not only the good fortune of winning much personal esteem, but also of being considered a man of genius, and one of our best educated surgeons. If the possession of the highest credentials which colleges and universities can bestow be a proof of learning, he must certainly be a profound classical and medical scholar, being, I believe, a graduate in arts and a doctor of medicine of Trinity College; but of these advantages he has as yet evinced none of the usual signs, having left his admirers as destitute of evidence to maintain their meritorious faith in his transcendent perfections, as the prophet of Mecca left his followers of miracles to support their belief in his divine mission. Talent is but another name for the power of production, and the inductive philosophy of modern times teaches us to rest satisfied about the absence of a cause where an effect cannot be discovered. It is certainly drawing too freely on the kindness of his friends to afford them negative proofs only of his merits; and ungrateful to leave them but the poor consolation of quoting from Gray,

'Some mute inglorious Milton here may rest',

if it should so please Providence to remove him in the present stage of his career. He is now connected for a length of time with a situation which daily reminded him of exertion, and supplied the means of professional literature; but we are still thrown on the pleasing though perhaps futile alternative of looking forward to futurity for that fruit which has yet scarcely put forth a blossom. During a long period of probation we do not find his name among composers, compilers, essayists, or any other of the thousand appellations of literary operations, which mark the march of mind in this most wonderful of all ages. One small work indeed rejoices in his name, but its tiny form would be alike endangered by the weight of censure or of panegyric. Viewed even through the lens of partiality, it is impossible to magnify the act of reducing into a legible form, discourses which had been spoken on one branch of anatomy daily for many years, into a solid basis of professional reputation. Even this diamond edition of the dissecting room, was not hazarded before the public until out and polished by the critical hands of the late Mr. Todd; or without an invidious attack on the labours of his colleague, Mr. Shekelton, one of the most industrious and promising cultivators of natural science whom Dublin ever saw. If we turn from the medical literature of the day to search for records of his taste and dexterity in the museum, we shall find as few monuments of the industry of his scalpel as of his pen; there being, I believe, scarcely a single preparation in that quarter of the College produced by his labour, or impressed with his name. It is possible Mr. Harrison might have performed all he has omitted, and that reasoning on his latent capabilities from negative data, is like attempting an analysis while the crucible is empty. Once, however, and only once, I had the pleasure of hearing him put forth his strength in a studied discourse, in which it was expected his learning would be equalled only by his oratorical powers, for which, as a descriptive anatomist, he is so justly celebrated. It was on the death of Mr. Todd. The course of lectures then in progress being interrupted by that melancholy event, Mr. Harrison was called on to complete them; the occasion naturally suggested a panegyric on the deceased, and it was consequently expected that the orator would prove himself worthy of succession by the talents displayed in the apotheosis of his friend and predecessor. The audience was certainly predisposed to indulge in emotions of sorrow, the event which called them together being still fresh on the public mind, and at all times indeed there is a strong sympathy between Pat's tympanum and his tears. Presuming on his sensibility, the Pericles of the dissecting room plunged at once into the depth of elegiac passion; epithet followed epithet; figure entwined with figure; virtue pressed on virtue; talent expanded into genius, until the immortal spirit of the deceased, decked with a rhetorical garland of all the perfections of humanity, was, by one commanding flourish of the pencil, dashed on the canvass in the act of creating the Royal College of Surgeons, and breathing infallibility into every part of its infant frame. Whether it is that the human heart is so capricious an organ, requiring such a peculiar delicacy of tact to elicit its finer tones, or that the unskilfulness of the minstrel, the antidote which his features, exhilirating grief itself like one of those cherubs that smile through the grim trappings of the hearse, supplied against melancholy, or that some inconcealable defect in his subject for eulogy prevented the signs of premeditated woe, it is certain that the conclusion of the climax excited an untimely titter through the benches, one or two laughing outright; and it is said that Sir Peter Courtenay, then engaged in the Museum, saw the bust of Dease tremble on its pedestal at the moment of the awful annunciation which transferred the glory of his labours to Mr. Todd. For the accuracy of this rumour I cannot vouch, Sir Peter being sometimes subject to superstitious indulgencies of the spirit, might, in one of his gloomy anticipations of being assassinated by the hands of a papist, have conceived, in the awe-inspiring presence of bottled monsters and ghastly skeletons, that the marble of the Popish lithotomist and founder of the college was actually rising in arms against his life. I cannot say, however, that I experienced on the occasion any of those thrills of feeling which true eloquence will sometimes produce; or discovered in the texture of his discourse any of those classical spangles with which learning supplies genius to ornament its woof. It is not, however, to be inferred, because he may not have pleased the perhaps whimsical taste and extravagant expectations of the writer, that he is not liberally educated in the ordinary acceptation of the phrase, an useful teacher of his profession, and highly endowed with the faculty of conveying his ideas on familiar topics, for nothing could be more incorrect, or more foreign to my views, than to lead my readers to any such conclusion. In medicine as in heaven there are 'many dwellings', and Mr. Harrison may take up his abode in the dissecting-room as the best demonstrator in Dublin, and as far as I can collect from the most intelligent of the English and Scotch students here, perhaps in Great Britain. Whatever of anatomy is known, he unfolds to his pupils in the most minute and comprehensive manner, being, on anatomical subjects, perfectly at home; and if there be any fault in this respect it arises from a redundancy of description and a rapidity of utterance, errors which can only spring from a thorough knowledge of his duties and a perfect command over the vocabulary of technical expression.

It is not, therefore, on the grounds of any incompetency to discharge the duties for which he has been chosen, or on the supposition, that the electors did not act conscientiously in appointing him, that any objection can be made to his elevation to a professor's chair, for the court could not have selected a more efficient teacher of anatomy; but, for the obvious reasons, that a mere teacher of anatomy was not the person wanted to advance the interests of the College, that family influence had been used to secure his election, and that the system of election itself is grossly erroneous in principle. Of mere practical anatomists and anatomical stuff of every description, we have more than a superfluity. Our proverbial wealth, in this species of chattel, has long enjoyed much the same kind of vague and useless celebrity, as the mountains of Peru for their unwrought ores. Our resurrection men, the most accomplished certainly of that much-abused race, have, I believe, done as much for our fame as all our surgeons together, and Bully's Acre diffused our scientific reputation as widely among the civilised nations, as our Dublin hospital reports. By professional literature alone, we can be rescued from this poverty of authorism in the midst of abundance of intellectual materials; and it is, consequently, with some qualms of patriotic displeasure, that we see a man, not likely to remove this imputation, raised to an office which should be filled by one whose master mind, operating on our unworked treasures, would impress them with his own image, and by their diffusion bring our name into more general circulation. With still less of passive endurance can we see places, which should be filled by such men, disposed of by a system of family influence, which if not checked in its spreading progress, threatens to exclude talent from its right, and, in its stead, to make

'Dunce the second, rule like dunce the first'.

For one, I cannot agree with Mr. Abernethy's latest theory, of breeding professors; or, of even procuring by the force of art, those qualities in a teacher which can be the fortuitous gifts of nature alone. The project, indeed, may succeed among cattle and kings — among 'South Downs' and 'Bourbons' — whose virtues are always hereditary; but that the best anatomical sire, though ever so perfect in all his points, can transmit his own excellencies to his progeny, 'guid faith, he mauns fa that'. But, as long as our present mode of election continues in operation, there is too much reason to fear that expostulation is vain, and that it will only prove the cradle of a long line of 'infant anatomists'. Under such a system, college, like custom-house oaths, will soon become proverbial for their violation, and a pass word of deception. But admitting even that these electors conscientiously discharge their obligations, how is it possible that they can return a fair verdict, without an examination of the parties? What man, on his oath, can affirm which of two, three, or half a dozen of candidates, of whose competency to teach he knows nothing more than from public report, or personal representation, is the most talented, or possesses the most extensive information? Impossible in effect, and blasphemous in principle, such a system arrogates the omniscience of heaven, by pretending to a knowledge of the secrets of the human mind without the human labour of scrutiny, and necessarily involves its supporters in the foul crime of perjury by presumption.

ERINENSIS
Dublin, October 1827

# 16

# MR. JACOB'S INTRODUCTORY LECTURE

THE revolution in the arrangements of our college, which was detailed at some length in a late communication, terminated yesterday in an exhibition, attended by circumstances which demand a specific notice from their peculiarity, and I might add, their importance, at least in this remote part of the empire, where trivial incidents sometimes assumes the dignity of events. Divested, however, of the adventitious amplification with which our provinciality naturally invests ordinary occurrences, the occasions was one of intrinsic interest in the records of our scientific movements; one in which our national feelings were deeply embarked, and rendered still more momentuous by the shipwreck of these anticipations. The sound of the hammer for more than twelve months, had launched us in an agreeable voyage of hope, while the appointment of several approved pilots at the helm, promised a favourable conclusion to our speculations. In fact, after the toil and expense laid out on the decoration of the college, the addition made to the numerical strength of its functionaries, with various other supplementary provocations to excitement, it was not to be wondered at, that the hour, when matter and mind were to reflect mutual splendour on each other, and our appetite for information on certain topics was to be allayed, should have been awaited with an intensity of anxiety, for which my experience furnishes no parallel. In short, it

173

was to be an era in the history of the establishment; or to borrow a technicality from the periodical craft, (no offence, I hope,) the institution was to commence a 'new series', under more propitious auspices. Great changes had certainly been made in its different departments; others, equally considerable, were supposed to have been in contemplation; divided in its councils on questions not only involving its own interest, but even that of our metropolis, to which, 'fallen! fallen! from its high estate', the casual aims of science are now an object of some consequence; it was expected, that out of these circumstances some superior spirit would arise, and comprehending the exigences of the crisis, would satisfy public curiosity, by an ample explanation of the past; and while sketching the intensions of futurity, would give an earnest of their wisdom in the execution of the draft. Though not an admirer of the policies adopted, in many instances, by the active agents of the college, nor convinced of their capabilities to give weight to prudent measures, by the authority of literary merit, I confess I permitted the repose of my incredulity to be broken by the popular current, and believed that for once, the obvious indications of the case would force them into the right path of conduct; and that the very pressure of expectation would have extracted from sterility itself, something worthy of the temper of the times.

Willing to be deceived, I resigned myself, like many others, to the pleasing reveries of hope, and in my way to the place of their fulfilment, had the singular merit of sketching in my mind, insensible to the commotions of Grafton Street, and the seductions of shop-windows, the 'ideal' of the discourse, and of the individual by whom it should be delivered. He should, I imagined, be at least six feet high, imperial measure, with a genuine Milesian face, the 'front of Jove himself', an eye of lightning, a powerful arm, voice more loud than sweet, a rich fancy, strong intellect, sound judgment, genius to conceive, taste to execute, fortitude to deliver what a heart in the 'right place' suggested, with his mind plentifully stored with classical, miscellaneous, and medical information; in short, a well-built, talented, honest, fearless Irishman, who had risen to eminence by force of character alone, having a consummate contempt for all trickery and corruption; and with a degree of liberality quite uncommon to persons of my creed in Ireland, I conceived he would have been improved by a slight twang of the 'brogue', and by not eating meat on Fridays — the nation, of which I thought he should have been a perfect specimen, being, I fear, in spite of the 'new reformation', irrevocably addicted to ichthyophagyon two days of the week. The discourse should, in all respects, correspond with the characters just described; be bold in conception, and fearless in execution; applaud where approbation was due, and condemn, without mercy, where vices provoked reproof; expose defects, reckless of all personal considerations; and propose remedies, regardless of the profits or losses of individuals; convince the wavering, awe the corrupt, and elevate the minds of the young to a just perception of the extent and respectability of the profession in which they were about to embark, by the liberality of its views, and the depth of its scientific intimations. The sounds of approbation with which such a manifesto would have been received, began to swell on my ear; I saw the eyes of the multitude kindle into enthusiasm; as their hearts expanded to the influence of truth; I traced their impressions communicating, as they spread wider and wider from their source, a healthy agitation to the public mind, like the divergent undulations of a lake when disturbed at its centre; while fancy, in another corner of the picture, presented Mr. Colles writhing under the infliction of the orator; Sir Peter Courtenay holding a bottle of ammonia to Mr. Harrison's nose; Porter biting the dust in actual convulsions; Palmer and Auchinleck running down York Street as if the 'tip-staff' was at their back; and the rest of the crew hiding 'their diminished heads' under the benches, with their heels up, and calling on the mountains to cover them, as if the blast of the last trumpet had thundered on their ears. Lawrence — Armstrong, hurling one of their annual missiles, plumed with wit and pointed with justice, which bear death yearly among the ranks of corruption, involuntarily mingled with my associations; and even our own Carmichael, wielding with his gigantic arm the truncheon of reform, and prostrating its opponents at every blow, started up on the canvass to supply my imaginary desideratum. Absorbed in these perhaps malicious abstractions, I passed through Grafton Street, unconscious, as if it had been another Palmyra, until striking my shoulder against the college, I awoke from my dream — cast an eye on my watch — it was nearly ten o'clock. I looked round, and taking in Mr. Jacob in the distance, the delusion vanished, and I entered in a state of despondent collapse, equal to my late excitement, to work out a seat in the best manner I could.

A long attendance at professional meetings of every description, enables me to say, that I never witnessed any thing of the kind equal to the vast concourse of spectators by which I was now surrounded. Long before the appointed hour, a theatre capable of containing a large assembly originally, was found, though lately enlarged nearly to twice its former dimensions, quite inadequate to the accommodation of the crowds which sought admission. From the top to the bottom of this spacious receptacle was filled even to suffocation; and as I turned up to inspect the congregation of Scotch pebbles, English spar, and Irish diamonds that glittered on all sides. I instinctively recoiled from the comtemplation of the moving mass that heaved in the tortures of pressure and perspiration above my head. The contagion of curiosity seemed to have transcended the pale of the medical world, for I observed that the condensation of the multitude had been completed by a liberal influx of the representatives of every other profession and grade of society. The physical sensations excited by such a concentration of humanity, would probably have propagated themselves to the minds of the same number of persons of any country under similar circumstances; but amongst Irishmen, such a provocation naturally elicited more than an ordinary display of their proverbial restlessness. For some time the stimulus to inquietude expended itself in critical anticipations of the person and performance of the expected orator, and in occasional ejaculations of corporeal suffering. These complaints and commentaries sometimes assumed rather a grotesque character from their contrasted combination, and to such questions, answers, and remarks as these I could not be inattentive:— 'Is Erinensis here to day?' — 'Oh! my leg; to be sure he is.' — 'Lord have mercy on poor Jacob! Up with the windows.' — 'We'll have it all in *The Lancet*. Oh! my country, all I suffer for your sake.' — 'Do ye think he'll play the monkey to-day as well as at his first appearance in Park Street? D–n all lectures, past, present, and to come. What brought me here?' — 'Amen. Tom, will you send an os frontis whizzing right through the glazier, and let in a few zephyrs from the Green? Here he comes, the great little man in the spectacles.' — 'No, faith, but his master; and now for a regular round to knock the dust out of your "kids."' The dialogue ended, the door opened, and the hero of the Richmond entered. A momentary pause of silent respect, like the calm preceding a storm, ensued, in which the energies of the spectators seemed to have been collecting only to burst on him with increased violence in the tornado of applause, amidst which he moved to his seat. However our studious visitors might look upon such tumultuous eruptions of feeling, I could scarcely regret that they were so ardently and loudly lavished on one by whom they were so well deserved. Fortunately for the preservation of the temper of the audience, their growing impatience found an outlet in many such boisterous explosions, as some favourite examiner, or member, took his seat below in the space allotted for them apart from the students. In a moment, however, of partial repose, the object for whom all eyes had been so long and anxiously looking out, rushed in from a side door, followed by a confusion of sounds, in which the most experienced ear in popular vociferation might be at some loss to determine whether ridicule or applause predominated. Accidentally recognising the table, in the rapidity of his flight, he as precipitately drew himself up to the highest pitch of his altitude, and, pausing for a moment, stared through the spectacles at the living mass that towered above him, as if confounded by its magnitude and the deafening peals by which he was assailed. Having assured himself that he had taken a right position, and waiting with the occiput almost in opposition with the dorsal vertebrae, until the alarming tumult had subsided, he squared his elbows, and, turning to Mr. Cusack, addressed him as president, by stating, that he stood there, by order of the College, to make some remarks preliminary to the course of lectures, and, in an under-tone of submissive humility, assured the honourable members, that they were not there to receive instruction, but to preside over its administration to others. By what agency Mr. Jacob performed the feat of courtery displayed in his obeisance, I have been at a loss to determine, and equally so, why Mr. Cusack should have worn his beaver on, unless Sir Peter Courtenay had assisted the former by some astute contrivance in the floor, and that Sir William Bitham, 'Ulster King at Arms', has made out some family connexion between the latter and the noble house of De Courcy. Its deep shadow, however, I thought improved rather than injured the expressive inanity of the president's visage, which seemed as intensely vacant as if he had been meditating a trip to Gretna with the goddess of the Dunciad, or ruminating on the gloomy prospects of Park Street, brought to his memory so forcibly by the presence of his quondam associate, Mr. Jacob, who, having thus laid the first-fruit offering of his gratitude with all due servility at the feet of his electors, proceeded to address the audience indiscriminately.

The subjects of Mr. Jacob's lecture were extremely heterogeneous, their diversity disdaining the dull toil of judicious selection, and snapping the thread of the discourse by perpetual transition. I must be, therefore, as abrupt as my original, in noticing his production, which might be read from the middle, the end, or any other given point, without injury to its arrangement of intelligibility. The late alterations in the College, and the local advantages of the Irish school, were themes of too prominent a character to have escaped the attention of a less accurate observer than Mr. Jacob. Occupying their proper place, and represented in suitable colours, they might have given force to the effect which he intended to produce; but when Mr. Jacob determined on asserting that the College was at length a perfect institution, and that the school of Dublin was now the first in the world, I fear he erred materially in his estimate of the powers necessary for the discussion of such important subjects. Dublin is certainly not the best school in the world, but it is quite beyond Mr. Jacob's qualifications to do justice to its merits. The fact which he selected to make good this point, that there are now in our city accredited agents from London and Edinburgh for the purpose of pickling and casking dead bodies, was certainly a good one, but in his hands liable to many objections. The fertility of Bully's Acre, which has shed such a halo of glory around the school of Dublin, is purely accidental, and it consequently required a degree of logical tact in the management of the argument, by no means possessed by Mr. Jacob, to found a claim to superiority on a mere casualty; merit, in ethical reasoning, being always associated with moral exertion. I grant, of course, the vast importance of the silent instruction of the grave, and that the dead professors of Bully's Acre are infinitely more eloquent than many of our living ones; but did Mr. Jacob imagine that he was capable of eulogising the illustrious defunct that slumber in their 'narrow beds' around the monument of Brian Boirhome? I have myself got as far as the twenty-second book of an epic poem on the

Golgotha of the Hospital fields, with Peter Gerahty, the prince of resurrection, for its hero; but after so many hours expended on the celebration of this theme, and with a thorough knowledge of its magnitude, I should, in a concerted discourse, hesitate to venture on its praise, or to make it the basis of a panegyric on the school of Dublin. The reasons adduced by Mr. Jacob for attempting a defence of our school, were equally unfortunate, and as badly handled; these reasons were, that he was an Irishman, addressing an Irish class, and that a Doctor Somebody, in his enumeration of various cities celebrated for the facilities of professional education which they afforded, omitted all mention of the capital of the West. Now, in the first place, I deny that Mr. Jacob is, in any one essential quality, an Irishman, except his being born in the Queen's County; and if he have any doubts on the matter, I beg of him to read my description of one; then look into his dressing glass, and if he be not convinced of his mistake, I would recommend him to consult his tailor without a moment's delay. Were he really an Irishman, the Dr. Somebody, who had the temerity to insult by his silence the school of Dublin, would be, instead of being as I suppose he is at present, committing legitimate murder among his fellow men, as dead and rotten as any patient he ever poisoned in his life. With respect to the appointment of additional professors, proving the perfection of the College, I do fear that he furnished, on this occasion, the most conclusive evidence of the fallacy of the allegation in his own person and performance. Two sheeps' heads are most unquestionably better than one, the axiom being as true in metaphysics as in the manufacture of broth; but that the concentrated essence of all the heads that were ever exposed for sale in Ballinasloe, would produce any thing like the flavour and excellence of one bowl of turtle soup, any more than that all the inhabitants of Timbuctoo, if made into one man, would be equal to one white, is what I must dispute. That Mr. Macnamara is an invaluable auxiliary in point of longitude is undeniable; of Mr. Harrison's agility no one doubts, having stood the test of experiment; and that Mr. Jacob is willing to exercise whatever faculties he may possess, I do not intend to dispute; yet I should pause ere I asserted in his place, that their united strength, physical and mental, was a proof that the College had at length been perfected. Besides, the assertion was indirectly a bitter sarcasm on Mr. Jacob

and his own party, who, to my certain knowledge, have been saying, for many years, that the College required no improvement;
indeed I never recollect an introductory lecture in which its infallibility was not maintained, but like all other infallible bodies, it has
changed with the times.

The question of the abolition of apprenticeships, which has been
for so long a time a bone of contention among the profession in
Dublin, was a topic on which some explanation was required from
the representative of the College on the present occasion. So much,
however, has been said on this subject, the system of apprenticeship has been so often demonstrated to be one of the imperfections
of our perfect College, that I should be tempted to leave it to its
fate, but for the novel and ingenious defence made by Mr. Jacob in
its support. His arguments will speak for themselves, which are in
substance, as well as I can recollect, as follows:— 'As masters
cannot attend to dressing and minor operations, these duties necessarily devolve on their apprentices; though the complaints of the
negligence of masters are sometimes well founded, incalculable
advantages are derived to pupils, from the opportunities which they
afford for private instruction; if you look to the men who have
succeeded in their studies and in life, and trace the causes of their
success, you will invariably find these fortunate individuals have
served apprenticeships; and, lastly, that an apprenticeship made the
student go through a more systematic course of education.' If
bleeding and bandaging, cupping and cauterizing, were actually to
cease with the abolition of apprenticeships, I would reflect
seriously before I deprived the afflicted of the assistance of dressers
by the adoption of such a measure; but then when one looks to
other countries, where these duties are performed without a single
indenture, there surely can be no apprehension that ulcers would
run wild in Ireland, even though indentures were abolished. The
balance struck between the neglect and attention of masters to their
pupils, may be a nice point to decide, particularly where such a
considerable quantity of the heaviest of all metals is placed in one
of the scales; and so to the professional prosperity of apprentices
depending on scientific instruction, or the ordinary influence of
mere interest, as it is called, Mr. Harrison, I presume, and many
others, could decide the point for ever. On the supposition that
apprenticeship is the most systematic course of education, it would

be unnecessary to dogmatise, there being so many living examples of the system at present in Dublin. Mr. Jacob's arguments and facts were, however, far exceeded by his illustrations, of which, I think, the following is a fair specimen:— 'The system of professional education (said he) may be considered as a race course, at the end of which a stone wall of fearful dimensions is erected; the course is intersected with hedges and ditches; many enter on it with enthusiasm, lashing and dashing at every obstacle, but before they go far, find themselves merged in a drain; others wander off the course, never to return: but view the apprentice, he proceeds with an uniform speed and undaunted courage; he flies over every impediment, or should these be insurmountable, he goes round to the gap; nothing diverts him from the course, until at length he reaches the wall, and clears it in good wind, never failing to find the king's plate on the other side.' Shouts of laughter of course followed the delivery of this parable, culled from the 'Racing Kalender'; and when the noise a little subsided, the Solomon of the 'stand-house' thus explained his meaning: 'The wall is the examination, and the public are looking from behind it, betting on the winner, and waiting to reward the victorious.' The peals of laughter were now renewed with redoubled violence; waves of mirthful fat were seen undulating along Mr. Wilmot's ribs; Mr. Harrison chuckled knowingly at the sad condition of his sporting colleague; and Mr. Colles, whose lips seldom divericate beyond the legitimate range of a sneer, seemed in some danger of dislocating his jaw from excessive agitation. Had Mr. Crampton cracked off this parallel in the theatre to the sound of a hunting whip, no one would have been surprised, it being quite in character with the nimrod of the county Dublin, but for Mr. Jacob to attempt it, who would as soon bestride a Bengal tiger or a crocodile, as any charger of common spirit, and whom the veriest heart-broken hack on the 'rock road' would brush off his back like a gad-fly on a summer's day, was really unaccountable. The novelty of the comparison promises him, at least, the immortality of a cant, into which it has already passed, the wags of the dissecting room asking each other, 'Who takes Jacob's stone wall next?' This part of the discourse being obviously intended for Mr. Carmichael, I amused myself in contemplating the visual encounter of the parties, and nothing could be more melancholy than the plight of poor Mr. Jacob, as he cast a side glance at his opponent, whose scornful looks of contempt, mingled with pity and the might of conscious rectitude, seemed to have reduced the speaker to one half his dimensions. He next adverted to the disinterestedness of the College in the proposed admission of members without serving an apprenticeship, and making some distant allusions to a new charter, suddenly restrained himself, as if he had recollected Horace's address to his muse:—

'Quo musa tendis? desine pervicax,
Referre sermones deorum', &c.

or feeling, perhaps, that he had in this respect exceeded the letter of his instructions, left us to conjecture his mysterious misgivings on an obviously uncongenial theme.

About three quarters of an hour were occupied in discussing these important matters; and then proceeding in his peroration, made some remarks on the course of lectures to be delivered, as he observed, by order of the College, on comparative anatomy; descanted on the utility of this branch of science, the necessity of a knowledge of Greek for its attainment; and, as an exemplification of his own proficiency in that language. How, said the little linguist, (who, I suppose, has performed the Herculean task of mastering the gospel of St. John, and a few dialogues of Lucian,) could Cuvier have fallen into the error of including the horse in the genus Pachydermata? for his skin is remarkable for its *smoothness*, not for its *roughness*; as if the qualifying epithet of the generic compound had any thing to do with the defining of smooth or rough surfaces, being interpreted by Schrevelius, I believe, as expressive of thickness. But notwithstanding this profound display of Greek, horse-skin, and comparative anatomy, he assured his junior audience that they could not spend twelve short hours more profitably than in learning this science; a space of time which might be looked on as rather short for attaining a knowledge of so extensive a subject, if the abilities of the teacher were not taken into consideration. I regret I cannot speak even in terms of common respect of this performance or its author, for the ordinary language of critical denunciation would be misapplied in noticing either. Whatever he attempted to praise, was quite beyond the reach of his approbation; his censure merely displayed the strength of its object, and the helpless weakness of the assailant; his criticism, turning back on himself, demonstrated his ignorance; in short, whatever faults could be committed in the conception, execution, and delivery of one discourse, were concentrated in this production, which has excited the indignant contempt of the surgical profession in Dublin.

ERINENSIS
Dublin October 30, 1827

# 17

# THE PRIVATE SCHOOLS OF DUBLIN

*. . . ridentem dicere verum Quid vetat?*

Hor.

'WE WERE now,' says Dr. Johnson, in his Journey to the Hebrides, 'treading that illustrious island which was once the seminary of the Caledonian regions, whence roving clans, and savage barbarians, derived the benefits of knowledge, and the blessings of religion. This island, which was once the metropolis of learning and piety, has now no school of education, or temple for worship. That man,' he continues, in a tone of sublime sentiment worthy of its author, 'is little to be envied, whose patriotism would not gain force on the plains of Marathon, or whose piety would not grow warm among the ruins of Iona. Perhaps, in the revolution of ages, Iona may be some time again the instructress of the western regions!' Who, in this descriptive prediction of the fate of Iona, does not see the three stages of bloom, decay, and regeneration, which the literary reputation of Ireland has undergone? — that country to which Iona itself is indebted for its founder and its fame. The first to diffuse the light of learning through the isles, it became the Iona of scientific recollections, amidst whose ruins the philosopher wept, and is now again, in the fulness of time, restored to the honourable ascendancy of being that 'School of the West', which it was called by Dr. Johnson, in one of his letters to O'Connor, the historian of Bellenegane.

Persons superficially read, and still less observant, have been strangely puzzled to account for the sudden supremacy which the schools of Ireland have lately attained over their competitors. They cannot conceive, poor blind mortals, how pupils from civilized countries can, in the face of barbarism and insurrection, venture to live in Ireland. Now, if they only recollected the hint implied in Dr. Johnson's prophecy of Iona, they might at once perceive that what happened once may happen again. William of Malmesbury, too, could have informed them, that, about 1000 years ago, 'Students resorted from England to Ireland in such crowds as to require whole fleets to carry them over; Ireland being then a blooming country of scholars, whose students you might as well enumerate as reckon the stars of the sky'. Put 'corraghs', constructed of wicker-work and horse-skin, for our steam-boats, — and students in arts for medical pupils, — and what change has taken place in the studious intercourse of Ireland and its neighbours? so true is the exclamation of Solomon, that 'there is nothing new under the sun'! So far were the students of those times, more than those of the present day, from being deterred from visiting Ireland, that Bede, the father of British history, represents its inhabitants to have been then, what, we can assure our calumniators, they are still — 'Gens innoxia, et nationi Anglorum semper amicissima!' Alas! that the innocence and the love should have been all upon one side, — the hatred and the guilt on the other! But we must not wander from proofs to politics. So fashionable was it for pupils to come to Ireland in those days, just as they do now, that the usual answer to inquiries after one being missed from home, was — 'Amandatus est ad Hiberniam;' or, as it is more elegantly expressed by the poetical biographer of Sulgenus:

'Exemplo patrum commotus, amore legendi,
'Ivit ad Hibernos, sophia mirabilo claros'.

One essential difference, indeed, there was in the circumstances of this studious immigration, — that the pupils were fed, clothed, and educated, gratuitously, by the Irish; a fact which it may be necessary to point out, as the national hospitality has certainly degenerated so far, that it may not be prudent to venture over without a trifle of money now. For this important information we are indebted to George Lord Lyttleton, who says:- 'We learn from Bede, that, about the seventh century, numbers, both of the noble and second rank of English, left their country for Ireland, to study there; and all these, he affirms, the Irish most willingly received and maintained at their own charge; supplying them with books, and being their teachers, without fee or reward!' Yet is it a matter of surprise, with the ignorant calumniators of Ireland, that pupils should resort there; and that the descendants of men who were susceptible of the most enlightened generosity recorded in the history of any nation, should not only establish schools at home, but still send missionary professors, by dozens, to England at the present time. Let us but just touch these delusions with the magic wand of history, and mark how they vanish like the mists before the morning sun. Wonderful wonder, indeed, that Irishmen should still be the founders of schools at home and abroad! Why, the three greatest British universities have been founded by Irishmen, and several on the Continent. Johannes Caius, in his 'Cantabrigiensis Academiæ Antiquitates', positively asserts, that our illustrious ancestor, 'Johannes Scotus Erigena, was one of the founders of the academy of Cambridge;' Fabius Ethelwardus, and the Saxon annals quoted by Usher, state, that 'three Irishmen came over, in the year 891, to Alfred — Dufflanus first, Macbacthus second, and Magilmuminus third, — to superintend the three first colleges in Oxford'; and it is quite a mistaken notion, to suppose that Trinity College, Dublin, was established by Queen Elizabeth, for it had been founded, long before her reign, by Alexander Bignor, Archbishop of Dublin, and confirmed by Pope Innocent XXII. The French, indeed, have the candour to admit, that their University of Paris was instituted by Irishmen, as well as several of the continental seminaries of education. Thus we find the compiler Moreri, so highly complimented by Boyle, asserting, that 'Ireland has given the most distinguished professors to the most famous universities of Europe — as Claudius Clements to Paris, Albuinus to Pavia, and Erigena, our namesake, to Oxford'. To this honourable testimony we are happy to add the authority of Mosheim, who says:-'The learned men of Ireland discharged, with the highest reputation, the functions of Doctors, (*mark that*), in France, Italy, and Germany'; and also of Scaliger the younger, who writes:- 'For 200 years after Charlemagne, all the truly learned men were from Ireland'. In the same spirit, we find Henricus Aristisiodorensis writing to Charles the Bald:- 'Why should I mention all Ireland, with its crowd of philosophers, despising the dangers of the sea, and flocking to our shores'?

In one particular, indeed, we fall short of our ancestors in the number of our authors, for we are informed by Sir James Ware, that there were, from the 5th to the 16th century, 156 Irish writers; and the 10th age was called the 'sæculum obscurum et infelix', on account of the few emiment men it produced. Where, then, is the wonder that our Abernethys, our Lardners, Bennets, Quains, and Dermots, *cum multis aliis*, should still be the instructors of England? and that Ireland, whose very soil is made up of the *ditritus* of Parnassus, and the mould of philosophers, and whose very atmosphere has been inspiration to its inhabitants, should now, resurgent from its ashes, realize the phenomenon of that bird of Asiatic fiction, from whose remains an offspring is reproduced, with all the beauty and attributes of its parent? But what, it may be inquired, has all this vain parade of antiquarian lore to do with the subject indicated in the title of this paper? We may answer this impertinent interrogatory in the Irish way, by asking, in our turn, what was it that gave the preceding superiority to Ireland, and what has done so again? We answer, Private Schools made Ireland the 'Island of Saints': they have now made it the 'Island of Doctors'; and for this inestimable blessing, we are most certainly indebted to John Timothy Kirby, on the dome of whose theatre, in Peter Street, we shall, with the reader's permission, pitch our telescope, while making a critical survey of the private schools of Dublin.

Peter-Street School, the first, we believe, established in Dublin, as late as 1810, still continues to maintain a numerical superiority of pupils over its junior contemporaries, and a higher place in public estimation. The impulse of talent and vitality communicated in the '*nisus formativus*' of its birth, still invigorates its maturer years, and promises a perpetuity of its original strength and soundness of constitution. Like a new-made planet, hurled into space by the hand of Omnipotence, — '*parvis compone magna*', — it has shone on through time with unclouded splendour among its associates of the scholastic zodiac of Dublin. It has certainly the merit of great simplicity of construction; and singleness of purpose, without being obstructed in its movements by a complexity of objects, and a multitude of teachers. Anatomy, physiology, surgery, and pathology, are the only sciences taught; and are not these quite enough to be taught in one private school? We confess, we think that Mr. Kirby's imitators have not acted wisely, in attempting to unite the tuition of every branch of medical science in their schools; for they have but encumbered themselves with numbers, without increasing, in many instances, their strength. Mr. Kirby, it is true, must be considered 'a host in himself', and needed not the adventitious aid of a long train of scientific sutlers to his establishment, in

order to make a show; while the peculiarity of his manner, and the
felicitousness of his elocution, render the task of learning, from
him, less a toil than a pleasure. In our early days, when our young
blood made us, perhaps, more chivalrous than prudent, we tilted
off some of the more gaudy trappings of Mr. Kirby; but we always
conceded to him the possession of sterling abilities and much useful information. And, after all, though these eccentricities are
fair food for characteristic delineation, it is possible that, without
such qualities, his talents might never have become so extensively
useful. Genius, without artifice to buoy it into popularity, often
perishes in the husk; while, possessed of this extensive quality, it
diffuses its beneficial influence to all around it; like those seeds furnished by Nature with wings of down, which, wafting them into the
air, beautify the surrounding fields, and furnish food, both to bird
and bee, by their fruit and flowers. It is more than probable, that,
in our profession at least, some such buoy is indispensably necessary to float merit into notoriety; the distorted vision of our artificial society being no longer able, or indeed inclined, to discover
ability in its naturally unpresuming retreat, — like the pearl in its
humble shell. We are, at all events, pretty certain that, had not
Mr. Kirby's gold been combined with a little of the volatility of
mercury, it could never have enriched so many; and that the latter,
alone, could never have been circulated so extensively without the
weight and worth of the former metal. Such as Mr. Kirby was, he is
still, in person and accomplishments; for we can by no means agree
with those who conceive that his beauty has been injured by a late
attack of strabismus; on the contrary, the obliquity of vision produced by it has improved his appearance, by throwing into his
countenance a certain degree of humorous archness, which admirably consorts with certain passages of his lectures. We have some
suspicion, indeed, that Mr. Kirby has discovered the elixir of Paracelsus, and that he will never die. Just as all Dublin was lately looking out for his professional demise, on the death of his late partner,
Mr. Daniel, out he comes in a pamphlet advertisement, which does
honour to that fashionable species of literature, announcing,
instead of his resignation, his intention of conducting the whole
establishment by himself. There can be no doubt but, from the
versatility of his talents, he would have been fully able to perform
his promise; but his subsequent selection of a partner to share his

toils, happily relieved him from this obligation. In Mr. Ellis he has found all the advantages which extensive experience in private teaching, unremitting industry in the study and practice of his profession, and most respectable talents, can bestow. We congratulate Mr. Kirby on the selection he has made; but, indeed, he is peculiarly fortunate in finding *partners*, whether professional or matrimonial. The demonstrators, Mr. Brenan, and Mr. Young, are yet untried men; should they deserve that meed of approbation which the public voice has already conceded to them, and which their appointment, in some measure, justifies, we shall be happy to record the realization of these hopes; for, of all the duties which fall to our critical lot, that of twining the laurel around the brow of youthful desert is the most grateful. The establishment is furnished with a considerable museum, an useful library, and, with Mr. Kirby at its head–

'Nil desperandum auspice Teucro'.

Turn we then our glass across the water, on Moore Street. The object is certainly small, but extremely brilliant. Albeit our eyes are weak, and, being dazzled by its splendour, we shall not venture on a simile of a diamond, minute, and highly polished; but proceed to consider it as a medical school, without the illustration of a parallel. It is essentially different in character from any of the other private schools of Dublin; being smaller, and conducted principally by one individual, Mr. Wallace, though amply compensating for want of size, by the talents of its proprietor, and the objects to which he directs the attention of his pupils. We know, indeed, no professor in Dublin, who has struck out a more original course of cultivating medicine, or one more calculated to extend its boundaries, than that adopted by Mr. Wallace. Instead of directing the energies of his mind on the great mass of science and disease, he has separated fragments from this mighty pile, and committed them to the crucible of experiment, with the judicious hope of being able to analyze their nature in this more manageable form. Disease of the skin, for the treatment of which his establishment has acquired a deserved celebrity, is one of those subjects which he has thus considered experimentally; and his lectures promise to throw much light on the obscure nature of this topic. Besides these points of pathology, which, by an exclusive attention to them, he has made his own, in some measure, in Dublin, his laudable zeal prompts him to test the doctrines and practice of others, as they come before the public, and to add their utility by some improvements of his own. He is consequently less of the routine practitioner, and keeps up with the rapidly-increasing intelligence of the day, better, perhaps, than any of his contemporaries in our city. Mr. Wallace's various and numerous contributions to medical literature will bear us out in this estimate of his character. To all students who aspire beyond the application of their art, who, in short, would extend its limits by pathological experiments, and learn the proper manner of conducting them, — we would, by all means, recommend an acquaintance with Mr. Wallace and his excellent institution.

How we should have been so long looking out for the Richmond School, and not have found it, appears to us a little odd; unless, indeed, the filth and smoke among which it is placed should have obscured our telescope. We have now, however, a very distinct view of this bulky object, thanks to a rich gleam of sunshine that has just dissipated the darkness around it! This vast repository of science and disease, which in the extent of its wards, and the number of its teachers, may remind the English student of the great London hospital schools, has a mean, if not a dreary aspect. It contains, however, within itself, vast resources for the support of a medical school, greater, undoubtedly, than any other place of the kind in Dublin. One way or other, we believe, there are connected with it about three hundred patients; from among which, that pupil must certainly be an epicure in nosology, who could not select appropriate objects for observation, while its relation to the House of Industry facilitates a constant supply of the materials for anatomical pursuits. Its list of professors seems to be ably filled up, at the head of whom is Mr. Carmichael, whose name conveys a higher panegyric than even now, in a paroxysm of admiration of all the private schools of Dublin, we are able to indite. With Mr. Reid, to whom a part of the surgical course, we perceive, has been consigned, the readers of this Journal must be acquainted, through a short notice of him in our sketch of Mercer's Hospital, of which he is one of the surgeons; so that it is unnecessary to renew here the favourable impression conveyed of his transcendant merits on that occasion. Attached to this school, as professor of chemistry and materia medica, there is an individual of very rare attainments and

singular manners, of the name of Donovan. He is the only exception that we have ever known to the universal ignorance and worthlessness of that body to which he belongs — the apothecaries of
Dublin — a body from the nature of whose pursuits so much might
be expected, and from whom so many splendid discoveries in
science have emanated in other countries. In person, Mr. Donovan
is a short, square built, dark-looking man, without, apparently, a
single ray of talent illuminating the gloomy disc of his countenance.
His physiognomy, indeed, is the very antithesis of intellectual
expression; and but for a certain morose abstraction of look, as if
wholly absorbed in the intensity of his speculations, and that his
countenance is rendered still more sombre by a dark cosmetic seemingly composed of the dust of the laboratory, with the oily dews of
laborious cogitation, he might pass without being remarked by the
most expert disciple of Spurzheim and Lavater. His demeanour
corresponds pretty much with his personal appearance. His stern
features are seldom or never seen to relax even into a smile, or to
assume, for a moment, any one shade or modification of the
expression of painful or pleasurable emotion. Go where he will, his
face, like certain points of our earth, however it may revolve, is
shrouded in perpetual darkness. His conversation, from the philosophic orbit in which his mind travels, is stiff and formal as his
appearance. His words flow from him with the regulated punctuality of a pendulum, and his descriptions conducted *a la* Euclid. We
have frequently heard him describe, geometrically, his passage
from Apothecaries' Hall to his residence in Townsend Street, and
reduce the circumstances of a visit to one of his patients into a
sorites of syllogisms. He speaks on all subjects, and on all occasions, as if he thought Newton should supersede Blair; and that
prosody, or the doctrine of verbal quantities, is the only part of
Belles Lettres which should be consulted in conversation. Mr.
Donovan, however, is a gentleman of undoubted ability, and his
eccentric manner has been remarked only because it is allied with
superior qualifications. The same devotion to descriptive accuracy
which distinguishes his phraseology, is conspicuous in his compositions, of which he has given many, on very opposite subjects, to the
public. His first and largest work on the history of galvanism, with
a new theory of his own, was honoured with the prize of the Royal
Irish Academy, and is less known than it deserves. Since his com-

munion with the lightning of heaven, most of his productions have been of a more terrestrial cast; and like Benjamin Franklin, who could grasp the bolt of Jove, and philosophize with a boy's kite, Mr. Donovan has descended from the clouds to the kitchen, and adorned the humble labours of the cook with the splendour of science. We recollect reading, not long since, (and we regret we cannot now refer to the page for the sake of all lovers of the brau of Mocha,) in the Dublin Philosophical Journal, an Essay on the Roasting and Infusion of Coffee, by him, which is, perhaps, the best written on that thought-inspiring beverage, not excepting the culinary lucubrations of Count Rumford. In the same journal may be also found the description of a rain-gauge manufactured by him, which may give some notion of the patience of his demonstrations, and an idea of his great mechanical invention. The instrument itself is an extraordinary curiosity; one of those automatons of art, which, in the multiplicity of its operations, and the regularity of their performance, mimics the animated contrivances of nature. They are generally toys, and Mr. Donovan's is scarcely an exception. Having admired the wonderful accuracy with which is executes its various functions, our next feeling will be surprise, how man could have taken such immense trouble for the trivial object of measuring the height of water which descends on the earth in a year. There is also, in the same journal, a review of the last Dublin Pharmacopœia attributed to him, in which a multitude of errors are corrected, which have escaped the notice of other critics; thus showing the superiority of the working man of the laboratory, over those sciolists who concoct reviews in their closets for the medical journals. But we must have done with this interesting personage, by pointing out his high qualifications for discharging the duties assigned to him in the Richmond School, while we turn our instrument back upon the Park Street School.

This school, which was described at some length, along with its principal founder, Mr. Jacob, comprises teachers of many of the branches of medical science, some of whom are men of considerable merit. From this number we must exclude Mr. Cusack; for in every quality, except a practical knowledge of surgery, he appears to us defective as a teacher. Whatever success may attend his exertions as a stage manager, he should never venture the audience side of the curtain. Having himself the command of a respectable school of his own apprentices, and a consummate knowledge of fees and the funds, we would, by all means, recommend him to remain satisfied with exerting his ability in this way, and, for the rest, indulge in the luxurious privileges and immunities of a "sleeping partner" in the concern. Mr. Porter, his new collaborator, might, we fear, be stretched on the same couch. He succeeded Mr. Jacob "by purchase," as the Government Gazette has it, and, at least, promised a vast deal on his appointment. The rumour of the surgical lectures which he was to have delivered at the time is still painfully tingling in our ears, like the booing of a bull-frog. But blustering of this kind generally subsides into a monotonous calm. We cannot, at our pleasure, command information, for it can be acquired by long and gradual application alone; nor instantaneously transmute our dulness into talent, which is the gift of nature only. It is easy to excite expectation — how difficult to realize! By a little artifice we may readily awaken the curiosity of men; talent alone can keep this capricious passion alive. Mr. Porter's representations of himself to his private friends, have, we believe, disappointed the public. His success convinces that there must be something more than pounds and pupils to ensure the success of a school; indeed, we suspect this jointstock system of organising didactic establishments is liable to great abuse. The natural origin of such institutions is, that where they commence with perhaps a single individual, whose confidence in his own resources prompts him to, and, in some measure, justifies so arduous an undertaking. To such training in the open field of competition, where merit should rise without extraneous assistance, we would rather look for excellence, than to those hot-houses of mushroom professors, forced into a sickly pre-eminence by the sheer influence of interest and affluence. With respect to the other arrangements of this school, we see nothing which calls for our censure or our praise, except that by a singular valuation of talent, the two cleverest men in the establishment, Mr. Hort and Mr. Alcock, have been placed at the bottom of the list. With anything like a fair portion of those advantages which assist the ascent of talent up 'the steep of fame', and without which the task is always difficult, and sometimes fatal, we have no doubt but these two men, who are now at the bottom, would soon rise above their presumed superiors. With their useful exertions, and many other advantages which this school possesses, we have no doubt of its success, which we have no intention of marring by our preceding remarks.

So much have we gazed at the private schools, that we fear our sight will not stand us for the examination of a class of teachers of a different character, but whom we could not find in our heart to omit, in this panegyric on private instruction. There is, of course, in Dublin, as in all other great medical schools, species of tutors vulgarly called "grinders', who, like gypsies, practise their leger-demain art without any fixed habitation. Without theatres, museums, libraries, dissecting-rooms, or any of the other ostensive chattels of medical schools, these wonderful men undertake, from their own exclusive resources, to perfect pupils in all the arts. and sciences, or what answers precisely as well, to get them diplomas. There is something really so bold in the enterprise — so heroically romantic in the lives of these men, that they disarm criticism of its terrors, and reconcile us, by their extravagance, to their imposture. Yet, though this practice savours so strongly of charlatanry, still we are not hostile to it in the abstract, however grossly it is abused. It is, after all, but the application of the most useful form of educa-tion — private instruction; and if, in some instance, it is made sub-servient to bad ends, it might puzzle more expert casuists than we pretend to be, to apportion the just quota of crime which belongs to the pupil and the preceptor. We fear the balance of guilt would be oftener found on the side of the former than on that of the latter. Besides, it should be recollected, that it affords a respectable subsistence to many young men, and an useful employment of their time; for, to be under the necessity of explaining a subject to others, is one of the most powerful stimuli to make us understand it ourselves. Among this interesting class of men, there is, in Dublin, one of the name of Dr. Davis, who is a very perfect representation of the singular genius to which he belongs. He has certainly attracted great attention by the indefatigable industry and amazing ingenuity of the devices displayed by him in the prosecution of his multifarious avocations. He seems to have taken up the idea, prob-ably from that compounder of paradoxes, Mr. Hazlitt, that a man is estimated by the world at his own price, on the supposition advanced by this writer, that all men of genius have been invariably . men of confidence and assurance. Of this very questionable doctrine, Dr. Davis affords the most amusing illustrations. Though really young, he has contrived, by a well-designed costume, and a simulated manner, to bury all indications of youth beneath a broad-brimmed hat, a cravat seemingly tied by the very fingers of decrepitude, a suit of black of a designedly obsolete cut, and a look of mysterious profundity. Meet him at any hour in the street, and you are sure to find him in what we call in Ireland, a 'jog trot', such is the heavy tax which the support of a foolish and feigned character imposes on his unfortunate locomotive apparatus. Instantly he stops in the street; reads, perhaps, a slip of paper, and off with him again at his toilsome career. Should you be so kind to him as to stop him for a moment, and to break the current of his public meditations, he is sure to assail you with complaints of his restless existence and his inculculable profits; he cannot, in fact, comply with one half the demands made by the public on his professional skill, nor is the bank able to receive as fast as he can pour in the emoluments of his practice. Private society, however, is the sphere in which these demonstrations of laborious prosperity are manifested with the most elaborate assiduity for the production of effect. We recollect being at a party one night in Dublin, where Dr. Davis was one of the invited: he arrived, of course, fashionably late; he had not been long seated, when the noise of a carriage rolling up to the door seemed to threaten the house with instant destruction; the rumbling of the wheels had scarcely ceased, when a breathless lacquey appeared at the door, vociferating, with the utmost appearance of anxiety, 'Surgeon Davis — Surgeon Davis — Surgeon Davis'; in a tone of trepidation still more awful, 'Alderman Apoplexy, of Turtlesoup Square, has just fallen out of his standing! Christ save us'! The bow of old Timotheus, 'placed amid the tuneful choir', instantly sunk from his hand; the ladies, appalled by this unexpected intrusion of the voice of death amidst their merriment, stood motionless in the quadrille, like the fair dames of Egypt, warned of their mortality amidst their mirth, by the introduction of a garlanded corse, while Surgeon Davis, pressing his side pocket to ascertain the presence of his instruments, rushed through the estonished multitude, apologizing to his fair hostess and her spouse for the interruption, in the well-known line of Horace:

'Serius aut ocius, metam properamus
      ad unam'.

One, perhaps, of his best schemes to deceive the world into a belief of his imaginary business, may be witnessed at the examinations at the College of Surgeons. Generally within about ten or fifteen minutes before the business of the meeting is over, the door opens abruptly, and in struts the Doctor at his accustomed pace, and, wiping the big drops from his fevered brow, instantly all eyes are turned on the Doctor, and all watches are out to ascertain whether he has deviated by a minute from his usual time of executing his farce. He seems to enjoy as tribute of admiration, what is really intended for a sarcasm; and, after felicitating himself for a few moments, with a look of melancholy satisfaction, he suddenly starts up, looks profoundly on a billet or his tablets, mutters over the words of some address with a look of distraction, and, as if the genius of restlessness had taken possession of him, is off again on his never-ending excursions to his ideal patients. It may well be supposed, after this slight insight into the Doctor's innocuous and pleasant habits, that his pretensions as a teacher equal, at least, his success in personating a practitioner. They far, indeed, exceed his other exertions; for, like Orator Henley, there is no science of which he is not master, and which he does not profess to teach. We know of no means by which we could describe his pretensions to universal knowledge, as by the publication of one of his advertisements, which, we suspect, may be even mutilated by some accident or other. In order to give a stronger relief to this extraordinary document, we shall contrast it with the play-bill of the celebrated mimic and ventriloquist, Mons. Alexandre, whose wonderful versatility enabled him to represent in rapid succession, a vast number of characters. We shall, therefore, place the announcements of the performances of these celebrated rivals to reflect light on one another, and leave our readers to judge whether the Doctor does not beat the ventriloquist hollow:

| Rogueries of the Doctor | | The Rogueries of Nicholas | |
|---|---|---|---|
| Anatomy | Dr. Davis | Lord Mayor | Mr. Alexandre |
| Physiology | Dr. Davis | Alderman Orlington | Mr. Alexandre |
| Pathology | Dr. Davis | Tom Lovemore | Mr. Alexandre |
| Theory of Surgery | Dr. Davis | Sir F. Durable | Mr. Alexandre |
| Institutes of Medicine | Dr. Davis | Nicholas | Mr. Alexandre |

| Practice of Physic .. Dr. Davis | Moses Israel ... Mr. Alexandre |
|---|---|
| Chemistry ......... Dr. Davis | Archer ....... Mr. Alexandre |
| Botany ............ Dr. Davis | Crip .......... Mr. Alexandre |
| Materia Medica .... Dr. Davis | Grogan ....... Mr. Alexandre |
| Medical | |
| Jurisprudence .... Dr. Davis | Mrs. Orlington . Mr. Alexandre |
| | Miss Tirilda ... Mr. Alexandre |

Here we must separate these illustrious competitors, the Doctor having beaten the ventriloquist, by the support of the following additional characters:

Midwifery ....................... Dr. Davis
Diseases of Women and Children ..... Dr. Davis
Toxicology ....................... Dr. Davis
Practice of Humbug ............... Dr. Davis

But we must take our leave in peace of this medical Mokanna, sincerely hoping that our innocuous attempt to raise his 'silver veil', may not lessen the number, or diminish the faith of his followers, in his miraculous attainments; for the point of our pen admonishes us that we have written more than the lawful extent of a sketch. We shall merely remark, that the anatomical market of Dublin promises to be abundantly supplied this season at the usual low prices. We ourselves, indeed, in order to insure attendance, have taken the trouble to organise a *cordon sanitaire* of resurrection men around the churchyards of the capital, in order to protect them against foreign invasion. To any Scotch or English bone-grubber found trespassing on these prohibited grounds, the penalty will be burial alive in the very first grave he violates. Having made this proclamation, we shall conclude by wishing success to all private schools, private teachers, grinders, &c., and may they increase like the Israelites and the Irish in bondage, until they burst the chains in which corporations have bound them, by their merit and multiplication.

ERINENSIS
October 25, 1828

# 18

## OPENING OF THE MEDICAL SESSION IN DUBLIN

THAT portion of the medical year usually devoted in Dublin to introductory lectures, terminates with this day. Though marked by few circumstances demanding especial observation, except that the number of our pupils, and the exertions of our professors, promise a perpetuity of that prosperous change in the affairs of our school announced by us last session; still we deem even these few particulars of too much importance to pass over without commemoration. For our provincial dulness and insignificance, we hold, should not deprive us of the right of making the most of our littleness; while, to the great luminaries of the seat of science and of empire, it may not be uninteresting to see how we contrive to be stupid and common place in this distant part of the realm, as Gulliver was amused with the serious trivialities of the inhabitants of Lilliput. We shall present, for their philosophic recreation, such features of last fortnight's proceedings as we can conveniently condense within the accustomed limits of one of these papers, and as appear to us most deserving of record.

Mr. Kirby, as you must be aware, from occasional illustrations of his character in *The Lancet,* is always first in the field; for, like time and tide, he waits for no man. Justly relying on his own fertile resources, he proceeds to business without any reference to the rival attractions of other theatres simultaneously opened with his own. On Monday, the 3rd of November, therefore, being the eighteenth anniversary of the celebrated school of Peter Street, he presented himself before a numerous auditory, proud, apparently, of the success and longevity of this offspring of his talent and enterprize. Whether it was owing to his recent invigoration by the summer amusements, and the genial zephyrs of Wicklow, of whose salutary influence his person bore extensive traces, we know not, but we rarely saw him evince, at the commencement of a winter campaign, a greater elasticity of motion, or a more redundant flow of animal spirits. Perhaps, too the grateful reflection excited by seeing himself thus surrounded at the close of so many years, by so respectable an assembly in the scene of his early glory, may have, in no small degree, contributed to the manifestation of this buoyancy of demeanour, and stimulated his feelings to a more than ordinary display of their strength. Indeed, we could evidently perceive, on his entrance, that his look assumed the expression of that humid or lachrymal radiance of the eye described by Homer, with which a parent is wont to meet an absent and injured child; and that his Hessian boots, in which Mr. Kirby always delivers his introductory lectures, by the volubility of their movements, seemed intent with the determination of treading in triumph over the authors of his persecution. Nor were we deceived; Mr. Kirby having come prepared to proclaim the defeat of his opponents, and to point out the present flourishing condition of his school. He accordingly indulged largely in that humble but proud strain of eloquence, uniting the pathos of complaint with the defiance of ovation, which a man, who is conscious of having been injured, and is assured of victory, is so likely to employ in an autograph of his own exploits. At the onset of his labours, as he observed, a dark conspiracy, originating in the jealousy of the College of Surgeons, was formed to put him down; but, Antæus-like, he rose refreshed from each attack, and conquered his enemies in despite of all their efforts to put him down. Corporate hostility, however, was not the only grievance of which he had to complain; he subsequently became the victim of private plunder, and had the mortification of seeing the fruits of his anatomical industry conferring celebrity on an individual to whom they did not justly belong. The first to teach anatomy on the French system in Dublin, with many improvements of his own, notetakers were employed by a person who was ashamed of attending his lectures, and the information thus surreptitiously obtained, was subsequently published (there is no use in mincing the matter,) by Mr. Harrison, Professor to the College of Surgeons, in his late work on the Surgical Anatomy of the Arteries. Great as this hardship undoubtedly was, we could perceive that Mr. Kirby is of a most relenting disposition, and that, from the style of his remonstrance, he seemed more than repaid for the robbery committed on him, by the pleasure which he felt in contrasting his own scientific wealth with the intellectual poverty of his plagiarist.

These, and a variety of other topics, of which Mr. Kirby himself formed the 'Alpha' and 'Omega', constituted the substance of his discourse, and embellished, as they were, in his best style of eloquence, contributed to the obvious gratification of his audience.

While Mr. Kirby was thus, like all luminaries, revolving, Mr. Harrison was preparing to exhibit before the College of Surgeons, to whom, by an arrangement among the professors of that institution, the duty of delivering the first lecture was assigned this season. Mr. Harrison, we confess, astonished us, as much as Mr. Kirby amused. The delivery of his lecture was one of the most extraordinary feats of memory, we ever happened to witness. He spoke for about an hour and twenty-five minutes, without manuscript, memorandum, or any other compass, to guide him through this vast ocean of verbiage, not missing a single syllable of text, or quotation, prose, and poetical included. The whole discourse was repeated with the precision of a barrel organ; not a look, gesture, or intonation of the voice, during this wonderful effort, indicating the slightest lapse or labour of the memory, each word, we are sure, having been uttered precisely in the same order it was written, and committed to rote. Had Mr. Harrison, we thought, lived in the days of the good old kings of Celtic Ireland, when events were preserved by tradition, he would certainly have been worth his weight of gold as a 'Seneassie', or living history in the royal halls of Tara or Kinhora. Genealogies from Milesius, to the most distant ramifications of this royal stock; descriptions of battles from the hoisting of that awful signal of Irish warfare the 'Crantara', or burned branch dipped in blood, to the destruction of an entire sept; and the glories of the chace, from the first blast of the bugle to the death-yell of the wolf-dog over the dying stag, would have flowed in an uninterrupted narrative, even to the minutest particulars, from the lips of this Irish Teramorz, for the amusement of the Lalla Rookhs and Abdallahs of the wigwam palaces of Ireland. Had the poems of Ossian, indeed, been transmitted to us through so retentive a channel, the challenge of Dr. Johnson to Macpherson, would have been a piece of down-right impertinence; for, conveyed down through so faithful a chronicler, the aid of printing or writing would have been an absolute superfluity. In the matter, as well as delivery of Mr. Harrison's lecture, a surprising power of recollection was manifested. To us, it appeared to have been all derived from without — nothing from within. In our ears it sounded as the confused echo of multifarious impressions made by extensive reading, without being enriched by one idea deduced from original inspiration. Like the parody of the mocking bird, giving all the variations of the aviary, but without its sweetness or spirit; it was a tissue of philosophical common-places, selected without taste, and arranged without order. Nothing, indeed, can be more ludicrous, than those ill-assorted mixtures of thought and expression which we annually see compounded by mediocrity of talent, and flavoured with those common essences of wit, deprived of their aroma by frequent use, and supplied by a smattering of literature from lying on its surface. With just enough of invention to arrive at a caricature of a just design, and of belles-lettres to clothe it in borrowed dress, such writers produce medleys of ideas and diction, which, if composition were to be valued, like Turkey carpets and mosaics, for contrasts of colour, it would be beyond the power of critic to estimate their value. It is nothing uncommon to see the speculations of Newton, and the wit of Sir Roger de Coverly — the discoveries of Sir Humphry Davy, and the humour of My Uncle Toby, justle each other for precedence in these unnatural combinations of the style of sentiment with the matter of science. Mr. Harrison's discourse was a masterpiece of eloquence, if these models of mixed composition be assumed as the standards of oratory. With the borrowed wings of philosophy he soared, but the moment he laid aside his pinions, he was floundering on the earth again, and plentifully bestrewed his paths with those figurative forms of speech, which bore much the same relation to the ornaments of genius as the tarnished flowers of a milliner's window to the fresh productions of an April morning. He had probably been reading, some time ago, the Introduction to the Library of Useful Knowledge, by Mr. Brougham, on the Pleasures of Science; and imagined that while the impression of that curious paper was floating in his mind, he was really composing something as good for the College of Surgeons. It was certainly pitched on the same key, but we need scarcely add:

> 'Nam neque chorda sonum reddit, quem
> vult manus et mens
> Poscentique gravem persæpe remittit acutum'.

For, in this coincidence, the similitude ended. In justice, however, to Mr. Harrison, we should, perhaps, as a counterpoise to our criticism, observe that his lecture was most numerously attended, listened to with respectful attention, applauded in several passages, and, with many, raised his character still higher as a fluent talker, than it had been even before. Of the tendency of the medical politics advanced in the conclusion of his lecture, we would not have space to consider the danger and erroneousness, if the relation in which he stands to the College, and the gratitude which he owes to its corruption, did not render such a task unnecessary, by explaining the motives of his servile doctrine and adulation.

On the day following the Richmond School opened. Mr. Carmichael, for what reason we cannot positively assert, declined the delivery of the introductory lecture there this season. It is more than probable, as has been intimated in a strong and well-written letter signed 'Lennox', in a late *Lancet*, that Mr. Carmichael has some notion of withdrawing himself from a concern, for performing the duties of which, his other professional avocations afford him little time. Having been instrumental, as 'Lennox' (whose statements are, we understand, facts) observes, in sending pupils to the Richmond School, we owe it to ourselves and this Journal, in whose representations the public place so much confidence, to state that our recommendation of that establishment was founded partly on a conviction of Mr. Carmichael's capability of communicating instruction, and partly on a supposition that his known integrity was a sufficient guarantee for the performance of any duties which he might undertake. In the latter hypothesis, we perceive that we have been deceived, probably for the reasons assigned above; but we must say that it is unworthy of Mr. Carmichael's character, to induce pupils to any institution by the high celebrity of his name, whom he does not intend, or rather, cannot find time to instruct. We shall have no Stanley and Abernethy bonds in the hospitals and schools of Dublin. There is also a vague report, originating in a casual expression dropped by him at one of the Committees of the College, that Mr. Carmichael has changed his opinions on the policies pursued by that body. This we do not believe, though we can readily explain. Mr. Carmichael finding himself opposed by the majority of the College, may think it more prudent to stand out of the current of corruption, than to become a martyr to its force and its filth. The late elections for the disposal of offices in the College, must have given him a tangible intimation of the malignant effluvia which the publication of his lecture on medical education had conjured up around him, as the warmest and brightest sunshine is sure to awaken the rankest essence of the mire; and to convince him that, however just and prudent his views have been, a further promulgation of them might not be safe among such company. Though abstract principle demands a struggle even where victory is dubious, yet the number and malignity of Mr. Carmichael's opponents, afford at once an explanation and apology for his silence on the present atrocious proceedings of the College; and we must remain content with hearing the voice of reason and liberality thus drowned in the famished screams of a parcel of poor, young, hungry members of that body, crying out from their 'first-floor lodgings' for a monopoly of place and practice, with all the yearning ferocity of a litter of young wolves, yelling for more blood from their dens. In his absence this season, a Mr. Adams, one of the surgeons of the Jervis Street Infirmary, delivered the introductory lecture at the Richmond School. Of this gentleman and his discourse, we cannot pretend to speak with the precision of an actual observer. The day happened to be one of the dullest that even Ireland is able to produce; and as we always sympathize with the state of the atmosphere, never attempting, for instance, to demolish a lecturer when there is a single cloud in the sky, it may be readily supposed that out 'listless length' was scarcely stretched on a bench, when our eyelids (which, however, are so extremely thin, that we can see imperfectly through them) were hermetically sealed. How long we may have remained in this state, we know not; but we have an indistinct impression, like that left by a dream, that after being roused a little by clapping of hands and scraping of boards, a gentleman, of rather short stature, with black bushy hair, a degree of affrighted expression in his looks, a few of what we call in Ireland 'grog-blossoms' scattered over his face, and dressed in a suit of seedy black, entered the theatre, and proceeded to read a paper certain sentences, the import of which the unparalleled rapidity of their recital entirely prevented us for some time from learning. Exercising that faculty of seeing and hearing while asleep which the constant habit of critical vigilance has endowed us with, we endeavoured to catch the tenor of discourse, but all in vain, until the announcement of the name of Hippocrates warned us of the approach of a history of medicine for about five-and-twenty centuries, and of the propriety of indulging ourselves in the luxury of insensibility to so terrible an infliction, through the means of a sound sleep. In this happy state of suspended animation we always continue, when lectures, which profess to give an account of the healing art for nearly the age of the world in one hour, are in the progress of delivery; until the name of the 'immortal John Hunter', with which these boobies generally conclude, strikes on our ear, and assures that we may safely venture to awake. Of all that was, therefore, contained in Dr. Adams' discourse between these two rhetorical guides, Hippocrates and John Hunter, we cannot, of course, pretend to speak; but we presume it was as bad as any we ever heard spoken, and as detestably delivered as any we ever saw, whether asleep or awake.

Our readers will please to consider the interval of a week as annihilated, and accompany us on the Monday following to the theatre of anatomy, in the University of Dublin, to hear Dr. Macartney. There is this vast difference between the Doctor and many of his Dublin contemporaries, that his opinions are generally his own; his illustrations derived from actual observation; his language is artificially elegant; and his delivery always that of a gentleman. There is no assumption of a character foreign to his habits; no straining after effect through clumsy compilation; and, consequently, always agreeable by the single but all-redeeming virtue of simplicity. The matter of his discourse was admirably selected for enforcing the object which he had in view — the diminution of those prejudices which exist in the public mind against the practice of dissection. A disquisition on organic and inorganic matter, and their mutual transmutations into each other, with an account of the various systems of sepulture in use among ancient and modern nations, constituted, it must be admitted, a natural preface to the proposition with which he intended to conclude. The silly antipathies of the public on this subject were rallied by all the arguments of reason, and pleasantly ridiculed by all that dry, quaint humour, and philosophical anecdote of which Dr. Macartney is so perfect a master. Preparations, exhibiting the foul ravages of the various agents of decomposition on the human body, in the different forms of sepulture, were next produced, and comparatively inoffensive process of the anatomist contrasted with the disgusting operations of rats, maggots, gradual putrefaction, and all the other foul invaders which await us in the grave. At the conclusion of this antiquarian and scientific notice of the different ways in which we are to be finally reduced to our 'native earth', Dr. Macartney drew forth, from the glass pyramid in which the preceding monitors of our mortality were enshrined, a roll of parchment, on which was inscribed that resolution of himself and others, consigning their bodies after death to dissection, and produced by him in his execrable evidence before the Anatomical Committee of the Commons. This testamentary document, signed by many respectable persons, and promising to render its author immortal for its absurdity, is but one of those whims with which the Doctor sometimes dilutes his more serious and philosophic pursuits. Allowing the published determination of a few individuals to have their bodies dissected all the influence which such a decree is likely to exert in diminishing the disgust excited by human anatomy, that *all*, we fear, will be but little, as long as this practice is coupled in the public mind with the commission of crime. The time and attention, therefore, bestowed on this singular legacy would have, we think, been much better employed by the Doctor in convincing the legislature, through petitions, of the necessity of dissociating dissection and the gallows in the public mind, for while the one is linked with the other by the law, argument may well be suspended.

On the same day the lectures of the School of Physic were given in the theatre of Sir Patrick Dun's Hospital. They were commenced by the new Professor of the Practice of Medicine, Dr. Grattan, the gentleman on whom you have so severely but justly animadverted in a late leading article of *The Lancet*. You could never, indeed suspect, from his youthful and timid appearance, that he could have been the author of the furious extracts from his letter published on that occasion; or that, having composed them, he would ever have the courage of following them up by a thorough exposition of the abuses of the College of Physicians. An extreme pallor of countenance, marked by a sickly lividity under the eyes, a broad and smooth forehead spanned at the base by a pair of spectacles; a very weak and pharisaically modulated voice, with a general aspect of devotional abstraction, would stamp him rather as an expounder of the Gospel than a commentator on Celsus or Cullen. Had Lavater been beside us, we would expect to find the Rev. physiognomist taking down Dr. Grattan's face in his sketch-book, as a perfect specimen of the phlegmatic temperament, in which the *vis vitæ* was all but extinguished in a redundancy of the 'humours'. Though the cranioscopical divine would have been justified, by appearances in doubting the possibility of the fire of genius burning within so watery a tenement, yet we could correct his speculations so far as literary exertion was implied in his prognostication, by assuring him that the Doctor, as long as we remember, has been a most assiduous contributor to the press in the shape of letters, pamphlets, and essays, on all manner of subjects, professional, political, and statistical. His lecture being on the hacknied subject of medical history, we of course exercised our peculiar prerogative of criticising it asleep, and can only say, that it at least had the merit of evincing an acquaintance with the original authorities from which those encyclopædiac compilations are drawn, which furnish information to other lecturers, such as Mr. Adams, at second-hand. How far Dr. Grattan may advance the reputation of that body to which he has been so singularly united we know not, but were we to conjecture, from this specimen, we would say, that while he was, perhaps, capable of instructing his pupils in all that belongs to his department, he does not appear to possess that necessary animation and enthusiasm of manner to stimulate their industry, and awaken their ambition, to prosecute science in its more difficult but profitable forms.

Dr. Grattan was succeeded, at a short interval, in the same theatre by the Professor of the Institutes of Medicine, a gentleman of a very different appearance and cast of mind. Had we not been aware that Dr. Graves and the supreme honour of being born in Ireland, we would be inclined to set him down for a native of the South of Europe. His colour is a rich bronze, or brown olive, far too deep to be burned on by the coy sun of Ireland, which shrouds his glory too often in an impenetrable veil of clouds to darken the fair complexions of his children. His hair is of that intense jet and glossy texture, which is found to vegetate in perfection in warmer latitudes only; while his keen black eye, sparkling in its socket, would indicate a descent from some more ardent regions than the chilly clime of Ireland. The configuration of the countenance is also too lengthy, and its different organs too highly raised into 'relief', not to induce the observer to suspect, that the professor of these characteristics is a stranger, or at least an exception to the fair, fleshy physiognomies of his native land. There is, indeed, an air of foreign formation about his whole aspect, which induces us to believe that the family of the Graves are not sufficiently long settled in Ireland to be formed according to the standard of the native beauty of that country. After passing through five or six generations more, they may probably arrive at that honourable distinction, and appear indigenous plants of the soil. Dr. Graves, however, has excited much attention, and strong hopes of eminence in his profession, since his appointment in the School of Physic. The course of study to which Dr. Graves has submitted himself for this purpose, in some measure justified these anticipations. Having exhausted our British schools, he visited the continental seminaries, and came home deeply impressed with a conviction of the superiority of their system of medical education, and with a determination of carrying it into effect in his native country. An opportunity soon presented itself for the accomplishment of this design, in his appointment to the Meath Hospital on his return. An attempt to transplant this system was accordingly made by him; but, with all his care, it has not, we understand, turned out a very successful experiment. Something was certainly done, for which he is entitled to the gratitude of all who take an interest in the improvement of medical education. The novelty of a regular case-book, and of the delivery of occasional clinical remarks, was introduced by him, though poorly executed in that institution. As to the other parts of the German and Italian system, particularly that of consigning a certain number of patients to the care of more advanced pupils, they never were, nor perhaps ever can be introduced into any of our hospitals, under existing circumstances. In Edinburgh, where the closest approximation to this excellent ordinance has been made, the professors confess that any further extension of this mode of tuition is really impracticable among the pupils and patients of Great Britain. The former are necessarily a migrating body in this country, different parts of their education being acquired in different schools, so that they cannot well comply with any well-organised plan of instruction; and the latter are, perhaps, too deeply imbued with that restive selfishness, generated by free political institutions, ever to suffer themselves to become the passive instruments of experiment for the benefit of students. These are obstacles, to the removal of which, even the laudable zeal of Dr. Graves could not be supposed competent. He still, however, persists, with the most praise-worthy perseverance, in the prosecution of his design, and has, we are told, relinquished, in a great measure, his private practice, since his election to a professor's chair, that he might have more leisure to follow up his favourite pursuits. Such a disinterestedness, at least, indicates that Platonic affection for science which generally co-exists with the power of extending its boundaries. His manner, indeed, during his discourse, struck us as being in perfect harmony with the enthusiasm of his disposition, and his love of communicating as well as of cultivating science. He passed to the professor's chair with an alacrity of motion, and opened on his audience in a tone of impassioned perusal from a manuscript, which, to persons accustomed to less enthusiastic modes of address, and unacquainted with his warm temperament, might be painfully startling. His countenance, naturally expressive of much latent emotion, even in a state of quiescence, when thoroughly excited, as it then evidently was, by the working of his feelings, together with the accompaniment of a husky, sepulchral voice, strained to its highest pitch, and let loose on his audience without much regard to modulation, struck us, we confess, with a degree of surprise, a little too electric to be agreeable. His desire to impress the truth of his opinions on his spectators was obviously too powerful to be restrained by his taste and his judgment, for, during the whole of his discourse, he swept over the aching senses of his auditory in a whirlwind of enunciation, exhibiting all the tumult of a storm, without its grandeur or its force. The style of his lecture, which was principally physiological, partook a good deal of the faulty manner of its delivery. The whole was plentifully interspersed with profound reflections, which, in sentiment and diction, might put the three-piled periods of Goldsmith's Animated Nature, or of Herder's History of Man, to the blush. He dealt, too, pretty largely in those flowers of rhetoric, or elaborate figures of speech, so common to Irish writers, but which, in his inexperienced hands, appeared to us to have been no other than 'potato-blossoms'; and, by way of being sublime, alternately passed from earth to heaven, now grubbing out wonders from the one, and next soaring among the prodigies of the other. In one of those flights to the stars, towards the conclusion of his lecture, we could not help contrasting his position in the firmament, searching for the sublime, with that of Professor *Alciphron*, described by Mr. Moore, in his *Epicureun*, while suspended by the brazen ring from the sky, and buffetted about by all the agents of elemental strife.

Of the other introductory lecturers, the necessarily hurried composition of this sketch prevents us from taking any notice. We shall, therefore, merely state, for the present, that they were all dressed in well-cut blackcoats, and acquitted themselves entirely to the satisfaction of their respective audiences.

ERINENSIS
November 8, 1828

## 19

# THE DUBLIN COLLEGE OF SURGEONS
# AND ERINENSIS

*'Hos ego versiculos feci, tulit alter honores.'*

MY re-appearance, for the third time, in the pages of *The Lancet*, has been followed by manifestations of resentment, among a certain portion of the profession in Dublin, in which, it is to be feared a troubled conscience may have some share. The exertions, at least, of this party to discover me, strongly partake of the embarassing timidity of guilt; foolishly supposing that if they could tear off my mask, my strength, like that of Sampson shorn of his locks, would instantly vanish. In their blind zeal, it may be readily imagined, they have fallen into mistakes which, if they might not prove mischievous, would be calculated only to awaken a smile. If, indeed, to conceal myself from their threatened hostility, at the expense of the unoffending, were my present object, I could not adopt a more judicious plan for its attainment then to permit these blunders to pass by in silence. Humbly, however, as I think of my own labours, I value them sufficiently not to wish that any individual should be burthened with the credit or reproach of having composed these Sketches, much less that any person should suffer by being considered their author. These feelings alone, independent of egotistical speculations, induce me to attempt (notwithstanding the little confidence usually reposed in the assertions of anonymous writers speaking of themselves) to show the extreme folly of conjecture in matters of this kind, by its perpetual contradictions.

When the first of these papers was published, rumour, from the mere analogy of title and topic, detected the writer of them in the person of Mr. Cross, author of the excellent Sketches of the Medical Schools of Paris, a calumny on that gentleman in which I certainly had the better part. Having subsequently described scenes of which Mr. Cross, residing, I believe, in Norwich, could have known nothing, I had next the supreme honour of finding myself and Dr. Macartney one and the same person, in the suspicions of the day, for the unconscious benefit of whose celebrity I here beg leave, most heartily, to thank him. Well, the portrait of the Professor of Anatomy, the University of Dublin, appeared soon after; the delusion was, of course, as quickly dissipated as it was diffused; but I had the consolation of being immediately united to Mr. Kirby, an union, by the way, in which I may remark, I also felt highly flattered. Had my labours ceased here, they might still have retained all the splendour of Mr Kirby's fame; but, Marplot as I was, I should pencil a likeness of my illustrious representative, which, unfortunately, deprived me of the advantage of being synonymous with the founder of Peter Street School. Puzzled to find a fit and proper person to identify me with, the public now launched into the licentiousness of unlimited conjecture; and, will it be believed, that the Royal College of Surgeons in Ireland supposed they saw grounds for accusing Sir Astley Cooper of the composition of the Sketches, who, it was sagely whispered, was actually jealous of the rising fame of that institution? This report, however agreeable to my vanity, was, I regret, of too delicate constitution to live long; but as it was quite certain I must be some-body, and as nothing better presented at the time, surprise fixed, for awhile, the odium excited by my lucubrations on a candidate for 'letters testimonial', who has been rejected about this time on the principle, I presume, replied in the satirical precept — 'Facit indïgnatic versum'. This inglorious alliance carried in its improbability the seeds of its own dissolution; and I now turned out to be no less a personage than an Apothecary, whose claims to a connexion with me rested on the simple fact of his having penned some ingenious 'puffs' in the newspapers, in a style which (horresco referens) was said to bear a strong resemblance to mine. I was soon relieved from my disreputable association with the Apothecary and his 'puffs', to be identified with the *Sub*-Editor of a Popish morning journal, who, opportunely for the gratification of the public taste for gossip, had recently 'thrown physic to the dogs', and commenced practising without a license on the moral diseases of his native country. He did not long, however, enjoy a monopoly in my fame; a new candidate was started, in a reporter to a Protestant morning paper, who, I believe, was serving in the capacity of a surgeon at Sierra Leone, while I was writing these Essays in Dublin. This fact, when made known, threw me once more on the wide waste of anonymous existence, from which I was, in due time, delivered by identification with a melancholy looking pupil of Mercer's Hospital, who, having no apparent business on hand, the public should find him in employment, in the composition of the Sketches. Not satisfied with this adjustment of the question, the public divided on my identity, one party strenuously maintaining (risum teneatis amici?) that I was really Mr. Jacob, who, by virtue of his office as demonstrator to a rival institution of the College of Surgeons, should then be a medical Whig as he is now a Tory, a professor of that establishment; the other as arduously contending that my familiarity with Camper, Spurzheim, and Lavater, in my descriptions of professors' heads, was a demonstrative proof of my being a certain pupil of the Meath Hospital, who, about this time, became such a craniological enthusiast, that he actually combed back his hair to render his forehead a more convénient reference for the elucidation of his favourite doctrine. My metamorphoses, hitherto strange as they were, had not yet ended; they were now to be far surpassed, my sex (a point on which, like most men, I felt particularly sensitive,) being now changed by Mr. Tom Egan, according to whom I had absolutely entered the sacred premises of the Lock as a 'woman of the town', to watch his spiritual practice in that establishment, while my old friend, Mr. Cusack, as positively asserted that I must have the omniscience of a 'witch' to know that he had been in the habit of purchasing tumours for operation in Stevens' Hospital. This, indeed, was the very climax of transformation, at which a Pythagorean might rejoice; but I had still further trials to undergo. Characters being now a good deal exhausted in Dublin, the sphere of speculation was enlarged, and I had now the pleasure of finding myself in the person of Mr. Quain, of London, to whom report assigned the ingenious merit of making up these articles, out of materials transmitted by post to the metropolis. How long Mr. Quain may be allowed to enjoy a reputation of which, I presume, he would be no ways ambitious, I cannot say, so capricious is that spirit of conjecture which has made me, in succession, Mr. Cross, Dr. Macartney, Professor Kirby, a rejected Candidate, a puffing Apothecary, a Popish Editor, a Protestant Reporter, a Green-horn of Mercer's, Sir Astley Cooper, Mr. Jacob, a Phrenological Madman, Mr. Jones Quain, a Witch, a Woman of the Town; and, of course, it will be duly discovered, that in addition to all these I am the 'terræ fillius' of the next institution of which I may chance to give a description. The enjoyment of the privileges of immortality on alternate days, by the twin Sons of Leda, or the contortions of Proteus in the hands of Aristæus, were but plain matter of fact transactions, compared with these more than mythological transformations of character.

But to be serious, even though it 'exceed all power of face', how are these contradictions to be explained? Simply, because each of them has been the offspring of error. No person ever originated one of them, who are not conscious that he had no other foundation for his belief than mere conjecture; for, up to the present time, no individual could prove the authorship of these papers but the Editor of this Journal. The absurdity of these suspicions (and I have enumerated all that reached an ear naturally attentive to rumour) is manifest from the names on which they have fallen, as it is obvious that some of the men specified could not, and the rest would not, write these articles though they possessed the ability. So much for the consistency of guessing. As the articles themselves have given uneasiness, I think the character of some of the complainants, and the nature of the charges, entitled to some consideration. I have been generally taunted with writing anonymously — upbraided with the cowardice of concealing my name. To this I answer, I have a right to use my discretion, or my taste, in withholding my name. Having taken the right of disclosure into their own hands, and passed me through all the stages of degrading transformation, the demand of my identity comes with rather an awkward grace from these men. Until it be my pleasure to set them right, I will leave them to their suspicions, in which they have so liberally indulged, for I am not to be bullied into concession, or deceived by their shallow stratagems into the revelation of my name. The propriety of the task which I have undertaken has also been made the theme of condemnation; but, I answer, that I have taken no liberties with public characters, or used any precautions for concealing myself, for which I am not prepared to furnish hundreds of examples in the literature of this and of every other age. The whole periodical literature of the present day, not to include former times, is anonymous, and made up, in a great measure, of strictures on living character. The talented Sketches of the Irish Bar, Peter's Letters to his Kinsfolk, and several other essays of the same description, furnish at once a pertinent example of personal and nameless composition. To the charge that I have abused this right, by partiality in my representations of professional merit, I reply, that if I injured any person, the instrument, a free press, by which the wound was inflicted, was open to them for redress. I do not consider it an answer to this observation to say, that some men cannot defend themselves in print, if wronged, and that others think their time better employed than in replying to anonymous attacks. The man who does not defend his own character (and there are few who cannot write all that is necessary for this purpose) violates his own principle, and abuses as much, or more, the press by not correcting its licentiousness, as the man by whom he pretends to be injured. Social duties are obligatory on all. With any individual, however, whose name has been mentioned by me, or with any institution which I have described, I affirm I have no connexion whatever: my estimates may, indeed, have been wrong, but the imputation that they were biassed by improper motives I reject with contempt. In asserting this, I but claim the right of being judged by the general conduct of mankind in similar circumstances. The basest villain will act fairly without a motive to the contrary: I had none for being unknown, and, necessarily, so, no act of mine could be reflected back with interest on its author. With respect to the insinuation that my opinions have been influenced by politics and religion, I may merely remark, that I aspire to no higher distinction in either than that of being an Irishman and a Christian. I wish I could say so much for my accusers. Their own suspicions, which, along with coupling me with every grade of intellect, have confounded me with persons professing every and no form of religion, sufficiently acquit me of all sectarian predilections. As to the threats muttered against me by a faction in the College of Surgeons, this party might, if they had only common discrimination, perceive, in the nature of these Sketches, that I despised the consequences of detection. Having given them so much negative information, I will now affirmatively inform them, that no act of theirs, however base, or remote in design, can possibly reach me. With Niobe I may say, without, I hope, being turned into stone by the angry glances of these Apollos, for a reluctant intimation of my circumstances:

Tutum me copia fecit.
Major sum, quam cui possit fortuna nocere;
Multaque ut eripiat; multo mihi plura relinquet.

But why argue the question with them thus? They say they know me; I take them at their word, and ask them, why wait for additional evidence to justify the execution of their threats? If I am a member of their body, their new charter furnishes them with a congenial instrument of revenge; and since they have not the candour of men to be silent when uncertainty renders reports criminal, let them act consistently with their past conduct, and display, at least, the courage of the assassin, — I Dare Them To The Attempt.

ERINENSIS
Dublin, November 29, 1828

# 20

## MR. CUSACK

### Park-Street School

SOME TIME about the year 1825, a proposal for the establishment
of a private medical school was made by the late Mr. Thomas
Rooney of *the Meath*, to Mr. Cusack, of *Stevens' Hospital*. Mr.
Rooney, who viewed scientific pursuits through the sober medium
of political economy, persuaded himself, after a diligent series of
experiments on the credulity of patients and apprentices, that he
had at that period acquired a surplus of knowledge and reputation
which might be profitably employed in the instruction of the rising
generation of surgical students in Ireland. In applying to Mr.
Cusack, he fancied he had found a partner worthy of the enterprise; and in all other respects, save that of estimating Mr.
Cusack's sagacity at too low a rate, the selection was founded upon
correct principles of calculation, and a clear perception of character. Fortune, aided by his own exertions, had placed Mr. Cusack
in pretty much the same predicament of means and motives for
pushing his conquests farther, as Mr. Rooney himself; and it may
be readily supposed that he received the proposition with alacrity
and favour, however different his opinion might be of the mode of
carrying it into execution. A crisis in his circumstances had arrived,
and adopting Shakespeare's motto, that

> 'There is a tide in the affairs of men,
> Which, taken at the flood, leads on to fortune',

216

he boldly resolved to turn the advantages of the surgeoncy of *Stevens' Hospital* to the best account, and to prove to his indulgent patrons, the Governors of that Institution, who so generously had compounded with their consciences in his appointment, that these advantages were not conferred in vain. Directing his attention to his own position — the point to which most of Mr. Cusack's thoughts tend — he saw himself surrounded by not less than forty apprentices, the expenses of whose education, though once discharged, were only about to commence; and, if directed into some more appropriate channel, must of course flow into the College Treasury. Friendly as Mr. Cusack has ever been to the College of Surgeons, it was not to be expected that he would separate for its benefit the double tide of taxation to which pupils were then subjected, when it might be so conveniently diverted into one little 'Pactolus' of whose 'golden sands' he would be the sole trustee. Independently of these considerations, so natural to one in his condition, it is highly probable that he may have felt himself adumbrated by the shadow of Mr. Colles, which concealed him more than he thought was meet from the public view; and what made this reflection the more poignant was, that there existed little

Park Street School 1824–1849.

hope of the too-enduring substance which enveloped him in its shade being removed within any reasonable period of successional expectancy. As the 'nearest and dearest friends' will decide in such cases for their own welfare in parting, that moment is generally considered the best for separation, when the resulting benefits of movement wear the most autumnal aspect. With so many motives for attempting experiment, it was not wonderful that Mr. Cusack should adopt with avidity the advice of his friend Mr. Rooney: it was however but the project, not the partner, of which he approved. Requesting time — that dangerous 'integer' in all diplomatic transactions — Mr. Cusack employed the hours of deliberation with effect; and it was only by the sound of the mason's hammer in Park-street, and the publication of a prospectus of its school, from which his name was excluded, that Mr. Rooney's simple dreams of fame, fortune, and alliance with his honourable friend, were at length dissipated into thin air!

The appropriation of Mr. Rooney's project unincumbered by any connection with its legitimate parent, was not however the only difficulty which Mr. Cusack had to overcome. That indeed was an effort which any vulgar mind might have accomplished; but the choice of associates to secure success, and the provision against loss in the event of failure, were subjects which required somewhat higher qualities of address for their attainment. The yoking in of a single restive spirit in the new academic team, might derange if not impede altogether its future progress; while cheap as human labour has always been in Ireland, bricks and mortar, timber and slates, do not move into architectural coaptation without the encouraging smiles and dulcet notes of the financial Orpheus of College-green. It consequently became a point of the first importance with Mr. Cusack, to devise a plan by which the building might be made disposable without loss to the proprietors, in the event of failure bringing it under the 'House-Agent's' dominion. Several suggestions were offered on the point; one would have it built in the shape of a respectable dwelling; another in that of an hotel; a third, and so on, would have it assume the form of a manufactory of some kind or other; at all and each of which Mr. Cusack nodded one of his characteristic negatives. The originality of his mind carried him far out of the beaten path of common-place expedients; and turning the helm of invention into those loftier regions of discovery and humbug, in which on other occasions he had been so fortunate, he at length hit upon a plan worthy of his genius and of adoption. The plan upon which Mr. Cusack settled in this instance, is so characteristic of his mental resources, that a word or two on its origin may not be out of place. About the time of which we are speaking, the Protestant principle seems to have been undergoing one of its periodical movements in Ireland; the spirit of multiplication was vigorously stirring within it; and promised daily to shatter the unity of the Irish Church into all the religious forms and fragments of Christianity expected from the 'Second Reformation'. Here was an opening vista in which Mr. Cusack beheld with pleasure the new edifice of Park-street safe from the fluctuations of the 'market' and the contingencies of the 'hammer'. To provide for the new-born communities of Christians called into being by the labours of the 'Propaganda' of Cavan, convenient places of worship, was both a laudable and a safe speculation. Mr. Cusack, following up this happy idea, proposed at once that the new building should be constructed so as to be convertible at any future period into a snug dissenting 'Meeting-house', by the mere removal of the profane accompaniments of anatomy! The thought was so obviously a masterpiece of sagacity, that it was unanimously agreed to; a draft of the building thus 'contrived a double debt to pay' was forthwith ordered; and, in its circular-headed windows and gabled front, it still preserves the provident stamp of Mr. Cusack's genius.

Mr. Cusack was equally happy in the selection of his fellow-labourers. Various circumstances combined to point out Dr. Jacob as an eligible and willing agent in the concern. Notwithstanding his often and ardently-expressed admiration of Dr. Macartney of *Trinity College*, Dr. J. was weary of the subordinate character of Demonstrator; and probably conceived he had acquired sufficient knowledge and credit by his own connection with that eminent Professor, to undertake the part of a principal in a smaller establishment. Besides, he must have felt that in an institution as restricted by the statute-book to one undeviating course, as a planet to its orbit by the laws of gravitation, and, indeed, fully as little subject to human influence, there was no prospect of opportunities occurring for the exercitation of those peculiar qualities, of which Dr. Jacob has since given to the world so many convincing testimonies. His heart panted for a wider scope of exertion — his 'borrowed plumes' trembled for migration; and like the youthful Norval who 'had heard of battles and longed &c.', he only required to hear the roll of the recruiting drum, to enlist in the ranks, and it must be allowed that he met with a chief worthy of his high destination. The *corps dramatique* of the establishment was soon completed by the addition of congenial associates, selected by Mr. Cusack on a principle, the operation of which in this institution shall form, should we have space, the sublect of our concluding remarks.

While many of these, his earlier companions, have transferred themselves to the 'rich preserves' of the surgical corporation of Dublin, Mr. Cusack, ambitious of the most exalted station in that head-quarter of corruption, 'bides his time'; and awaits in decent silence the fulfilment of that arrangement which rumour, at least, has established between him and Mr. Colles, for succession to the chair of surgery. Upon his qualifications for this important office, there is some difference of opinion, but it is owing no doubt to a misunderstanding of the nature of the duties belonging to the situation, and of his character as a surgeon. It is true he holds a high place with many in the mechanical medicine of Dublin, and that if a prompt and judicious application of surgical science, in all cases requiring its interference, be intended by this estimate, his merits have not been overstated. With all the manipulations of surgery, and all those signs by which surgical diseases are recognised, long experience and observation must have made him familiar. Neither will it be disputed that he is conversant with the writings of most British surgeons, and that he has from time to time tested the value of their doctrines in the wards of *Stevens'*. The proofs and concessions however which establish his competency to serve his patients, do not necessarily apply to the case of his pupils, there being no greater fallacy than that which assumes that an efficient practitioner must be a good teacher. Every student who has attended Mr. Cusack's lectures, must have observed in them a practical refutation of such an hypothesis. Educated in a school which restricted surgery within the narrowest possible limits, and almost entirely excluded the aid of rational speculation in treating the subjects of that science, Mr Cusack's duties as a surgeon, and interests as a partisan of that school, have only confirmed him in the errors of his times, and, it is to be feared, they incapacitate him from taking his place among the philosophic professors of the present day, who would illustrate, by a knowledge of principles, the dark mysteries of empiricism. He scarcely takes the trouble to conceal the opinion (which, in despite of all profession to the contrary, would still be obvious from his discourses), that surgery has for some time arrived at the acme of perfection; and that all attempts to extend its boundaries, or to innovate on the method of studying it in Stevens' Hospital, are but the mere dreams of modern enthusiasts. Even in the everchanging empire of science, Mr. Cusack would be a tory; and fling upon the irresistible current of improvement, the feeble fetters of authority, and the usages of past ages. The consequences of this tone of mind assume an amusing aspect in the lecture-room. Believing, as Mr. Cusack does, that a surgical education consists in a knowledge of certain operations, and an acquaintance with certain morbid phenomena, it may well be supposed that he has devoted little attention to the arrangement of his lectures, or to the subjects of which they are composed. Most lecturers, too, condescend to respect the quality, and even the quality, of their language, as a necessary means of communicating their ideas. Mr. Cusack pursues an opposite course, and enters the theatre as if determined to substitute pantomime for all the 'parts of speech'. Others attempt to conceal their poverty of· ideas by a profusion of words; Mr. Cusack rejoices in the converse of the device, and leaves his auditors to infer the depth and extent of his knowledge by the parsimony of his phrases, and the exuberance of his physiognomical expression. His face serves as a sort of 'chapel-of-ease' to his tongue, the muscles of the one most faithfully undertaking the performance of half the duties of the other. The narration of a train of symptoms, or the description of a morbid appearance, commenced in an impressive tone, is not unfrequently concluded through the myological medium of Mr. Cusack's speaking countenance. He may now and then proceed as far as the first or second member of a sentence in describing a disease, or delivering an opinion; but it rarely happens that he does not finish the effort by a certain knowing contradiction of the external canthus or a profound protrusion of the under-lip, in which much of Mr. Cusack's mute eloquence appears to reside. With these silent auxiliaries of his descriptive powers, we have seen him *ogle* half the history of a 'fungus hæmatodes'; and go through no inconsiderable portion of an operation, with the sole assistance of the 'orbicularis oris'. It is not, however, to be supposed, that Mr. Cusack's face is remarkable for the mobility of its structure, or a playful variety of expression so often connected with high intellectual endowments. No greater mistake could arise out of our imperfect representation, as the few peculiarities we have stated are only rendered conspicuous by standing out in isolated relief upon the broad and unsymmetrical disk of a torpid and common-place physiognomy. We recollect nothing, indeed, in fiction or in reality, which can so well convey to the mind of one who has not seen the original in his intercourse with his class, a correct notion of Mr. C.'s manner and appearance, as the account of Swift's philosopher in the academy of Laputa, who undertook to supersede the use of language in the communication of knowledge, by a bundle of symbols to represent words and ideas.

The *disjecta membra poetæ*, may, indeed, be recognised now and then in his dislocated sentences and dark innendoes, but it would require a commentator with the talent of a Cuvier for reconstruction, to patch them up into an intelligible form. There are occasions, however, when Mr. Cusack can put off the dull lineaments of affected wisdom, and be roused into turbulent excitement, when the passions of self-interest and ambition assert their natural sovereignty in his breast, over the artificial assumptions of equanimity and moderation. We recollect having witnessed one of these glowing, but incautious triumphs of temperament over the frail and fictitious virtues of design and cultivation. The metamorphose of the wily simpleton into the coarsest partisan was complete, and indicated abilities worthy of higher objects and a better direction. The cause of medical reform had been then making rapid progress in Dublin, and was openly and ably advocated in some of the private schools. It was thought prudent to attempt to stop its further advances, by opposing to its march the once effectual barriers of corporate authority and professional *prestige*. Mr. Cusack was chosen to carry the onslaught on the reformers into fatal effect. He entered the theatre, followed by a mob of exulting retainers, who degraded even the humble duties of vassalage by the mean and ferocious malignity of their conduct. The long and vacant gaze of universal acquiescence with the opinions of all men, habitual to Mr. Cusack in his intercourse with the world, was seen to lower, as he commenced the charge, into a lurid expression of cowardly irritation; and the regulated phases of his features, with which he was wont to veil from view his private convictions, to be fixed in a spasmodic impersonation of powerless rage. A torrent of pointless vituperation on all those who opposed to that system of which he stood forth the characteristic advocate, came to his relief, and, in the course of some time, with the apathy of his auditors to the frantic appeal, restored him to the tranquil indulgence of his taste in buffoonery beyond which it is not quite safe for him to venture to rise. Not many years have elapsed since this furibund but futile effort was made to strangle medical reform in its birth in Ireland; but few as these years have been, they are sufficient to teach Mr. Cusack and his satellites the folly of endeavouring to preserve by such means the rotten outposts of corruption against the innovating influences of time and thought. The party who then smiled encouragement to their leader, — who hallooed him on like a mastiff on his prey, are now, together with him, as tamely as so many spaniels, crouching beneath the lash of reform; and humbly, but treacherously, beseeching its triumphant advocates at the seat of government, to preserve a little longer in some mitigated state of corruption, that institution which mercy itself cannot rescue from the punishment due to, and incurred by, its crimes.

In general Mr. Cusack, however, commands his temper, and dissimulates with success. His college intrigues are cleverly conceived, and conducted with prudence, seldom giving his opponents an opportunity to obviate his plans, and carrying them into execution without any squeamish regard for the means. No one knows better than he, how to insinuate the advantages of conservative principles in College politics, or to lull into repose the rising scruples of juvenile independence about a vote on a field-day in Stephen's Green. If fair words do not win over the reluctant youth to his objects, a well-timed intimation of promotion being shortly in the way, relaxes resistance, and seldom fails of bringing him within the fortunate ranks of one of Mr. Cusack's 'majorities'. By these and similar means he has got at the head of a party in the College, through whose agency that institution has been effectually usurped. Its treasury, property, and professorships, are now wholly at their disposal, and converted to their own purposes without the slightest regard to justice or public opinion. Since Mr. Cusack established this league between his own and the College school, the professorships in the latter, which an honest and independent profession would hold sacred as the sources of scientific instruction, and as the appropriate and honourable rewards of talent and industry, have been without exception given away as compensation for services rendered in the support of this ruinous confederation. Through a reform along of medical law, relief, is now to be sought from the evils of a combination which includes within its vortex a disposable force of corruption far beyond the controlling power of any liberal party which could be formed in the College in its present state. To this remedial change every eye is now turned; and, as in all probability the conditions of it will be shortly announced by the Government, we shall take an early opportunity of developing at greater length the scheme adopted by Mr. Cusack to frustrate that measure, and of adding a few suggestions on some essentials which, to be efficient in Ireland, *it must contain.*

ERINENSIS
Dublin, March 25, 1836

# APPENDIX

The Sketches, letters and related correspondence of Erinensis in *The Lancet* 1824–1836 arranged chronologically. Those marked * are reproduced in the text.

* 1. Royal College of Surgeons in Ireland.          Jan. 11, 1824.
* 2. Mr. Colles.                                     Feb. 15, 1824.
* 3. Mr. Todd.                                       Mar. 21, 1824.
  4. Royal College of Surgeons in Ireland —
     Letter from Vindex.                             Mar. 28, 1824.
* 5. Dr. Stokes.                                     Apr. 10, 1824.
* 6. Mr. Kirby.                                      May. 15, 1824.
* 7. Mr. Crampton.                                   Jan. 8, 1825.
  8. Letter from A. Colles.                          Jan. 29, 1825.
  9. Erinensis and Mr. Crampton.                     Feb. 19, 1825.
 10. The Fly Trap.                                   Mar. 5, 1825.
*11. Mr. Jacob.                                      Mar. 12, 1825.
 12. Jemmy Copland.                                  Apr. 9, 1825.
*13. Mr. Macartney.                                  Apr. 23, 1825.
 14. Erinensis introduces Mr. Crampton's
     Lectures.                                       Jun. 25, 1825.
 15. Jemmy Copland.                                  Jul. 23, 1825.
 16. Dublin Hospitals, letter from a pupil
     of R.C.S.I.                                     Aug. 13, 1825.
*17. Mr. Macartney, continued.                       Aug. 27, 1825.
 18. Letter from Mr. Macartney.                      Sep. 10, 1825.
 19. Mr. Macartney and Erinensis.                    Sep. 24, 1825.
*20. Dublin Hospitals.                               Nov. 26, 1825.
 21. Mr. Crampton's Lithotomy Instrument —
     letter from Francis L'Estrange.                 Dec. 9, 1825.
 22. Mr. Macartney and the Board of Trinity
     College.                                        Jan. 7, 1826.
 23. Mr. Crampton's Lithotomy Net.                   Jan. 14, 1826.
*24. Mr. Carmichael.                                 Mar. 4, 1826.
*25. Stevens' Hospital.                              May. 6, 1826.
*26. Mercer's Hospital.                              Jul. 15, 1826.
*27. Mercer's Hospital.                              Jul. 22, 1826.
 28. 'The King and Queen's College of
     Physicians in Ireland'.                         Aug. 10, 1826.
 29. Fever in Ireland.                               Aug. 26, 1826.
 30. Baron Larrey's visit to Dublin.                 Sep. 2, 1826.

*31. Mercer's Hospital.                                    Oct. 21, 1826.
*32. Letters from Eminent Characters, with
     Comments etc.                                         Nov. 25, 1826.
 33. The Court of Examiners.                               Dec. 4, 1826.
*34. Mr. Wilmot.                                           Jan. 13, 1827.
 35. The late Proceedings of the College.                 Mar. 17, 1827.
 36. Reduction of the Present Term of Medical
     Graduation in the University
     of Dublin considered.                                 Jun. 16, 1827.
 37. *As above.*                                           Jul. 5, 1827.
 38. *As above.*                                           Jul. 12, 1827.
*39. Mr. Harrison.                                         Oct. 20, 1827.
*40. Dr. Jacob's Introductory Lecture.                     Oct. 30, 1827.
 41. Examination of Dr. Macartney's Evidence
     to the Anatomical Committee
     of the House of Commons.                              Mar. 20, 1828.
 42. College of Physicians in Ireland.                     Sep. 1, 1828.
*43. The Private Schools of Dublin.                        Oct. 25, 1828.
*44. Opening of the Medical Session in Dublin.            Nov. 8, 1828.
*45. The Dublin College of Surgeons and
     Erinensis.                                            Nov. 29, 1828.
 46. James Johnstone, M.D.                                 Jan. 17, 1829.
 47. On the Contemplated Projects for
     supplying Subjects for Dissection.                    Feb. 4, 1829.
 48. James Johnstone, Post-Office M.D.                     Feb. 27, 1829.
 49. On the Exportation of Dead Bodies from
     Ireland to England and Scotland.                      Mar. 14, 1829.
 50. On Roderick Macleod's 'necessary system
     of things'.                                           Sep. 23, 1829.
 51. Periodical Obituary.                                  Oct. 17, 1829.
 52. The Zoological Gardens, Dublin.                       Sep. 21, 1834.
 53. The School of the Royal College of
     Surgeons in Ireland.                                  Oct. 18, 1834.
 54. Medical Patronage.                                    Nov. 30, 1834.
 55. The Concours.                                         Dec. 13, 1834.
 56. The Dublin Medical Press.                             Apr. 10, 1835.
 57. Dr. Litton, — The Glasnevin Botanic
     Garden.                                               May. 16, 1835.
 58. Erinensis to Dr. Johnson.                             Jul. 10, 1835.
 59. Dr. Johnson's reply to Erinensis.                     Jul. 18, 1835.
 60. Royal Dublin Society.                                 Mar. 10, 1836.
*61. Mr. Cusack, Park Street School.                       Mar. 25, 1836.

★ ★ ★

| 62. | Editorial in *The Lancet* | Dec. 29, 1827. |
| 63. | Editorial in *The Lancet* | Jan. 5, 1828. |
| 64. | Editorial in *The Lancet* | Jan. 12, 1828. |
| 65. | Editorial in *The Lancet* | Oct. 17, 1829. |
| 66. | Editorial in *The Lancet* | Apr. 12, 1834. |
| 67. | Editorial in *The Lancet* | Jul. 25, 1835. |
| 68. | Editorial in *The Lancet* | May. 7, 1836. |

# NOTES

## CHAPTER ONE

# THE ROYAL COLLEGE OF SURGEONS IN IRELAND

The Royal College of Surgeons in Ireland received its Charter on February 11, 1784, and appropriately first met at the Lying-in Hospital (Rotunda). Under the terms of its Charter it established a medical school and appointed professors, who at first lectured in their own homes without any fee. In 1789 the college acquired its first home — a small building at the back of Mercer's Hospital. No trace or picture of this building survives, apart from a ground plan in the Longfield Collection in the National Library of Ireland, where it is styled the Surgeons' Theatre. Between 1806 and 1810 a new home for the College was built at the corner of York Street and St. Stephen's Green on part of a burial ground not then in use. This simple, rather austere building was extended between 1825 and 1827 to the magnificient College we know today.

WILLIAM DEASE 1752–1798, was one of the original members of the Dublin Society of Surgeons, and was the most energetic of the founders of the Dublin College and its medical school where he was its first Professor of Surgery. Originally Surgeon to the United Hospitals of St. Nicholas and St. Catherine and later to the Meath Hospital, he had an extensive and fashionable practice and resided with the nobility of Sackville Street. Of his many publications, his *Treatise on Surgical Injuries of the Head* was perhaps his greatest work, and gained him an international reputation. He was President of the College in 1789, and has long been styled 'The Father of Irish Surgery'. He died suddenly in the Rebellion year of 1798.

JOHN HALAHAN 1753-    , was one of the original members of the College, and the first Professor of Anatomy in the Surgeons' School, 1785–1794, and again between 1799–1804. He was also the first Professor of Midwifery, 1789–1795. In 1804 he was succeeded in the Anatomy Chair by Abraham Colles.

SIR PETER COURTNEY, was clerk and housekeeper of the College until his death in 1832. He was a non-medical man and his baronetcy was inherited.

GEORGE RENNY 1757–1847, was a Scot and a graduate of Edinburgh University who after a military career settled in Ireland in 1783, eventually becoming Surgeon-General to the Forces. His influence in government circles benefited the College in the early

228

days of its history. He was President of the College in 1793.

JAMES HENTHORN 1744–1832, was one of the founder members of the College, its Secretary for 48 years and its President in 1822.

CHAPTER TWO

## ABRAHAM COLLES 1773–1843

Abraham Colles was a licentiate of the Surgeons' School and an arts graduate of Trinity in 1795. He graduated M.D. Edinburgh University two years later. In 1799 he was appointed Resident Surgeon at Dr. Steevens' Hospital, which was to be his professional home for some 40 years. In 1804, Colles was appointed to two Chairs — anatomy and physiology, and surgery in the Surgeons' School, which he was to occupy for 23 years and 32 years respectively. He was the greatest professor of his College, and in his day the leading surgeon in Ireland. He was President of his College in 1802 and 1830.

He is the subject of a recent biography*.

CHAPTER THREE

## CHARLES HAWKES TODD 1782–1826

Charles Hawkes Todd was a licentiate of the Surgeons' School, Surgeon to the House of Industry Hospital, and President of his College in 1821. He apparently was the first to suggest the cure of aneurysm by compression. He was co-professor with Colles in the College Chairs from 1819 until his early death at age of 44. His wife and 16 children were not provided for, and the subscription list for these by his Dublin colleagues was given able support by *The Lancet* publicity. His second son, Robert Bentley Todd had a distinguished medical career in London, becoming Professor of Physiology and Morbid Anatomy at King's College Hospital Medical School. He was also Physician to the Hospital and his statue now adorns its forecourt.

CHAPTER FOUR

## WHITLEY STOKES 1763–1845

Whitley Stokes was distinguished in many fields of scholarship, a Fellow of Trinity, and a member of the Society of United Irishmen. The latter he did not deny in 1798 when accused by the notorious Lord Clare; the sentence was that for three years Stokes was not to be elevated to a senior fellowship of Trinity. Later he was to resign his Trinity fellowship, but this was for religious reasons as he could no longer subscribe to the tenets of the Established Church. He

*\*Abraham Colles* by Martin Fallon, Heinemann, London 1972.

joined the 'Walkerites'. The Reverend John Walker, a fellow and tutor of Trinity at that time, was very unorthodox in his religious beliefs, also resigned his fellowship to found an extreme Calvinistic sect in Dublin. The 'Walkerites', following the teaching of St. Paul, greeted one another with a kiss, which naturally led to confusion and ribaldry in practice. The movement later faded out in splinter groups of 'Osculists' and 'Non-Osculists'. Stokes employed Walker as a private tutor to his family, who, not without significance were not to graduate from Trinity. Trinity, to their credit still recognised the greatness of Stokes in appointing him to a new and lucrative chair in Natural History, and it is in this capacity that Erinensis meets him. Stokes' other appointments were: King's Professor of the Practice of Medicine 1798–1811; Professor of Medicine in the Surgeons' School 1819–1828; Physician to the Meath Hospital in 1818; and the Regius Chair of Physic in Trinity in 1830. In the latter two posts he was succeeded by his son — the better known William.

Stokes wooed the Muses, and not unsuccessfully. Of painting and music he was an excellent judge, and his poetical compositions, though few, entitle him to a place among the minor poets. The following lines on the Shamrock were written on the occasion of the entry of George IV into Dublin in 1821, though not the best of his compositions, at least show his patriotic spirit:

> Fair plant, beloved with rooted truth,
>     And watered by my tears,
> The bitter trial of my youth,
>     The solace of my years,
>
> Lov'd, honor'd, plant, too long oppressed,
>     Beneath the foot of pride;
> At length unfold thy beaming breat,
>     And cast the dust aside.
>
> Belov'd, revive — your King appears,
>     To wipe your tears away;
> The sorrows of a thousand years
>     Are vanishing to-day.
>
> His aged head thy grateful breast
>     Shall soothe to safe repose;
> Free from the thorns that still infest
>     The Thistle and the Rose.

CHAPTER FIVE

# JOHN TIMOTHY KIRBY 1781–1853

John Timothy Kirby was a remarkable figure, flamboyant and ornate in character as in the trappings of his famous coach. He was a licentiate of the Surgeons' School and an arts graduate of Trinity.

He became a demonstrator to Abraham Colles, but resigned that appointment in 1809, to open with Alexander Read a private medical school in Stephen Street, close to Mercer's Hospital. Part of the front of house was occupied by a laundress, whose signboard bore the words 'Mangling done here', and the wags of the day said that the sign did duty for Kirby and Read as well as for the laundress. In the following year the school was removed to Peter Street and styled the 'Theatre of Anatomy and School of Surgery'. Then Read retired and Kirby became sole proprietor until 1832, when he closed the school on becoming Professor of Medicine in the Surgeons' School. There was a tavern in the Dublin suburbs known as the 'Grinding Young'. Over its entrance, a sign-board represented a mill, into the hopper of which old crippled persons were precipitating themselves, whilst from the outlet on the other side of the mill a stream of vigorous, and healthy personages issued. This was to symbolise the youth-restoring, health-reviving properties of the liquor retailed within the edifice. A humorist produced an illustration representing Mr. Kirby grinding country bumpkins into surgeons. Awkward fellows, some with straw ropes round their legs, were placed by 'Miller' Kirby in his mill, and rattled out therefrom as Navy and Army surgeons decked out in suitable uniforms. This illustration had a large sale at home and abroad. Kirby's certificates were accepted by the Edinburgh and London Royal Colleges and by the Service departments, and to meet their further requirements he added to his establishment a small hospital of 12 beds (his opponents said there was only one bed!), which he dedicated to St. Peter and St. Bridget. The Dublin College refused Kirby's certificates until his hospital had 20 beds. Strange as it now appears, Kirby's School met all the requirements of the Services. Only a few decades before, John Hunter stated that 'it was hardly necessary for a man to be a surgeon to practice in the Army'; and Wellington's men, or 'The Article' as he was wont to call them, were pretty tough!.

Kirby left an interesting autobiography. Behind all the bombast and glamour, he was a very able and hard-working doctor with as large a medical practice as a surgical one. His wife died at the birth of their 16th child, leaving him with nine young children to bring up. He was President of his College in 1832.

CHAPTER SIX

# PHILIP CRAMPTON 1777–1858

Philip Crampton was one of Ireland's greatest surgeons. He was a licentiate of the Surgeons' School and an M.D. of Glasgow University. After a short Army career, and at an early age, he succeeded William Dease as Surgeon to the Meath Hospital. Elegant in dress, physique and manners, always moving in high society, he was nevertheless an able surgeon, and adorned the surgical practice of his hospital for many decades. In many ways he was a complete contrast and chief rival to Abraham Colles.

In due course, Crampton became a Fellow of the Royal Society, Surgeon-General to H.M. Forces, and President of his College on four occasions. He was created a baronet in 1839. In 1830 Crampton proposed a remarkable and spirited motion before his College against an obnoxious Act of Parliament which required the dissection of executed criminals, and stated, 'It is calculated to excite in the minds of the ignorant feelings of hatred and disgust towards the surgical profession because it associates the surgeon with the executioner in the performance of the most odious and degrading of all offices'. In 1838 he read a memorable and erudite paper on medical history before his College and a distinguished gathering. Erinensis was naturally amused and intrigued by Crampton's employment of the 'net' to retrieve the stone during the lithotomy operation. Later, Crampton was to abandon lithotomy in favour of the lithotrite, and he was the first surgeon in Dublin to employ the new instrument. The citizens of Dublin erected a memorial in the shape of a bronze fountain to his memory.

GEORGE STEWART 1752–1813, claimed to be of royal descent. He was Surgeon to the Charitable Infirmary (later Jervis Street), an original member of the College, State Surgeon in 1785, Surgeon-General to the Forces in 1787, and President of his College in 1792. It was Stewart who spotted the potential of the young Abraham Colles.

MR. OWBERRY       –1820. Ralph Smith Obré was one of the assistant surgeons at Dr. Steevens' Hospital, one of the original members of the College, its Treasurer for 27 years, and its President in 1792. Obré had been for many years extensively engaged in treating the Venereal, and when his junior colleague Abraham Colles asked him if he believed that the disease was ever propagated by 'sitting in a public privy', Obré shrewdly answered, 'that it was sometimes the manner in which *married* men contracted it, but *unmarried* men never caught it in this manner'!

## CHAPTER SEVEN
# ARTHUR JACOB 1790–1874

Arthur Jacob was the son of the County Surgeon of Maryborough, Queen's County, to whom he was apprenticed. Later, he was an apprentice to Abraham Colles, a licentiate of the Surgeons' School, and a graduate of Edinburgh University. On his return to Dublin he was appointed Demonstrator to James Macartney in Trinity, being succeeded there by Dr. Peter Hennis Green (Erinensis). In 1804 with his colleagues Cusack, Wilmot, Marsh, Apjohn, and Graves, he founded the Park Street Medical School, which was described as a 'Chapel of Ease' to the Surgeons' School, and to which most of its staff succeeded. Jacob was to ease his way there in 1827 when he succeeded Abraham Colles in the anatomy and physiology chair. He held many appointments in the College and was its President in 1837 and again in 1864. One of his few weaknesses was his notion that he alone of the professors should always give the introductory lecture at the commencement of the School session. With Henry Maunsell, Jacob established the *Dublin Medical Press* in 1838, and as editor he was much given to drastic polemical articles which frequently greatly irritated those against whom they were directed. He had much in common with Thomas Wakley, in his intense dislike of charlatanism and humbug of every kind. An austere figure he rarely indulged in even the mildest festivities, and devoted himself wholly to his professorial, professional, and editorial work, and to original research. Jacob was the first to describe the bacillary layer of rods and cones of the retina, which is now known as Jacob's membrane. He was also the first to describe rodent ulcer, which in Dublin is still referred to as Jacob's ulcer. Finally, he invented a special needle for cataract operations which was long in use.

CHAPTER EIGHT

# JAMES MACARTNEY 1770–1843

James Macartney was born in Armagh, and was apprenticed to Hartigan of the Surgeons' School, but two years later he transferred to the Great Windmill School of Baillie and Cruikshank. While still a student Abernethy appointed him a demonstrator in anatomy at St. Bartholomew's Hospital, and elevated him to a lectureship on his gaining the M.R.C.S. diploma. Macartney specialised in surgical or topographical anatomy, and Macalister tells us that when demonstrating and to give his students confidence, he would tie the femoral artery blindfold, and, upon occasion ligate the vessel successfully with his back to the subject. Macartney entered the Army as a surgeon, but continued his lectureship at St. Bartholomew's Hospital until 1811, in which year he was elected F.R.S., and in which year also he went to Ireland with his regiment. When this regiment was disembodied in 1812, Macartney decided to remain in Ireland, and in the same year he obtained the M.D. degree of St. Andrews University. In June 1813, Macartney was appointed Professor of Anatomy and Chirurgery at Trinity, which Chair he was to hold for 'twenty-four contentious years', and in which he *made* the Trinity medical school.

During the 'resurrectionists'' campaign and the grave public disquiet which followed their gruesome activities, Macartney in 1828 suggested a better and more noble method of obtaining bodies for dissection. In the School of Anatomy in Trinity there is a docu-

ment signed by him and some 277 others, including many distinguished scientists of the period, which reads:

We whose names are hereunto affixed, being convinced that the
study of anatomy is of the utmost value to mankind, inasmuch
as it illustrates various branches of natural and moral science,
and constitutes the very basis of the healing art; and believing
that the erroneous opinions and the vulgar prejudices which pre-
vail with regard to dissections, will be most effectually removed
by practical example: do hereby deliberately and solemnly
express our desire that, at the usual period after death, our
bodies, instead of being interred, should be devoted by our
surviving friends to the more rational, benevolent, and honourable purpose of explaining the structure, functions and diseases
of the human body.

We leave his career to his biographer Macalister, who said of him:
'He was an expert anatomist, a philosophical biologist far in
advance of his period, with a mind and memory stored with knowledge ...' Macartney resigned his Chair in 1837, following an
impossible row with his College and his colleagues, having previously sold the contents of his museum to Cambridge University
for an annuity of £100 a year for 10 years. He died in March 1843,
and the last words he wrote may form his epitaph:

The last great event is the extinction of the systematic functions
which is commonly called death. As soon as the vitality of the
tissue is lost, the body becomes subject to the laws of inorganic
matter. The greater part of it is exhaled and is carried by the
winds and clouds to distant regions, and finally they descend
with rains to fertilise the earth. We thus repay our great debt to
nature, and return the elements of our bodies to the common
storehouse. Thus ends this strange eventful history.

'All forms that perish, other forms supply:
    By turns we catch the vital breath and die,
Like bubbles on the sea of matter borne,
    They rise, they break, and to the sea return'.

## CHAPTER NINE
# DUBLIN HOSPITALS

In this Sketch Erinensis confines himself to the latest Dublin
Hospital — the new *Meath Hospital* and *County Dublin Infirmary*
which was completed in 1822. The original hospital was founded in
1753, and occupied various sites in the Coombe, and was intended
to afford medical assistance to the operative population of the
'Liberties' — that south-west corner of Dublin which for centuries
lay outwith the jurisdiction of the city: it was a thriving community
of small industries such as weaving, tanning, brewing etc., occupy-

ing what was originally the Earl of Meath's estate, but now an insalubrious area of the metropolis.

Of the hospital's physicians, Whitley Stokes was the subject of a previous Sketch. His son William — the 'great' Stokes had not yet arrived — he was to succeed his father in 1826. The reader will no doubt note the omission of the name of Robert James Graves — the most dynamic medical man ever produced by his country, who with the younger Stokes introduced clinical teaching and made the Meath Hospital famous in the annals of medicine. Graves, no doubt was Vindex who wrote that letter of March 28 1824 to *The Lancet*, and he probably then knew or suspected the identity of Erinensis.

TOM BOONEY i.e. CUSACK RONEY 1782–1849, was Surgeon to the Meath Hospital and President of the College in 1814 and 1828. Charles Lever has immortalised Roney in his amusing novel, *Confessions of Harry Lorrequer*. Dr. Finucane, pretending to be suffering from hydraphobia, tells Lorrequer that he has bitten off Cusack Roney's thumb, whereupon the doctor is left to the exclusive possession of the mail coach, whilst Lorrequer passes a rainy night upon its summit.

THOMAS HEWSON 1783–1831, was a licentiate of the Surgeons' School and an arts graduate of Trinity. He was appointed Surgeon to the Meath Hospital in 1809, and Professor of Surgical Pharmacy in the Surgeons' School 1819–1826. He was President of his College in 1819.

RAWDON MACNAMARA      –1836, was a licentiate of the Surgeons' School, and was for a time Demonstrator to Professor James Macartney of Trinity. He was appointed Surgeon to the Meath Hospital in 1819, and succeeded Thomas Hewson in his Chair at the Surgeons' School. He was President of his College in 1831, and his son, of the same name was President in 1869.

WILLIAM HENRY PORTER 1790–1861, was a licentiate of the Surgeons' School and a graduate in arts and medicine of Trinity. In 1819 he was appointed Surgeon to the Meath Hospital. His name appears in eponymous medical literature — Porter's sign — trachael tugging in aortic aneurysm. He died apparently from that lesion. Porter succeeded Colles in the chair of surgery in the Surgeons' School in 1836, and was President of his College in 1838.

FRANCIS L'ESTRANGE 1756–1836. Francis L'Estrange's medical education does not appear to have been recorded. In 1799 he was appointed Assistant Surgeon to Mercer's Hospital, later becoming full surgeon. He was also Assistant Surgeon to the House of Industry Hospital. Erinensis was very amused with his collaboration with Philip Crampton, the 'surgical Walton', in the production of the 'Dublin landing net' in the lithotomy operation. L'Estrange engaged in obstetrical and surgical practice, and was accoucher at the birth of the poet, Thomas Moore. He was President of his College in 1796.

CHAPTER TEN

# RICHARD CARMICHAEL 1776–1849

Richard Carmichael was one of Dublin's greatest surgeons. Educated at the Surgeons' School, he was President of his College in 1813, 1826 and 1845. His professional life was spent at the House of Industry (Richmond) Hospital, and at the Westmoreland Lock Hospital. It was at the latter hospital that he acquired his great knowledge of the Venereal, which gained him an international reputation. During his life-time, and again in his will, his College, the Richmond Hospital, and the Medical Benevolent Association benefited from his generosity. When he died, it was written of him:

> His epitaph should resemble that of Boerhaave in sublime simplicity. The tablet that marks the spot in the cemetery of St. George's parish, where all of him that was not immortal rests, should bear an inscription like this —
> 'Salutifero<br>RICHARDI CARMICHAEL<br>genio sacrum.'
> We were about to say that a brilliant light had been extinguished by the death of this great and good man. But it is not so. His bright example will long light congenial spirits in his profession to tread the path he trod, and encourage them to emulate the energy, the perseverance, the virtues, that made him an ornament to his profession, a credit to his country, an honour to human nature itself.

CHAPTER ELEVEN

# DR. STEEVENS' HOSPITAL

Dr. Richard Steevens was the son of a Wiltshire clergyman who had to flee his cure and his country to escape Cromwell and to settle in Athlone. Richard Steevens in due course graduated in Trinity, and rose high in his profession, becoming President of the Physicians' College in 1703, and again in 1710, in which year also he was appointed Regius Professor of Physic at Trinity. In the same year he died, aged 56, and unmarried. In his will he left his real estate to trustees for the use of his unmarried sister Grizel during her life-time, and after her death 'to provide one proper place or building within the city of Dublin for a hospital for maintaining and curing from time to time such sick and wounded persons whose distempers and wounds are curable'.

His sister however decided that her brother's wishes should be carried out in her life-time, but her efforts to obtain a site and patronage were hampered by Queen Anne's death in 1714. The site was procured in 1717 and the building began in 1720. Dr. Steevens' Hospital can thus claim to be the oldest voluntary hospital in these islands; in so far as it was the oldest in conception, and even more important, it is on the same site, practically in the same fabric, and serving the same function for which it was founded two-and-a-half centuries ago. It was the professional home of Abraham Colles and his son William for 100 years, and it was that famous team of Abraham Colles, Samuel Wilmot and James William Cusack that established the Hospital as the 'Home of Irish Surgery'.

Jonathan Swift, the great Dean of St. Patrick's Cathedral, who was appointed a trustee of the Hospital in 1720, was no doubt influenced by the success of the institution when as far back as 1731 he wrote his brilliantly cynical *Verses on the Death of Dr. Swift*:

> He gave the little wealth he had
> To build a house for fools and mad,
> And showed by one satyric touch
> No nation wanted it so much.'

Swift died in 1745 and in his will dated 1740, he directed his trustees to dispose of his fortune 'by purchasing lands of inheritance situated in any province in Ireland except Connaught and from the yearly profits of these to purchase a piece of land situated near Dr. Steevens' Hospital and to build a hospital there large enough for the reception of as many idiots and lunatics as the annual increase of the said lands and worldly substance will be sufficient to maintain, and I direct that the said hospital be called St. Patrick's Hospital'. In 1746, Swift's trustees approached the governors of Dr. Steevens' Hospital, who willingly gave up part of their ground for the creation of St. Patrick's Hospital (often referred to as Swift's Hospital), and ever since the two great institutions have worked side by side for the relief of those disordered in body and mind.

CHAPTER TWELVE
# MERCER'S HOSPITAL

Mary Mercer established a small stone house as a refuge for 20 girls in the grounds of St. Stephen's churchyard in 1724. 10 years later this was converted into a hospital of 10 beds for 'diseases of tedious and hazardous cure, such as falling sickness, lunacy, leprosy, and the like, or of such other diseased and infirm poor persons as the trustees think proper'. The hospital funds benefited from the proceeds of Handel's 'Messiah' which was first performed in Dublin in 1742. The hospital was rebuilt in 1757, and extended a century later.

ALEXANDER READ 1786–1870, was an arts graduate of Trinity and a licentiate of the Surgeons' School. He was Surgeon to the hospital and President of the College in 1825 and 1835.

WILLIAM AUCHINLECK 1787-1848, was born in Dublin, but his family were of Scottish extraction. He was a licentiate of the Surgeons' School, and was later appointed Surgeon to the hospital. He was President of the College in 1829.

MICHAEL DANIEL 1792-1837, was a licentiate of the Surgeons' School, and was later appointed Assistant Surgeon to the Hospital. He was Demonstrator in Anatomy in Kirby's School.

GERALD MACKLIN 1767-1848, was a licentiate of the Surgeons' School, and subsequently became a surgeon to the hospital. He was State Surgeon in 1806, and President of the College in the same year.

EDWARD HILL 1741-1830, was physician to the Hospital. He was Regius Professor of Physic in Trinity for 49 years and President of the Physicians' College on six occasions. He was not interested in clinical medicine and rarely attended the hospital. Hill was one of those brilliant scholars, more *grammaticus* than *medicus*, who could equally well have adorned a Chair in English literature. He was for many years engaged in an edition of Milton's *Paradise Lost*.

CHARLES RICHARD ALEXANDER LENDRICK      -1841, was the other physician to the hospital. He was King's Professor of the Practice of Medicine in Trinity, and President of the Physicians' College in 1828. It was his famous row with Macartney over the hours of lectures that led to the latter's resignation.

CHAPTER FOURTEEN
## SAMUEL WILMOT 1772-1848

Samuel Wilmot graduated in arts and in medicine in Trinity, and was also a licentiate of the Surgeons' School. He was a demonstrator in anatomy in Trinity, and acted as *locum tenens* during the illness of Professor Hartigan in 1812, but was defeated by Macartney for the Trinity Chair in the following year. Wilmot was then appointed Surgeon to Mercer's Hospital, but later transferred to Dr. Steevens' Hospital to found with Colles and Cusack a great surgical team. Wilmot was for a short while after Todd's death, Professor of Anatomy in the Surgeons' School, but continued as co-professor with Colles in the surgical Chair until 1836. He was also one of the founders of the Park Street School, and was President of the College in 1815 and 1832.

CHAPTER FIFTEEN
## ROBERT HARRISON 1796-1858

Robert Harrison was an Englishman who was educated and settled in Dublin. He graduated in arts and in medicine in Trinity, and was also a licentiate of the Surgeons' School. When qualified he was appointed Demonstrator to Abraham Colles, and in 1827 succeeded him in the anatomy and physiology Chair in the Surgeons' School. He was later to succeed to the anatomy and chirurgery Chair in Trinity on Macartney's resignation in 1837. Harrison was a brilliant anatomist and teacher, and made many contributions to medical literature. His *Surgical Anatomy of the Arteries* was a work of sterling merit and went to many editions. The famous *Dublin Dissector* first published under the *nom de plume* of 'M.R.C.S.I.' and later under his own name, also went to several editions and was for long a favourite manual in the American anatomy schools. He was President of the College in 1848.

ANDREW ELLIS 1792–1867, was a licentiate of the Surgeons' School, and after qualifying was attached to private medical schools, including that of Kirby in Peter Street. He was appointed Professor of Surgery in the Apothecaries Hall, and later to the same post in the Catholic University. He was Surgeon to Jervis Street Hospital, and President of the College in 1849.

WILLIAM HARGRAVE 1797–1874, was an arts and medical graduate of Trinity, and a licentiate of the Surgeons' School. He toured the surgical clinics of London, Edinburgh and Paris, and later established his own private medical school in Digges Street. He succeeded to the Chair of Anatomy in the Surgeons' School in 1837, and to the Chair of Surgery 10 years later. He was President of the College in 1853.

JOHN SHEKLETON 1795–1824, was apprenticed to Abraham Colles, and later his demonstrator in the Surgeons' School. In 1820 he was appointed the first Curator of the College Museum. He was a very able anatomist, showing considerable promise; he discovered a small muscle — the *compressor venae dorsalis penis* — which is occasionally present in man. Shekleton died rather tragically from a wound received in dissection, and an account of his case was reported by Abraham Colles.

CHAPTER TWENTY

# JAMES WILLIAM CUSACK 1788–1861

James William Cusack was one of Dublin's great surgeons, and ranks with Colles, Crampton and Carmichael. He was Obré's apprentice at Dr. Steevens' Hospital, and a student and licentiate of the Surgeons' School. Concurrently, he had a brilliant undergraduate career in Trinity, becoming a Scholar of the House and winning the Berkeley gold medal before graduating in arts and medicine. In 1813 he succeeded Abraham Colles as Resident Surgeon at Dr. Steevens' Hospital, which post he was to occupy until 1834 when he was promoted to Assistant Surgeon. The post of

Resident Surgeon was an important one, as Cusack now had an equal share of the 175 surgical beds with the assistant surgeons Colles and Wilmot. He was also the administrative head of the hospital, responsible its discipline and internal economy. All accident cases were admitted under his care, and he had to summon the assistant surgeons in difficult cases and where the patient needed a 'capital' operation. It was the custom that the whole surgical staff should visit the wards together on certain days and to present together at operations. It is of interest that Woodroffe, Colles and Cusack were Presidents of the College whilst resident surgeons at the hospital.

Cusack had a large surgical practice, especially after Colles' death when he became the leading surgeon in Ireland. He had an unusually large number of apprentices, due mainly to his connection with the Park Street school of which he was a founder. When his apprentices attained the number of 52, his pupils styled him 'Colonel of the 52nd'. He was a most hospitable man, particularly in the case of his former apprentices, and his home in Kildare Street formerly owned by Todd was always open to them. At one time 11 of the surgeons of county infirmaries were his past apprentices. It was the custom of Cusack like Prodicus the Cean of Athens, to make his pupils attend him in his bedroom each morning before he got up, in order to question them about their work and to give them such clinical instruction as he thought fit. This was Cusack's happy interpretation of 'bedside' teaching later to be successfully inaugurated by Graves and Stokes at the Meath Hospital. It was while Cusack was resident surgeon that Charles Lever the novelist was a student at Dr. Steevens' Hospital, and there he played many of his practical jokes which he described in *Charles O'Malley*. Although fond of practical jokes, Lever was a favourite with his teachers, and Cusack in particular seems to have allowed him great freedom.

Cusack worried much about his operations, and lay awake at night before his operation day, pondering over details of his cases. He published very little, but his ability as a surgeon cannot be questioned. In 1852 Trinity appointed Cusack to its second Chair — the University Professorship of Surgery, which title was altered to the Regius Chair during the tenure of its next occupant, Robert Adams (of the 'Stokes-Adams syndrome'). Cusack was President of his College on three occasions, in 1825, 1847 and 1858. He was Surgeon in Ordinary to Her Majesty the Queen in Ireland.

PARK STREET SCHOOL established by Cusack and his colleagues has already been referred to (*vide* Arthur Jacob). About 1824, Park Street was the abode of persons leading unvirtuous lives; and when in later years it was purified from its moral filth, its name was changed to Lincoln Place, which it still remains. The school was closed in 1849, when its principal proprietor, Hugh Carlisle, was appointed Professor of Anatomy in the newly established Queen's College, Belfast. The building in a later decade was converted into a hospital — St. Mark's Hospital, made famous as the professional home of Sir William Wilde, — T.G. Wilson's *Victorian Doctor*.

# BIBLIOGRAPHY

Brook, Charles W., *The Lancet* Oct. 6, 1973.

Cameron, Sir Charles, *History of the Royal College of Surgeons in Ireland*. 2nd Edn., Dublin, 1916.

Cope, Sir Zachary, *The Royal College of Surgeons of England*. London. 1959.

Fallon, Martin, *Abraham Colles*. London, 1972.

Gilborne, John, *The Medical Review*. Dublin, 1775.

*The Lancet*. Vols. 1823–1836.

Macalister, Alexander, *James Macartney*. London, 1900.

Macalpine, Ida, *et. al.* B.M.J. Booklet. London, 1968.

Sprigge, S. Squire, *Life and Times of Thomas Wakley*. London, 1899.

Wakley, Thomas, *Dictionary of National Biography*. London, 1909.

Widdess, J.D.H., *A History of the Royal College of Physicians of Ireland*. Edinburgh. 1963.

Widdess, J.D.H., *A History of the Royal College of Surgeons in Ireland and its Medical School*. 2nd Edn., Edinburgh, 1967.

Wilson, T.G., *Victorian Doctor*. London, 1942.

# INDEX

Aberdeen University  6
Abernethy, John  5, 14, 114, 172
Adams, Robert  203, 240
Alcock, Benjamin  193
Alexandre, Mons.  196
All Hallows  84
Anatomy Bill  7, 9
Anderson's Quarterly Journal  79
Apjohn, James  78
Apothecaries Company of Dublin  6
Apothecaries Company of London
   4, 6
Apprenticeship System  55, 120,
   121, 180, 181
Archbishop of Canterbury  7
Arygyll Street  1, 4
Athlone  59
Auchinleck, William  130, 137, 141,
   149, 154, 157, 175, 238

Bayton, Doctor  141
Bede  185
Bell, John  133
Belloc, Hillaire  2
Bishop Williams and May  7
B.M.A. Council  9
Bully's Acre  52, 171, 178
Burke and Hare  7, 14
Burns, Joe  98, 102
Bushe, Chief Justice  61
Brutus  7

Caius, John  186
Cameron, Sir Charles  8
Canning, George  3
Carmichael, Richard  12, 107, 111,
   112, 114, 115, 157, 175, 202, 236
Caroline, Queen  1, 2
Castlereagh  3
Cato Street Conspiracy  1
Charlotte, Princess  2
Clare, Lord  38
Cobbett, William  4, 20
Colles, Abraham  12, 19, 20, 21, 22,
   23, 32, 36, 67, 68, 75, 106, 107,
   116, 121, 126, 157, 165, 166, 168,
   175, 181, 216, 228
Congreve  85
Copland, James  6, 8, 11, 147
Cooper, Bransby  5

Cooper, Sir Astley  5, 8, 34, 51, 64,
   211
Courtney, Sir Peter  17, 36, 154,
   170, 175, 177, 226
Crampton, Philip  12, 24, 54, 57,
   60, 64, 100, 101, 104, 105, 121,
   153, 157, 181, 231
Court of Examiners, Dublin  9
Court of Examiners, London  6
Cross, Arthur  8
Cusack, James William  13, 71, 78,
   120, 125, 126, 149, 150, 158, 177,
   192, 216, 239

Dawson Street  60, 61
Daniel, Michael  138, 188, 238
Davis, Charles  194
Dease, Richard  142
Dease, William  16, 170, 228
Donovan, Michael  189
Dublin Hospital Reports  33, 34
Dublin University  6, 9
Dun's Hospital  100

Edinburgh University  6
Egan, Tom  111, 212
Ellis, Andrew  166, 189, 239
Erigena, Johannes Scotus  186
Erinensis  8, 12
Examiners, London  45

Fallon, Mrs. Ganly  60
Freemasons' Tavern  14
French Revolution  1

Geo. III  1, 2
Geo. IV  1
Gilborne, John  12
Greeks, The  14
Glasgow University  6
Grattan, James  141
Graves, Robert  71, 78, 206
Green, Peter Hennis  9
Greene, Herris  8
Golden Age of Irish Medicine  13
Goldsmith  85
Guy's Hospital  5

Halahan, John  16, 228
Halford, Sir Henry  6, 8
Hargrave, William  166, 239

Harrison, Robert 13, 24, 105, 116, 149, 153, 157, 163, 166, 169, 171, 175, 179, 181, 199, 200, 238
Henthorn, James 18, 111, 116, 226
Hewson, Thomas 101, 107, 163, 235
Higgins, Professor 71
Hill, Edward 138, 140, 141, 238
Hippocrates 133, 203
Hohenlhohe, Prince 47
Hort, Mr. 193

Isle of Leon 45

Jacob, Arthur 12, 70, 71, 73, 78, 158, 163, 173, 175, 178, 192, 219, 232
Jervis Street Hospital 143
Johnson, Doctor 17
Johnstone, James 6
Junius 8, 36
Juvenal 14, 57

Kirby, John Timothy 8, 12, 24, 43, 44, 47, 49, 50, 51, 52, 79, 153, 157, 187, 198, 211, 230
Kirby's Mill 45, 231
Kyle, Doctor 83

L'Estrange, Francis 140, 141, 143, 235
La Charité of Peter Street 45
Lancet, The 4, 5, 6, 9, 11
Lawrence, William 7, 34, 121
Lavator 108, 109
Lendrick, Charles 141, 238
Liverpool, Lord 1, 3
London College of Medicine 7
London Medical and Physical Journal 6
London Medical Repository 6

Macleod, Roderick 6
Macalister, Alexander 8
Macalpine 2
Macklin, Gerard 141
Macartney, James 8, 9, 12, 49, 82, 106, 204, 216, 233
Macnamara, Rawdon 101, 163, 179, 235
Magee, William 39
Mary, Queen of Scots 2
Meath Hospital 64, 66, 67, 100, 207, 234
Medical Act 7
Medical Profession in London 10
Medico-Chirurgical Review 6
Membury 3

Mercer's Hospital 8, 16, 100, 128, 130, 237
Mercer's Street 44
'Moll Flanders' 43
Morrison's Hotel 137

Napoleonic War 1
Natural History 39
Newgate 1

Obré, Ralph Smith 61, 232
Owen, Robert 41
Oxmantown School 99

Palmer, Abraham 98, 121, 143, 175
Parker, Tom 1
Park Street Medical School 71, 79, 192, 216
Parry 14
Patriot, Scholar and Irishman 12, 42
Peile, Robert 121, 126
'Peterloo' 1, 52
Peter Street 45, 47, 48, 187
Perrot, Sir John 84
Porphyria 2
Primrose, George 53
Porter, William Henry 98, 101, 122, 149, 151, 157, 193, 235
Provincial Medical and Surgical Journal 9

Quakers Burial Ground 16
Quain, James 8, 213

Radicalism 1
Race for the Succession 2
Regent Street 1, 4
Regent, The 4
Renny, George 18, 228
Read, Alexander 134, 237
Rees's Encyclopedia 87, 93
Richmond, Duke of 61
Richards, Solomon 59
Richmond Hospital Medical School 33, 189, 202
Romans, The 14
Rooney, Thomas 10, 126, 235
Rose, Mr. 44
Royal College of Surgeons in Ireland 7, 9, 15, 20, 44, 71, 90, 95, 156
Royal College of Surgeons in London 3, 4, 6, 8, 90
Royal College of Surgeons of England 7
Royal College of Physicians of Ireland 71, 99

Royal College of Physicians of
  London  4, 6, 8
Royal Dublin Society  9, 71
Royal Irish Academy  192

Sadler  14
School of Physic  88, 205
Shekelton, John  169, 239
Sidmouth, Lord  3
Shiel, Doctor  14
Sierra Morena  45
Steevens' Hospital  100, 117, 124,
  216, 236
'Stella'  124
Stewart, George  61, 232
Streeton, R. J.  9
Stokes Whitley  12, 35, 37, 39, 40,
  229
Stramonium  48, 153
Stringer, Surgeon  60
Surgeon Generalship  61
Surgical Stamp Office  59
Swift  85, 129, 237
Syntax, Doctor  39

Tierney, Sir Michael  64, 84

Thistlewood, Arthur  1
Thwaite's Soda Water  131
Thomas's St. Hospital  5
Todd, Charles Hawkes  12, 24, 26,
  27, 29, 31, 32, 33, 36, 49, 92, 116,
  156, 169, 226
Trinity College  38

United Borough Hospitals  3

Victoria, Princess  3

Wakley, Thomas  1, 3, 5, 8
Wallace, William  189
Warburton, Henry  7
Wardrop, James  7
Waterloo  2
Wellington  2, 14
Weekly Political Register  14
Westmoreland Lock Hospital  107,
  110
Wicklow Mines  41
Willis, Robert Darling  2
Wilmot, Samuel  13, 71, 73, 76,
  126, 127, 156, 158, 160, 163, 181,
  238